Giuseppe Riva, John Waterworth, Dianne Murray

Interacting with Presence: HCI and the Sense of Presence in Computer-mediated Environments

Giuseppe Riva, John Waterworth,
Dianne Murray

Interacting with Presence: HCI and the Sense of Presence in Computer-mediated Environments

Managing Editor: Aneta Przepiórka

Associate Editor: Pietro Cipresso

Language Editor: Matthew Coleshill

DE GRUYTER
OPEN

Published by De Gruyter Open Ltd, Warsaw/Berlin.

ISBN 978-3-11-040967-3
e- ISBN 978-3-11-040969-7

Bibliographic information published by the Deutsche Nationalbibliothek
The Deutsche Nationalbibliothek lists this publication in the Deutsche Nationalbibliografie; detailed bibliographic data are available in the Internet at http://dnb.dnb.de.

Managing Editor: Aneta Przepiórka
Associate Editor: Pietro Cipresso
Language Editor: Matthew Coleshill

www.degruyteropen.com

Cover illustration: © Thinkstock/denphumi

Contents

Introduction: Editors' Introduction to Interacting with Presence

Giuseppe Riva, John Waterworth, and Dianne Murray

Why "Interacting with Presence"?

This volume arose from a longstanding conviction that our subjective experience of information technology is profoundly affected by the extent to which we feel ourselves to be really present in the mediated worlds that the technology makes available to us. 'Presence' is just this "feeling of being inside the mediated world". It is a crucial and increasingly necessary element in both design and usage of many recent and developing interactive technologies. In the same way that 'feeling present', or consciously 'being there', in the physical world around us is based upon perception, physical action and activity in that world, so the feeling of presence in a technologically-mediated environment is a function of the possibilities for interaction.

A more advanced human-centred interaction with systems would provide users with a sense of being there, close to if not equivalent to the experience of actual presence. Creating this sense of presence remains a major challenge and is leading to the development of new interdisciplinary research, combining cognitive psychology, haptic (sense of touch) studies, computer graphics and multimedia design, advanced communication theory and socio-cultural issues. A theory of presence, emerging through this interdisciplinary research, that explores the cognitive and affective roots of sensory perception, is expected to give rise to the design of innovative systems that offer "richer" experiences than any current media and communication technologies.

This, however, is no easy task.

Many researchers, artists and designers have explored the role of the sense of presence in interactive experience. While there is still not a general consensus about what presence actually is, it is fair to say that most investigators agree about what it is *not*. Presence is not the degree of technological immersion, it is not the same thing as emotional engagement, it is not absorption or attention or action; but all of these have a potential role in understanding the experience of presence in interaction – the experience of *interacting with presence*. The feeling of presence is a crucial aspect of many recent and developing interactive technologies. The illusion of being present is the key ingredient that gives interactive media the power to affect people profoundly, to change them.

Due to the complexity of the topic, and the interest in this concept, many different attempts to explain the nature of mediated presence have been made. The most basic distinction concerns the issue of technology. For many researchers, mediated presence is a direct function of our experience as mediated by specific types of technology. Presence is often defined within this view as the *"perceptual illusion of non-mediation"* manifested as the disappearance of the medium from the conscious attention of the subject. For others, presence is seen as a broader psychological phenomenon – *"inner presence"* – related to the control of the subject and to social activity.

Presence is important and is a significant factor in so many different aspects of mediated life because it affects how we behave, what we pay attention to, and how we understand and remember events. The editors believe that, as with emotions, the ability to feeling varying degrees of presence is essential to our survival. Clearly, the experience of presence in a mediated environment is to no small extent a function of the possibilities for interaction, in the same way that feeling present in the physical world is grounded in perception, action and the body. Since these interaction possibilities can be manipulated by design, and in almost unlimited ways, we can conduct experiments in which we measure mediated presence to provide new insights into how and why we feel present in general. The mediated environments we are now creating mix the physical and virtual ever more closely in our experienced everyday lives. To survive and thrive in them, we believe that we will need to consider closely exactly when, to what degree, and in response to which situations we need to feel present - and how we can design our future applications and mediated worlds to achieve that.

"Interacting with Presence" provides an introduction and overview of this increasingly important topic. This timely edited volume presents a range of theoretic perspectives and empirical evidence casting new light on understanding and designing for presence in interaction. Because of its experiential impact on the user, presence is emerging as a key concept for understanding and predicting developments in diverse areas such as interactive entertainment, gaming, psychotherapy, education, scientific visualisation, sports training and rehabilitation, and many more.

With its roots in the development of virtual reality technology, the study of mediated presence has expanded into a range of application disciplines, as discussed in detail in this book. One of the most refreshing and stimulating aspects of presence research is the diversity of views and approaches brought to bear on its explanation and exploration. In tune with this state of affairs, the authors of the chapters in this book explore many different aspects of presence in relation to such topics as the use of tools, social interaction, the nature of mediated embodiment, wellbeing, personal identity and persuasion.

Structure of This Book

As editors, we have organised the 11 chapters in this volume according to five themes reflected in the sections of the book and outlined below. We have not sought to impose our own views of presence on the other authors. The chapters were chosen initially on the basis of the interest and relevance of the proposal to an understanding of presence as mediated through interacting with information technology. The chapters submitted were then reviewed, and most of those were then revised in line with the comments received from two reviewers and the editors. Following this, final versions were submitted and eventually made ready for publication in the book.

The book as a whole comprises a diverse collection of approaches to interacting with presence. What all the chapters share is a conviction that the sense of presence matters. Presence mediated by technology, whether in virtuality, in physical reality, or in some admixture of the two, is important - not merely as a by-product of interaction, but as an outcome with powerful effects.

An Introduction to Presence: Section 1

Section 1 introduces presence in two chapters that lay out the field as whole, essentially from the perspective of the editors themselves.

Chapter 1, by Giuseppe Riva and Fabrizia Mantovani, presents a general framework for understanding presence in mediated interactions, as 'Extending the Self through the Tools and the Others'. They suggest that presence has a key role in cognition by virtue of having three critical features that cannot be explained by other cognitive processes. Firstly, presence "locates" the Self in an external physical and/or cultural space: the Self is "present" in a space if he/she can act in it. Secondly, presence provides feedback to the Self about the status of its activity: the Self perceives the variations in presence and tunes its activity accordingly. Finally, presence allows the evolution of the Self through the incorporation of tools: tools do not only enable us to extend our reaching space, but may also become part of a plastic neural representation of our body that allows their use without additional cognitive effort.

They extend this analysis by pointing out that social presence enables the subject to identify the Other and to attribute to him or her an ontological status that is different from other objects perceived. Social presence allows interaction and communication through the understanding of the Other's intentions. Ultimately, they point out that social presence permits the evolution of the Self through the identification of "optimal shared experiences" and the incorporation of artefacts – physical and social – linked to them.

Chapter 2, by John and Eva Waterworth, outlines three progressive stages of interactive presence, and the main design challenges raised by each. The first category, termed altered embodiment, refers to the way technology allows us to experience the world with modified or enhanced senses. Echoing the previous chapter, the second category - expanded embodiment - refers to the ways in which technology can push the envelope of the mental body in which one feels present out beyond the physical body. This involves the incorporation of information technology as part of the Self, implying a change in the boundary between the Self and the non-Self, the Other that constitutes the world around one. Finally, distributed embodiment refers to how the sense of being present in the world can be separated from that of ownership of a particular body, through the development of new approaches to deploying the technologies of virtual realisation. It is suggested that these three stages of mediated presence are key concepts for understanding possible ways in which designed interactive experiences will affect and continue to change our experience of the world and of our own bodies in the future.

From the Body to the Technology to the Brain: Section 2

Section 2 provides a view of presence "from the body to the technology to the brain" with two chapters that attempt to ground the phenomena of presence within quite novel theoretical contexts.

We routinely think of mediated presence as a result of the simulation of perceived reality by computer. In **Chapter 3**, 'Measuring presence in the simulating brain', Daniel Sjölie focuses on how a description of the brain itself as an organ for simulating its environment can inform and illuminate the meaning of brain measurements taken in connection with the sense of presence. Suggested general principles for brain function, such as the free-energy principle, have implications for the ways in which presence can, or cannot, be measured in terms of brain activity. The chapter discusses the implications of accepting the simulating brain concept as a working hypothesis, rather than focusing on arguments for these theories of brain. Such implications are related to how measurements can be connected to some of the most common theoretical descriptions of presence, and to a brief review of previous brain measurement studies that have investigated presence. Overall, the chapter provides a way of interpreting the phenomena of presence, from a new perspective based in the general principles of brain function.

Chapter 4, 'A Framework for Interactivity and Presence in Novel Bodies', by Andrea Stevenson Won and associates, explores the fascinating topic of experiencing mediated presence by interacting with (what are perceived subjectively as) non-human bodies. Using trackers, users can control multiple avatar limbs in order to manipulate objects, move through space, and otherwise act in the virtual world. In this chapter the framework developed earlier by two of the authors, Antal Haans and Wijnand A. IJsselsteijn is used to investigate the experience of self-presence in cases of nonhuman avatars or avatars that otherwise differ in ability or control schema from the user's own body, such as avatars with more than two arms. The authors focus on cases where participants inhabit avatars in which the veridical mapping between tracking and rendering is disrupted.

Experiencing the Others through a Technology: Section 3

Section 3 examines social presence, the feeling of being engaged with, and connected to others, and the ways it may be mediated by technology.

In **Chapter 5**, John M. Carroll and colleagues analyse community awareness technologies in terms of their ability to make members feel more present to others and feel that others are more present to them, introducing the concept of "hyperpresence". They focus on place-based technologies and the exciting possibility that they may be used to amplify the sense of presence in the physical world. They draw upon several design investigations of supporting community awareness through the aggregation of RSS feeds and Tweets, digital cultural heritage, volunteer efforts, and fieldwork to understand community awareness designs in a health community.

Chapter 6, by Matthew Hudson and Paul Cairns, looks at the important topic of digital social games and how to measure presence there. Social presence is a key part of the playing experience in such games, but existing measures lack the sophistication to deal with these more diverse gaming situations. The chapter describes the development of a new questionnaire to measure the complex nature of social presence in digital games. The resulting questionnaire consists of 39 items with two main modules addressing competitive and collaborative components of social play.

Using Presence to Increase Wellbeing: Section 4

Section 4 then focuses on health and how presence can be a factor in efforts to promote improvements in wellbeing.

In **Chapter 7**, Henry Moller and his co-workers outline a novel paradigm in immersive media technology which is now within reach for clinical application. This seeks to enable an induced state of wellbeing, by creating uplifting states of consciousness rather than generating aversive stimuli or presenting cumbersome tasks for users. Demand for innovative and patient-centred care to alleviate stress-related and psychosomatic conditions is certainly high in medical settings. A mental health treatment modality that is effective, safe and free of adverse effects is a desirable set of criteria not only from a patient's perspective, but also from the perspective of clinicians who provide healthcare service to patients. In this chapter, positive experiential learning through inspirational/motivational shifts in consciousness through technology is presented as an important route for health promotion in the future.

Sheryl Brahnam (**Chapter 8**) looks at mediated psychotherapy, and specifically "the uncanny stranger in the room". Taking the perspective of the therapist, this chapter reflects on how, in distance psychotherapy using the telephone and videoconferencing technologies, both the lack of important physical cues and the addition of media artefacts (such as audio/video synchronisation problems and technological glitches) can potentially affect the therapeutic relationship and therapeutic presence. The chapter increases our understanding of therapeutic presence and how it is affected when mediated, which will put designers and developers in a better position to appreciate the necessity of supporting and of protecting presence when designing future systems for distance psychotherapy.

Chapter 9, by Villani et al., presents exposure therapy as an effective way to treat anxiety and stress, using Virtual Reality Exposure Therapy, so that the therapeutic experience can be precisely controlled. The authors point out that because of the increased availability of unobtrusive biosensors, and of their integration with other devices, it is possible to measure and take advantage of the sense of presence during the interaction - and so to overcome the limitations of existing protocols for psychological stress and anxiety. They suggest that presence - the experience of "being there" - is influenced by the ability of "making sense there" and by the possibility of learning, by living real experiences in computer mediated environments. They demonstrate that the concept of presence is a critical feature to consider when designing technology-mediated protocols, and describe how future investigations will give researchers and clinicians important indications about how to create increasingly effective virtual therapeutic experiences.

Individual Differences in Presence: Section 5

Finally, **Section 5** looks at the relatively neglected topics of individual differences in presence, and of presence as an outcome of persuasive technologies.

In **Chapter 10** Anna Felnhofer and Oswald D. Kothgassner confront gender, a personal characteristic that is widely considered to be very important, despite the dearth of substantial findings on the topic. The chapter outlines some of the past research that has been carried out on gender differences in both social and physical presence. Two studies are then described in detail. The first looks at male and female presence experiences in students delivering a speech in front of a virtual audience. The second focuses more broadly on gender differences in young and older adults, while interacting with virtual characters in a collaborative virtual environment. Overall, the results indicate a significant advantage of men over women for physical but not for social presence.

Chapter 11, by Jesse Fox and associates, explores three components of presence (self, social, and spatial presence) and how they relate to persuasion in virtual environments. Presence has often been studied as the mechanism explaining why a virtual environment is successful in persuasion. This chapter points to the importance of understanding the mechanisms that explain presence as an outcome in such persuasive environments. The authors outline an approach whereby virtual environments can be created to cultivate presence and more readily facilitate persuasive goals.

In Summary

The wide array of disciplines and applications described in the five Sections strengthens the idea of the importance of presence for real-life applications. As the field continues to grow, we eagerly expect larger on-the-field trials as well as comparisons to existing methods of practice, supporting continued growth of new applications.

Moreover, the book also outlines how the vision of 'optimal presence' can be a strong starting point for giving direction to interactive technology research over the coming five/ten years. Major opportunities to create an optimal presence landscape, based on advanced and intuitive interfaces, can be built in areas such as mobile communications, portable devices, systems integration, embedded computing and intelligent systems design.

Specifically, the book suggests that it is possible to combine the objective of optimal presence with enhancements in information and communication technologies in a move toward a new paradigm: 'Positive Technology'. The main objective of this new paradigm is to use technology to manipulate and enhance features of our personal experience for increasing wellness and generating strength and resilience in individuals, organisations, and society.

In particular it suggests that it is possible to use presence and technology to manipulate the features of our personal experience in three separate but related ways:

1. *By structuring personal experience* using a goal/meaning, rules and a feedback system;
2. *by augmenting personal experience* to achieve multimodal and mixed experiences;
3. *by replacing personal experience* with a synthetic/fictional one.

Nevertheless, the design goal of achieving positive technologies requires an interdisciplinary approach, integrating knowledge and ideas from disciplines such as neuroscience, social and cognitive psychology, multi-sensory perception, cognition, artificial intelligence, multimedia development, video compression or telecoms engineering. In order to build environments which can efficiently transmit remote presence, it will be necessary to incorporate and integrate ongoing insights from these fields into next-generation research for advanced, wideband multi-sensory services and novel telecommunications architectures.

Moreover, the concept of social presence also emphasises the social dimension of innovation, and the ability as well as the willingness of society to use, absorb or adapt to technological opportunities. Alongside technological and economic feasibility, the implications for issues such as social sustainability, privacy, social robustness and fault tolerance may in the longer run determine the success or failure of any presence-enhanced application.

In the end, we hope that the contents of this book will stimulate more research on technical, cognitive and human factors connected to the sense of "being there" and on how best to use it in communication, education, commerce, design and telemedicine. We thank all the authors for their great work in making this book what we believe it to be – a significant contribution to understanding the roles and importance of presence in a range of interactive situations. We hope our readers enjoy *Interacting with Presence*!

1 Extending the Self through the Tools and the Others: a General Framework for Presence and Social Presence in Mediated Interactions

Giuseppe Riva and Fabrizia Mantovani

Abstract: The concept of "presence" originated from and was diffused by a technological scientific community at the same time as the introduction of a unique piece of communication technology, teleoperators: robots controlled from a distance by a human operator. In this case the term telepresence refers to the human operator's sensation of being present in the remote location in which the teleoperator is situated. However, different recent neuropsychology studies suggest that presence has a key role in our cognitive processes: it is the the outcome of an intuitive metacognitive process that allows us to control our actions through the comparison between intentions and perceptions. Specifically, presence has three critical features that cannot be explained by other cognitive processes. First, presence "locates" the Self in an external physical and/or cultural space: the Self is "present" in a space if he/she can act in it. Second, presence provides feedback to the Self about the status of its activity: the Self perceives the variations in presence and tunes its activity accordingly. Third, presence allows the evolution of the Self through the incorporation of tools: tools do not enable us only to extend our reaching space, but when successfully mastered become part of a plastic neural representation of our body that allows their use without further cognitive effort (intuitively). In this way we can focus our cognitive resources on actions that are not only related to the here-and-now, improving the complexity of our goals. The concept of presence concerns the subject and his or her ability to act in the world: I am present in a real or virtual space if I manage to put my intentions into action intuitively. But how does one connect to the Other? How does the Other become present for the subject? The recent discovery of mirror neurons - a class of neurons that are activated both during the execution of purposeful, goal-related actions, and during the observation of similar actions performed by another individual - suggests the existence of a second selective and adaptive mechanism, "social presence", which enables the Self to identify and interact with the Other by understanding his intentions: it is the outcome of an intuitive metacognitive process that allows us to understand the actions of an enacting Other through the comparison between his/her expected intentions and perceptions. In other words, from an evolutionary point of view, social presence has three functions. First, social presence enables the subject to identify the Other and to attribute to him an ontological status – "the other similar to the self" – different from the other objects perceived. Second, social presence allows interaction and communication through the understanding of the Other's intentions. Third, social presence, permits the evolution of the Self through the identification of “optimal shared experiences” (Networked Flow) and the incorporation of artifacts – physical and social – linked to them.

Keywords: Presence, Social Presence, Self, Others, Mediated Interaction, Tools

1.1 Introduction to Chapter 1

The concept of “*presence*” originated from and was diffused by a technological scientific community at the same time as the introduction of a unique piece of communication technology, teleoperators: robots controlled from a distance by a human operator (Heeter, 1992). In this case the term telepresence refers to the human operator’s sensation of being present in the remote location in which the teleoperator is situated (Held & Durlach, 1992). But am I present only when I’m experiencing a telepresence system or a virtual reality environment?

Obviously the answer is no. However, many scholars still consider presence as a function of our experience of a given medium (Media Presence). The main result of this approach is one of the most known definitions of presence: the “*perceptual illusion of non-mediation*” (Lombard & Ditton, 1997). According to this view, presence in a mediated experience is achieved by means of the disappearance of the medium from the conscious attention of the subject. The main advantage of this definition is its predictive value: the level of presence is reduced by the experience of mediation during the action. So, to improve presence, I have to remove the medium from the attention of the user. The main limitation of this vision is what is not said. Is it a specific cognitive process? What is its role in our daily experience?

In this chapter we will draw on the recent outcomes of cognitive sciences to offer a broader definition of presence, not related to technology only (Waterworth, Waterworth, Mantovani, & Riva, 2012). For a long time cognitive science considered action, perception, and interpretation as separate activities. A recent trend in cognitive science is instead seeing cognition as *embodied:* our conceptual system produces dynamically contextualized representations (simulations) that support situated action in different contexts. In this context what is the role of presence?

As we will discuss in the next pages, the experience of presence can be described as the outcome of an intuitive metacognitive process that allows us to control our actions through the comparison between intentions and perceptions (Riva, 2007; Riva & Mantovani, 2012). Following this view, presence is a core neuropsychological phenomenon whose goal is to produce a sense of agency and control: I am present in a real or virtual space if I manage to put my intentions into action (enacting them).

However, while I can be present, at the same time, someone else can be present to me. This concept is well reflected by the definitions provided by the Merriam Webster dictionary: “presence” is both “the fact or condition of being present” and “the actual person or thing that is present”; “present” is “being in view or at hand” (Merriam-Webster, 2010).

Here we suggest that to fully understand the concept of presence, we need to connect it to its social counterpart: "social presence". A central objective of contemporary cognitive science is the explanation of "*Social Cognition*", the information-processing system that enables us to engage in social behavior. Specifically, social cognition addresses how people process social information: its encoding, storage, retrieval, and use in social situations.

But what makes a subject "present" within a group? And what happens when the others are not with me physically, such as in a shared virtual worlds?

The recent discovery of "mirror neurons" - a class of neurons that are activated both during the execution of purposeful, goal-related actions, and during the observation of similar actions performed by another individual - suggests the existence of a second selective and adaptive mechanism - "*social presence*" - which enables the Self to identify and interact with the Other by understanding his intentions. The experience of social presence (that someone else is with me) can be described as the outcome an intuitive metacognitive process that allows us to understand the actions of an enacting Other through the comparison between the expected intentions and the perceived actions.

In the following paragraphs we will endeavor to justify these claims and to underline their relevance for the design and usage of many recent and developing interactive technologies.

1.2 From Space to Action

In our daily life the experience of presence is strictly related to space (Spagnolli & Gamberini, 2005): I'm present *in* a space.

But how do we experience an external space? Cognitive sciences clearly demonstrated that our spatial experience is the outcome of the interaction of different spatial representations whose integrated activity give rise to spatial awareness (Matelli & Luppino, 2001). For example, the proprioceptive knowledge of our own body's location in external space (*the feeling of being in a given space*) requires that information about the angles of each joint be combined with information about the size and shape of the body segments between joints.

Specifically, evidence from clinical and experimental studies indicates that our spatial experience involves the integration of different sensory inputs within two different reference frames (see *Figure 1.1*) defined by our body model and related to its possibility of action (Longo, Azañón, & Haggard, 2010; Previc, 1998):

- *Egocentric* (body as reference of first-person experience). It is based on the body of the observer: it is defined by its three axes: front-back, left-righ, head-feet and within this frame the position of an object changes if the subject moves (Frith & de Vignemont, 2005). More, this frame defines the "*peripersonal space*", the

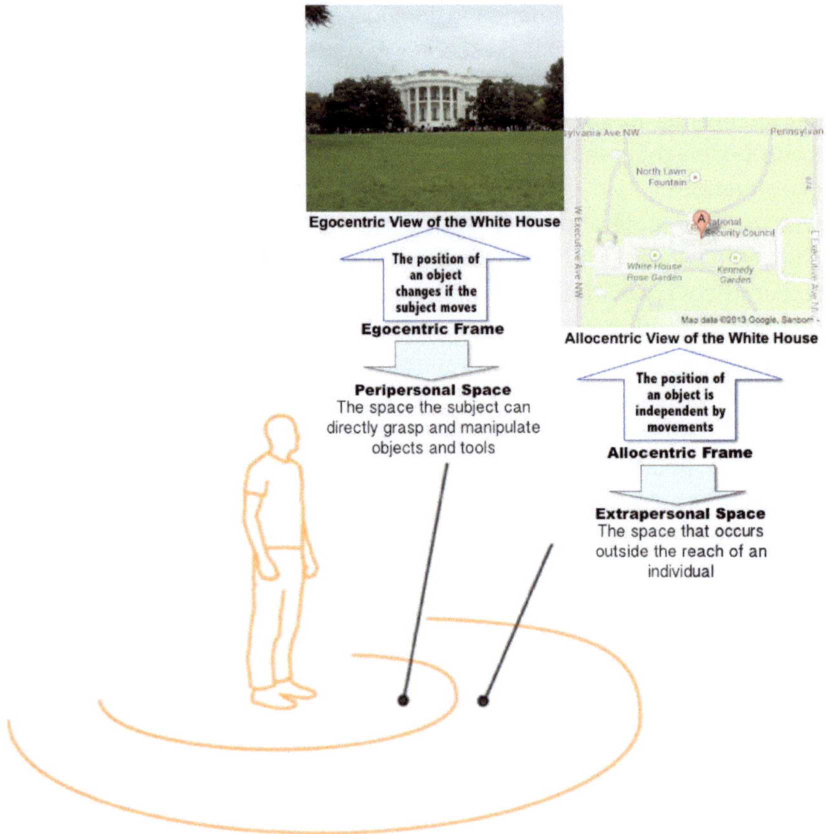

Figure 1.1: The experience of space

space immediately surrounding our bodies. Within this space the subject can directly grasp and manipulate objects and tools.

- *Allocentric (*body as object in a world*)*. It is defined by the spatial relations between the objects (*landmarks*) included in it. Within this frame the position of an object does not change if the subject moves, and the object exists even if there is no relation with the self or another person (Frith & de Vignemont, 2005). It is shaped around the "*extrapersonal space*", the space that occurs outside the reach of an individual.

This picture suggests that, even if we have a unitary spatial experience, we do not have a single global representation of space. More, we conceive places in terms of the actions we could take towards them: subjects have not a separate knowledge of the place's location relative to them, what they can do in it, and their purposes. An example can help in understanding this point. Retrieving an occluded object – e.g. when we lift a box to retrieve a sheet from under it – is an action taken on the basis of a belief about where the object (sheet) is located relative to the self. It follows that to know that the sheet exists when it is covered by the box is a matter of knowing what can be done to make the sheet visible. In other words, spatial perception is a dynamic operation that can be continuously modified and updated by the actions carried out by the subject.

1.3 From Action to Presence

According to Gamberini, Spagnolli and Mantovani, the sense of presence is linked to a subject's capacity for action and his ability to position himself within his physical and social space (Spagnolli & Gamberini, 2005). More precisely, for Spagnolli and Gamberini (2005): "Presence is the feature of the agent which is manifested through the creation of a space during action" (p. 8).

A similar, but broader view, was recently outlined by Riva and Waterworth (Riva, Waterworth, Waterworth, & Mantovani, 2011; Waterworth, Waterworth, Mantovani, & Riva, 2010). The idea proposed by these authors is the following: presence can be described as a selective and adaptive mechanism which allows the Self to define the boundaries of action by means of the distinction between "internal" and "external" within the sensory flow.

In other words, from an evolutionary point of view, presence has three functions:

- To check the efficacy of the subject's actions through the comparison of intention and the result of the action. As suggested by the *Covert Imitation Theory* (Knoblich, Thornton, Grosjean, & Shiffrar, 2005; Wilson & Knoblich, 2005), the brain instantiates a sophisticated prereflexive (non-intentional) simulation, based on motor codes, of the outcome of an action and uses it to evaluate its course. From a computational viewpoint, this is achieved through a forward-inverse model:
  - First, the agent produces the motor command for achieving a desired state given the current state of the system and the current state of the environment;
  - second, an efference copy of the motor command is fed to a forward dynamic model that generates a prediction of the consequences of performing this motor command;
  - third, the predicted state is compared with the actual sensory feedback. Errors derived from the difference between the desired state and the actual state can be used to update the model and improve performance.
- To permit the subject to position himself in a space – real, virtual or social – through the distinction between "internal" and "external" and the definition of a boundary: the Self is "present" in a space if he/she can act in it.

- To allow its own evolution through the identification of *"optimal experiences" (Flow)* and the incorporation of the artifacts – physical and social – linked to it. Artifacts do not enable us only to extend our reaching space, but when successfully mastered become part of a plastic neural representation of our body that allows their use without further cognitive effort (intuitively).

To sum up, we can define presence as *the pre-reflexive sensation of "being" in an environment, real or virtual, which results from the capacity to carry out intuitively one's intentions within that environment.* But what does it happen when these actions are implemented using a tool?

According to the Merriam Webster dictionary a "tool" is both "a handheld device that aids in accomplishing a task" and "something (as an instrument or apparatus) used in performing an operation" (Merriam-Webster, 2010). These definitions underline that tools are controlled by human action and that they exert an action upon external objects. But, as reflected by the two different definitions, the relationship between the human action, the tool and its final effect is not always the same.

For this reason, in this context we can distinguish between two different types of mediated action (Riva & Mantovani, 2012): *first-order or second-order* (see *Figure 1.2*):

- In *first-order* mediated actions the subject use the body to control a proximal tool (an artifact present and manipulable in the peripersonal space) to exert an action upon an external object. In practice, there is a direct spatial connection between the body of the subject, the tool and the external object. An example of first-order mediated action is the one of the tennis player striking the ball (external object) with the racquet (proximal tool).
- In *second-order* mediated action the subject use the body to control a proximal tool that controls a different distal one (a tool present and visible in the extrapersonal space) to exert an action upon an external object. In this situation there is a spatial disconnection between the peripersonal (near) space that contains both the body of the subject and the proximal tool, and the extrapersonal (far) space, that may be either real or virtual, where are located both the distal tool and the external object. An example of second-order mediated action is the one of the cranemen using a lever (proximal tool) to move a mechanical boom (distal tool in the real space) to lift materials (external real objects). Another example, more related to technology, is the one of the videogame player using a joystick (proximal tool) to move an avatar (distal tool in a virtual space) to pick up a sword (external virtual object). A possible, simpler variant of second-order mediated action is the direct use of the body to control a distal tool that exerts an action upon an external object. An example of this variant is the interaction with the Microsoft Kinect system: I move my body to move an avatar (distal tool) to pick up virtual objects.

Here we suggest that these two mediated actions have different effects on our spatial experience (*Figure 1.2*):

Figure 1.2: Mediated action and its effects on the experience of the subject

- A successfully learned *first-order* mediated action produces *incorporation*: the proximal tool extends the peripersonal space of the subject (the subject is present in the tool);
- a successfully learned *second-order* mediated action produces *incarnation:* a second peripersonal space centered on the distal tool (the subject is present in the extrapersonal space – telepresence);

- a successfully learned *second-order* mediated action associated to a spatio-temporal correspondence between multisensory feedbacks experienced by the user and the visual data related to the distal virtual body (avatar) produces *embodiment:* the user experiences a new body in the avatar (the subject is present in a different body - body ownership illusion).

Let's try to deepen these points. Since the seminal work of Atsushi Iriki on macaques and tools (Iriki, Tanaka, & Iwamura, 1996), many different studies demonstrated that, after a successful training, a proximal tool (*first-order mediated action*) is incorporated in the bodily experience of the subject (Farnè, Bonifazi, & Làdavas, 2005; Farné, Serino, & Làdavas, 2007). From a phenomenological view point, after the training *we are now present* in the tool and we can use it intuitively as we use our hands and our fingers.

But what does it happen when we learn to use a distal tool (*second-order mediated action*)? In a different experiment Iriki and colleagues trained macaques to retrieve food by watching their hand/arm movements through a real-time video monitor (Iriki, Tanaka, Obayashi, & Iwamura, 2001). In other words, in Iriki's study the monkey used the self-image in the monitor as a distal reference of hand movement, similar to when a human is using the Microsoft Kinect. The study showed that the identical neurons, which code the image of the hand in normal condition, responded in a similar manner to the image in the video monitor: here, again, the image of the hand is experienced as a direct an extension of the self. And this happened only after the acquisition of the new motor skill: before training no neuron responded to visual stimuli presented in the monitor screen. This required an integration of the visual data (the distal tool) with the proprioceptive/tactile data (the real hand moving the proximal tool): how are they integrated?

Different authors suggest that a *second-order mediated action* is based on the simultaneous handling of two different body models – one centered on the real body (based on proprioceptive data) and a second centered on the distal tool (visual data) – that are weighted in a way that minimizes the uncertainty during the mediated action (Jäncke, Cheetham, & Baumgartner, 2009; Wirth et al., 2007). Specifically, when the distal-centered peripersonal space becomes the prevalent one, it also shifts the extrapersonal space to the one surrounding the distal tool. From an experiential viewpoint the outcome is simple: the subject experiences presence in the distal environment (telepresence).

Recently a series of different studies (Guterstam & Ehrsson, 2012; Slater, Perez-Marcos, Ehrsson, & Sanchez-Vives, 2009; Slater, Spanlang, Sanchez-Vives, & Blanke, 2010) using a second-order mediated technology – virtual reality - have demonstrated that it is possible to use it for inducing a body transfer (Embodiment). This is achieved by a spatio-temporal correspondence between multisensory feedbacks experienced by the user and the visual data related to a distal virtual body (avatar). This correspondence may be produced both by the association between touch and its visual correlate (seeing the avatar being touched and experiencing the touch simultaneously) and by experiencing the first person perspective of a life-sized virtual human body that appears to substitute the subject's own body. See also Chapters 2 and 4 for a broader discussion of this point.

1.4 From Presence to Social Presence

The concept of presence concerns the subject and his or her ability to act in the world: I am present in a real or virtual space if I manage to put my intentions into action with or without the support of tools. But how does the Self connect to the Other? To answer this question we will analyze the implications of the "mirror" neurons discovery which we mentioned at the beginning of the chapter.

These neurons, discovered in the ventral pre-motor cortex of apes (area F5), have, amongst other qualities, that of activating not only when the animal performs a given action, but also when the animal sees another animal – man or ape – performing the same action (Rizzolatti, Fadiga, Gallese, & Fogassi, 1996; Rizzolatti & Sinigaglia, 2006). Therefore, the individual who observes is able to put himself in the shoes of the actor: I am able to understand what another is doing because when I watch him I experience, completely intuitively, the same neuron activity as when *I* perform that action.

The result is the creation of neural representations which are shared on two levels (Gallagher & Jeannerod, 2002):
- On the one hand, execution and observation share the same neural substratum in one individual subject;
- On the other, when a subject observes another subject's action, the same representations are simultaneously active in the brains of both subjects.

This means that at neural level, the action performed and the action observed are codified in a multi-subjective format, which does not recognize actor or observer. This process is, however, effective if the subject is capable of distinguishing between an action performed and an action perceived. At the moment in which the subject is able, through presence, to distinguish between him or herself and another, "an I and an Other are created". The "Other similar to the Self" thus becomes, together with the Self, one of the two relevant elements which the organism is able to identify within its perceptive flow.

This suggests the existence of a second selective and adaptive mechanism, social presence, which enables the Self to identify and interact with Others by understanding their intentions. In other words, from an evolutionary point of view, social presence has three functions:

- To enable the subject to identify the Other and to attribute to him an ontological status – "the Other similar to the Self" – different from the other objects perceived,
- To allow interaction and communication through the understanding of the Other's intentions; from the computational viewpoint, it happens using the same approach used by Presence:
  - First, the agent recognizes a motor intention, and identify the actor as another intentional self (Other);
  - second, an efference copy of the motor command is fed to a forward dynamic model that generates a prediction of the consequences of performing this motor command (goal);
  - third, the predicted state is compared with the actual sensory feedback. Errors derived from the difference between the predicted state and the actual state (break) can be used to update the model and improve performance.
- To permit the evolution of the Self through the identification of *"optimal shared experiences" (Networked Flow)* and the incorporation of artifacts – physical and social – linked to them.

In summary, we can define social presence (Biocca, Harms, & Burgoon, 2003; Riva, 2008; Riva, Davide, & IJsselsteijn, 2003) as the sensation of "being with other selves" in a real or virtual environment, resulting from the ability to intuitively recognize Others'intentions in our surroundings (see also Chapters 5 and 6, this volume).

From the combined analysis of presence and social presence, it emerges that the point of contact between these two processes clearly lies in the *intentions* and their codification by means of *motor representations of action* (Knoblich & Flach, 2003):
- On the one hand, presence verifies the effective fulfillment (enaction) of the intention in action;
- On the other hand social presence permits the identification of the Other's intentions through the analysis of his/her actions.

But how do we structure and manage intentions? An important attempt to explain the structure of intentions has been made by the French researcher Elisabeth Pacherie (2008). The main assumptions of this model, known as the *"dynamic theory of intentions"* are the following:
- It does not make sense to consider an action as an individual mental act. Intentions are a dynamic structure arranged on a number of levels.
- This organization is hierarchically structured on three mutually inclusive levels:
  - Motor intentions (M-intentions);
  - Proximal intentions, situated in the present (P-intentions);
  - Distal intentions, directed towards the future (D-intentions).
- The relationship between these levels is one of inclusion and organization. Specifically, a distal intention (to build a house) is composed of a series of proximal

intentions (to lay the foundations, build the walls), which are themselves made up of a series of motor intentions.

1.5 The Evolutionary Role of Presence and Social Presence

In his book, "*Descartes' Error: Emotion, Reason, and the Human Brain*", the neuropsychologist Antonio Damasio identifies the sense of the self as the essential nucleus of the conscious, the result of both interaction and the relationships between the organism and the object (Damasio, 1994).

The origin of the sense of the self lies in the "*proto-self*" (Damasio, 1994), "a coherent collection of neural patterns which map second by second the state of the physical structure of the organism in its various dimensions" (p. 189). The proto-self's main task, of which the subject is not aware, is "positionality", that is, to identify organism's physical boundaries by verifying somatic functions.

Through the evolution of the proto-self, two other types of self successively emerge – the "*core self*" and the "*autobiographical self* "– which are at the basis of conscious experience. The core self can be described as a conscious representation of the present in which there are three elements: the object of which the subject is aware, the position of the subject's own body in relation to that object, and the relationship which is established between the two.

The transition from the core self to the autobiographical self is made possible through the use of language. By using language we can create a story, our story, in which we position and structure the different experiences which we have had. It is through the development and awareness of this story that the self becomes self-conscious, aware of itself.

Starting from this view, the hypothesis discussed here is that each level of the Self is associated to *a specific ability to differentiate between internal and external* which increases the control that the organism has over its own activities, thus increasing its chances of survival (Riva, 2009; Riva, Waterworth, & Waterworth, 2004; Riva et al., 2011). Furthermore, the close link between the levels of the Self and the three intentional levels described by the *Dynamic Theory of Intentions* presented by Pacherie (2006, 2008) enables us to associate each level to a specific intentional capacity and a level of presence and social presence (see *Table 1.1* for a summary of the presented model).

Table 1.1: The presence model

Concept	Definition
Presence	A selective and adaptive mechanism which allows the Self to define the boundaries of action by means of the distinction between "internal" and "external" within the sensory flow. The feeling of presence is the outcome an intuitive metacognitive process that allows us to control our actions through the comparison between intentions and perceptions. Although presence is a unitary feeling, on the process side it can be divided into three different layers/subprocesses, phylogenetically different, and strictly related to the evolution of self.
Proto Presence	The first subprocess of Presence is related to the emergence of proto-self: the intuitive perception of successfully differentiating the self from the external world through action. It depends on the level of perception-action coupling (Self vs. non Self).
Core Presence	The second subprocess of Presence is related to the emergence of core-self: the intuitive perception of successfully acting in the external world towards a present Object. It depends on the level of vividness (Self vs. Present External World).
Extended Presence	The third subprocess of Presence is related to the emergence of extended-self: the intuitive perception of successfully acting in the external world towards a possible Object. It depends on the level of relevance (Self vs. Possible External World).
Object	The person, condition, thing, or event at which an action is directed. An Object is a psychological representation, and therefore actions can be directed either at objects of the world (present Objects) or fictions, the future, and other forms of virtuality (possible Objects).
Social Presence	A selective and adaptive mechanism which allows the Self to identify and interact with Others by understanding their intentions. The feeling of social presence is the the outcome of an intuitive metacognitive process that allows us to understand the actions of an enacting Other through the comparison between his/her expected intentions and perceptions. Although social presence is a unitary feeling, on the process side it can be divided into three different layers/subprocesses, phylogenetically different, and strictly related to the evolution of self.
Other's Presence	The first subprocess of Social Presence is related to the ability of recognizing motor intentions in other individuals. This capacity allows the Self to recognize an intentional Other (the Other in opposition to the Self).
Interactive Presence	The second subprocess of Social Presence is related to the ability of recognizing motor and proximal intentions in other individuals. This capacity allows the Self to identify the Other whose intention is directed towards him (the Other towards the Self).

Continued Table 1.1: The presence model

Concept	Definition
Shared Presence	The third subprocess of Social Presence is related to the ability of recognizing motor, proximal and distal intentions in other individuals. This capacity allows the Self to identify Another whose intentions correspond to his/her own. (the Other like the Self).
Optimal Experiences	Specific individual (Flow) and social (Networked Flow) situations in which the individual experiences *the maximum feeling of presence.*
Flow	There are exceptional situations – e.g., a tennis player who goes to the right (proto presence) before the ball bounces on the court to swing a winning forehand ground stroke (core presence) on a second set-point at the Wimbledon final (extended presence) - in which the activity of the subject is characterized by a high level of presence in all the three different subprocesses (Maximal Presence). When this experience is associated with a positive emotional state, it constitutes a flow state.
Networked Flow	There are exceptional social situations in which a group of subjects in a liminality phase (a state of transition, in which the earlier *positive* condition is no longer present, and the future *positive* condition has not yet come into) experiences the maximum level of social presence (the feeling of sharing objectives and emotions with others) and the feeling of being able through the their collective action of exiting from liminality (maximum level of presence).

1.5.1 The Three Levels of Presence

Even if Presence is a unitary feeling, the recent neuropsychological research has shown that, on the process side, it can be divided in three different layers/subprocesses phylogenetically different, and strictly related to the evolution of Self:

- *Proto Presence* (Self vs. non Self – M-Intentions);
- *Core Presence* (Self vs. present external world – P-Intentions);
- *Extended Presence* (Self vs. possible/future worlds – D-Intentions).

In sum, presence allows the Self to evolve by extending the boundaries of its actions through the acquisition higher levels of intentional ability.

The first level of the self, the *proto-self,* corresponds to "*proto presence*" *(proprioceptive),* the ability to enact motor intentions by moving the body (the boundaries of the Self's actions are determined by the body). This is made possible by the Self's ability to distinguish between internal and external states. This happens through *perception-action coupling:* the more the organism is able to *correctly associate stimuli to movement in sensorial flow,* the better it is able to differentiate itself from its external surroundings and thus increase its chances of survival (the Self as opposed to the not-Self).

The second level of the self – the *core self* – corresponds to *"core presence" (perceptual),* the ability to enact proximal intentions through the identification of direct *affordances* (the boundaries of the Self's actions are determined by the perceived world). This is made possible by the Self's ability to separate and couple representations and perceptions, picking out those which are relevant. Within the experiential flow, the Self separates intentional information from the real object. The better the organism is able to distinguish between imagination and perception, planning and action, the greater its chances of survival will be.

However, the organism must also be able to analyze and identify the perceptions which correspond to the intentional information (*relevance*). The more the organism is able to successfully connect intentional information to real-world objects, the greater the likelihood of fulfilling its proximal intentions and thus the greater its chances of survival (the Self in relation to the present world). In general, there are two elements which allow this distinction to be made: *vividity* and *multi-sensoriality.* In fact, mental images are much less vivid than perceptions, and are also characterized by the predominant visual component. Coupling, on the other hand, takes place thanks to *recognizability:* the capacity to associate a real object to a given intention.

The third level of the self – the *autobiographical self* – corresponds to *"extended presence" (reflective),* the ability to enact distal intentions through the identification of indirect *affordances.* This is made possible thanks to the Self's ability to analyze representations and identify those which are relevant. The better the organism is able to separate itself from the present and *identify within its own representations those most relevant,* the greater are its chances of survival (the boundaries of the Self's are determined by possible/conceivable worlds).

Extended presence is also the element which allows for the subject's "*absence*", that is, *its presence in an exclusively mental activity.* During an experience of absence, such as thinking, day-dreaming or meditating, the subject tries to separate itself as much as possible from the outside world and to concentrate exclusively on its own mental processes (the self outside of its external surroundings). In general, the more the subject believes that mental activity is important for its "internality", the greater its attempts will be to isolate itself from the outside world.

What is the link between the three levels of presence? They are evolutionarily organized – from the lowest to the highest – but functionally separate. This means that, in the case of injuries which may impair the subject's ability to activate one of the three levels, the others will still be functional. For example, in the case of a neurological disorder called *autotopagnosia* – the inability to localize parts of the body – the subject loses its *proto presence.* This does not prevent the subject from continuing to experience core presence and extended presence.

The three levels of presence are linked by their *simultaneous influence on the actions of the subject*: the experience of the action changes according to the presence of the subject on each of the three levels. It is important to note that the subject is usually unaware of the role of the three levels of presence in determining the characteristics of his or her actions. However, the subject is evolutionarily programmed to *consciously understand the variations* between the three levels and if necessary, to modify an action in order to return to its initial state. If, during a virtual reality experience, my arm moves and suddenly comes into contact with a cable, I immediately become aware of the change at the level of proto presence and I shift my attention from my virtual reality experience to the cable which is impeding my movement (Spagnolli & Gamberini, 2002)

The same is true for the other levels. If the reality TV show the subject is watching becomes boring or upsetting, the subject becomes immediately aware of the variation in the level of extended presence, and can decide whether or not to pick up the remote control and change channel.

1.5.2 The Three Levels of Social Presence

The study of infants and the analysis of their ability of understanding and interacting with people (Meltzoff & Decety, 2003) suggest that also Social Presence, on the process side, includes three different layers/subprocesses phylogenetically different, but mutually inclusive (Riva, 2008):

- Other's Presence (Other vs the Self - M-Intentions);
- Interactive Presence (Other toward the Self – P-Intentions);
- Shared Presence (Other is like the Self - D-Intentions).

The first level of imitative skills – the ability to imitate a human being – corresponds to *"Other's Presence"*, the ability to recognize motor intentions, which allows the Self to recognize an intentional Other: the better the subject is able to *recognize within the sensorial flow the stimuli which relate to "another similar to the self"*, the better he is able to carry out an intention, and thus increas his chances of survival (the Other in opposition to the Self).

The second level of imitative skills – the ability to identify a human being who is imitating me – corresponds to *"Interactive Presence"*, the ability to recognize motor and proximal intentions which allows the Self to identify the Other whose intention is directed towards him: the better the subject is able to *recognize within the sensorial flow the intention direct towards him by "an Other similar to the self"*, the greater the chances of successfully carrying out an action, and therefore the greater the chances of survival (the Other towards the Self).

The third level of imitative skills – the ability to recognize the intentions and emotions of a human being – corresponds to *"Shared Presence"*, the ability to recognize motor, proximal and distal intentions, which enables the Self to identify Another whose intentions correspond to his own: the better the subject is able to *recognize within the sensorial flow an "Other similar to the self" with intentions the same as his own,* the better he will be able to successfully initiate collaborative interaction or communication, increasing his chances of survival (the Other like the Self).

Shared presence permits the subject to feel empathy, *the capacity to see oneself in another person, to get inside another's thoughts and state of mind.* During the experience of empathy, the subject separates himself from his own intentional and emotional state, and identifies with that of another person (the Other merges with the Self).

What is the link between the three levels of social presence? As with presence, the three levels are evolutionarily organized: from the lowest to the highest. However, unlike presence, the levels of social presence are not functionally separate but mutually inclusive. This leads to two consequences. The superior levels also include the inferior levels: if the subject is able to understand distal intentions (shared presence), he is also capable of understanding motor intentions (other's presence). At the same time, it is impossible to activate the higher levels of social presence if the lower levels are not activated first: if I am unable to understand a subject's proximal intentions (interactive presence) then I will not be able to understand his distal intentions (shared presence).

The three levels of social presence are linked by *simultaneous influences on the subject's capacity for social interaction:* the way in which the interaction is experienced changes depending on the level of social presence experienced by the subject. It is important to note that, as with presence, the subject is unaware of the role of social presence in determining the characteristics of his actions. He is, however, evolutionarily programmed to perceive the shift from one level of social presence to another in social interactions. Furthermore, if this shift offers a valuable opportunity, the subject can act to increase his level of social presence. If a girl starts staring at me at a party, I immediately become aware of the shift from other's presence (the girl is at the same party as me) to interactive presence (the girl is looking at me). If the girl is interesting, I can approach her and talk to her in order to understand her intentions: is she looking at me because she likes me or because I have a stain on my jacket?

1.6 From Theory to Practice: the Development of Better Interactive Technologies

At this point, a possible comment from the readers of the chapter is this one: interesting stuff, but how can it help me in developing better interactive technologies?

The first deductions which can be made from what has thus far been discussed, is the existence of *a link between presence and the effectiveness of an action*: the greater level of presence a subject experiences in an activity, the greater the organism's involvement in the activity will be, and this increases the probability of the activity ending well (the transformation of the intention into action).

This concept is particularly important when the subject carries out the activity by using a tool, including media. The use of a tool compels the subject to modify his action, forcing him to adapt himself to the tool. In this case, given equal conditions and skills, the greater efficacy of the activity when carried out using a tool is linked to the tool's ability to facilitate the subject in increasing his level of presence. We shall give an example to explain this concept.

Imagine that we have a computer and have to copy a file from a disc onto a USB stick. We have seen that *proto presence* constitutes the first level of presence, which concerns the level of coupling between movement and perception. This means that an activity in which it is easy to immediately identify the result of one's own movements is preferable to an activity in which this is not possible. For this reason, the subject, all things being equal, will tend to choose a program which facilitates the direct perception of movement – *I move the file by dragging it with the mouse* – as opposed to one which does not – *the instruction "copy name-of-file a: b:"*. Likewise, using the arrow key on the keyboard to copy the file is preferable to using an instruction, but worse than using the mouse.

During an activity we are obviously not influenced by only one level of presence, but by all three levels together. For example, when we are doing a distance-learning training course, interaction with the mouse is preferred to interaction with the keyboard (proto presence); the use of multimedia equipment is better than making use of a simple text (core presence); undertaking tasks linked to experience and to the interests of the project is preferable to carrying out abstract tasks (extended presence).

But what happens when we have to choose between activities or artifacts which differ within the different levels of presence? For example, how do users choose between a distance-learning training course with interesting modules but which uses only texts, and another which makes extensive use of multimedia but which addresses less interesting topics? In these situations, the level of presence which is evolutionarily superior prevails: first extended presence, followed by core and then proto presence. Users will therefore choose the course featuring interesting topics but which only uses text.

A second consequence of the considerations made in the preceding paragraphs, is the existence of certain *"optimal experiences", in which the individual experiences the maximum feeling of presence at each of the three levels*. This experience, when it is associated with a positive emotional state (it is also possible to experience the maximum feeling of presence in emotionally negative situations, such as during an escape) is defined as *"flow experience"* (Csikszentmihalyi, 1990, 1994). This state is characterized by a high level of concentration and participation in the activity, by the balance of the perception of the difficulties of the situation and the *challenge*, and personal *skills*, by the distortion of the sense of time (the internal clock slows down, whilst the external one speeds up), and by a natural interest in the process which produces a sense of pleasure and satisfaction. More, flow has been associated to creativity and emotional wellbeing (Csikszentmihalyi, 1997).

In our model, optimal presence in a mediated experience arises from an optimal combination of form and content, able to support the activity of the user. At the higher level of activity, optimal presence arises when the contents of extended consciousness are aligned with the other layers of the self, and attention is directed to a currently present external world (Waterworth & Waterworth, 2006). However, this is a difficult task to achieve for a developer. He/She has to provide as much immersion as possible, integrating proto (spatial) and core (sensory) presence. To integrate extended presence, the events and entities experienced in the interactive system must have significance for the participant. The form must provide the means for a convincing bodily and perceptual illusion, but the content should be integrated with (and so attract attention to) the form for the illusion of mediated presence to happen convincingly.

Similar considerations can also be made concerning the concept of social presence.

First, there is a link between presence and efficacy of interaction: *the more often that the organism experiences a high level of social presence during interaction, the greater his ability to understand the other, and therefore the chances of the interaction being successful increase.*

Second, there is also a specific optimal experience for social presence – *"networked flow"* – the result of the association between (Gaggioli, Milani, Mazzoni, & Riva, 2011, 2013):

- *The maximum level of social presence:* the feeling of sharing objectives and emotions with others;
- *The group members' perception of being in a phase of liminality:* a state of transition, of being "about to...", in which the earlier *positive* condition is no longer present, and the future *positive* condition has not yet come into being.
- *The shared recognition of a possible common strategy for exiting from liminality:* everybody working towards a shared objective, which the group can change.
- *The maximum level of presence:* the feeling of being able, through the personal involvement in the group, of successfully transforming intentions – both individual and collective - in actions.

In this case, the maximum level of presence and social presence permits the subject to increase their self-efficacy and to find the motivation for change within the shared group activity.

This concept shares a number of similarities with the concept of the "nascent state" proposed by Alberoni. Subjects who go through this have a strange experience which causes them to develop an alternative interpretation of existence (Alberoni, 1977). *"Nascent state is an exploration of the boundaries of the possible, given a certain type of social system, with the goal of maximizing what is realizable within that experience and solidarity for oneself and others in that moment in time. The group of men amongst whom a nascent state is created will always attempt to construct a way of living which is completely different from the everyday institutional norm" (p. 31).* Alberoni's ideas highlight how the simultaneous union between high levels of presence and social presence make *networked flow* a *state of transition* which constitutes the specific conditions for social transformation. It is at this moment that the subjective intention becomes collective (*we-intention).*

This model provides relevant guidelines also to developers of collaborative mediated experiences (Graffigna, Barello, & Riva, 2013a; Riva, Banos, Botella, Wiederhold, & Gaggioli, 2012):

First, the more the communicative task is complex, the more are the intentional levels that have to be supported by the mediated experience to induce a high level of presence: it is difficult to induce social presence during complex cooperative tasks.

Second, the best avatars are those whom can express fully the intentions of the user: it is not critical to have a human-like avatar. Is more important to have the possibility to express intentions through them. According to communication and cognitive psychology, nonverbal cues (facial expressions and body movements) are critical to provide intentional cues.

Finally, we have the highest level of Social Presence when the environment is able to support the full intentional chain of the Other: if the Other is not able to express and enact fully his/her intentions through the medium the level of Social Presence will be low.

In conclusion the model offers us two general guidelines for developing optimal presence in a mediated interactive/collaborative experience:

- *To induce optimal presence, a mediated experience has to include/support recognition of the specific purposes of the users.* If the experience or the subjects involved are not able to identify the specific objectives of all the users they will fail in supporting his/her action, reducing the level of presence.
- *To induce optimal presence, a mediated experience has to identify and support the specific tools that mediate the activity of the users.* Most of the activity of the users is mediated by physical and social artifacts. The experience has to identify and embed in the system features to support the individual and shared actions of the users effectively.

Another important consequence of this model is that we can develop technologies – "Positive Technologies" - that are able to improve the quality of our personal experience by enhancing the level of presence and social presence experienced interacting with them (Graffigna, Barello, & Riva, 2013b; Graffigna, Barello, Wiederhold, Bosio, & Riva, 2013; Riva, 2012). Specifically, presence can be used to manipulate the features of an interactive experience in three separate but related ways (Graffigna, Barello, et al., 2013a; Riva et al., 2012):

- *By structuring it* using a goal, rules and a feedback system – *Extended Presence and Shared Presence* (McGonigal, 2011). The goal provides subjects with a sense of

purpose focusing attention and orienting his/her participation in the experience. The rules, by removing or limiting the obvious ways of getting to the goal, push subjects to see the experience in a different way. The feedback system tells players how close they are to achieving the goal and provides motivation to keep trying.
- *By augmenting it* to achieve multimodal and mixed experiences – *Core Presence*. Technology allows multisensory experiences in which content and its interaction is offered through more than one of the senses. It is even possible to use technology to overlay virtual objects onto real scenes (Rosenblum, 2000).
- *By replacing it* with a synthetic one – *Proto Presence*. Using VR it is possible to simulate physical presence in a synthetic world that reacts to the action of the subject as if he/she was really there. More, the replacement possibilities offered by technology even extend to the induction of an illusion of ownership over a virtual arm or a virtual body (Slater et al., 2010).

1.7 Conclusion to Chapter 1

The chapter presented the experience of presence and social presence as two neuropsychological phenomena, evolved from the interplay of our biological and cultural inheritance, whose goal is the enaction of the volition of the Self (Presence) and the understanding of the volition of the Other (Social Presence):
- "Presence" is defined as the non-mediated (intutive) perception of successfully transforming intentions in action (enaction) within an external world;
- "Social Presence" is defined as the intuitve perception of an intentional Other (I can recognize his/her intentions) within an external world.

Both Presence and Social Presence evolve in time, and their evolution is strictly related to the three-stage model of the ontogenesis of Self introduced by Damasio (Proto-Self, Core Self, Autobiographical Self). More, we can identify higher levels of Presence and Social Presence associated to higher levels of intentional granularity: the more is the complexity of the expressed and recognized intentions, the more is the level of Presence and Social Presence experienced by the Self.

How does this vision can help the development of effective interactive technologies? Here we suggested that the experience of the highest level of presence and social presence is associated to specific optimal experiences – flow and networked flow – that allow better individual and social activities. This suggests the development of optimal technologies – "Positive Technologies" - that are able to improve the quality of our personal experience by enhancing the level of presence and social presence experienced interacting with them.

Obviously, this chapter has its limitations: the framework here introduced is still in progress and some of the claims presented require additional theoretical work and an empirical confirmation. Nevertheless, quite independently of the intricacies of terminology and conceptualizations, we hope that the Presence framework discussed in these pages will help to disentangle the variety of claims and theories that characterizes interactivity and intersubjectivity research.

References

Biocca, F., Harms, C., & Burgoon, J.K. (2003). Toward a more robust theory and measure of social presence: Review and suggested criteria. *Presence: Teleoperators, and Virtual Environments, 12(5)*, 456-480.

Csikszentmihalyi, M. (1990). *Flow: The psychology of optimal experience.* New York: HarperCollins.

Csikszentmihalyi, M. (1994). *The evolving self.* New York: Harper Perennial.

Csikszentmihalyi, M. (1997). *Creativity: Flow and the Psychology of Discovery and Invention.* New York: Harper Perennial.

Damasio, A. (1994). *Decartes' error: Emotion, reason, and the brain.* New York: Grosset/Putnam.

Farnè, A., Bonifazi, S., & Làdavas, E. (2005). The role played by tool-use and tool-length on the Plastic Elongation of peri-hand space: a single case study *Cognitive Neuropsychology, 22(3-4)*, 408-418.

Farné, A., Serino, A., & Làdavas, E. (2007). Dynamic size-change of perihand space following tool-use: Determinants and spatial characteristics revealed through cross-modal extinction. *Cortex, 43*, 436-443.

Frith, U., & de Vignemont, F. (2005). Egocentrism, allocentrism, and Asperger syndrome. *Consciousness and cognition, 14(4)*, 719-738.

Gaggioli, A., Milani, L., Mazzoni, E., & Riva, G. (2011). Networked Flow: A Framework for Understanding the Dynamics of Creative Collaboration in Educational and Training Settings. *The Open Education Journal, 4*(Suppl 2:M2), 107-115.

Gaggioli, A., Milani, L., Mazzoni, E., & Riva, G. (2013). *Networked Flow: Towards an Understanding of Creative Networks.* Dordrecht: Springer.

Gallagher, R., & Jeannerod, M. (2002). From action to interaction. *Journal of Consciousness Studies, 9*, 3-26.

Graffigna, G., Barello, S., & Riva, G. (2013a). How to make health information technology effective: the challenge of patient engagement. *Archives of physical medicine and rehabilitation, 94(10)*, 2034-2035.

Graffigna, G., Barello, S., & Riva, G. (2013b). Technologies for patient engagement. *Health affairs, 32*(6), 1172.

Graffigna, G., Barello, S., Wiederhold, B. K., Bosio, A. C., & Riva, G. (2013). Positive technology as a driver for health engagement. *Stud Health Technol Inform, 191*, 9-17.

Guterstam, A., & Ehrsson, H. H. (2012). Disowning one‘s seen real body during an out-of-body illusion. *Consciousness and cognition, 21(2)*, 1037-1042.

Heeter, C. (1992). Being There: The subjective experience of presence. *Presence: Teleoperators and Virtual Environments, 1(2)*, 262-271.

Held, R.M., & Durlach, N.I. (1992). Telepresence. *Presence, Teleoperators, and Virtual Environments, 1(1)*, 109-112.

Iriki, A., Tanaka, M., & Iwamura, Y. (1996). Coding of modified body schema during tool use by macaque postcentral neurones. *Neuroreport, 7(14)*, 2325-2330.

Iriki, A., Tanaka, M., Obayashi, S., & Iwamura, Y. (2001). Self-images in the video monitor coded by monkey intraparietal neurons. *Neuroscience Research, 40(2)*, 163-173.

Jäncke, L., Cheetham, M:, & Baumgartner, T. (2009). Virtual Reality and the Role of the Prefrontal Cortex in Adults and Children. *Front Neurosci, 3(1)*, 52-59.

Knoblich, G., & Flach, R. (2003). Action identity: Evidence from self-recognition, prediction, and coordination. *Consciousness and cognition, 12*, 620-632.
Knoblich, G., Thornton, I., Grosjean, M., & Shiffrar, M. (Eds.). (2005). *Human Body Perception from the Inside Out.* New York: Oxford University Press.
Lombard, M., & Ditton, T. (1997). At the heart of it all: The concept of presence. *Journal of Computer Mediated-Communication [On-line], 3(2)*, Available: http://www.ascusc.org/jcmc/vol3/issue2/lombard.html.
Longo, M.R., Azañón, L., & Haggard, P. (2010). More than skin deep: Body representation beyond primary somatosensory cortex. *Neuropsychologia, 48*, 655-668.
Matelli, M., & Luppino, G. (2001). Parietofrontal circuits for action and space perception in the macaque monkey. *Neuroimage, 14*(1 Pt 2), S27-32.
McGonigal, J. (2011). *Reality Is Broken. Why games make us better and how they can change the world.* New York: The Penguin Press.
Meltzoff, A.N., & Decety, J. (2003). What imitation tells us about social cognition: a rapprochement between developmental psychology and cognitive neuroscience. *Philosophical Transactions of the Royal Society, 358*, 491-500.
Merriam-Webster. (2010). *The Merriam-Webster Dictionary*. Springfield, MA: Merriam-Webster.
Pacherie, E. (2006). Toward a dynamic theory of intentions. In S. Pockett, W. P. Banks & S. Gallagher (Eds.), *Does consciousness cause behavior?* (pp. 145-167). Cambridge, MA: MIT Press.
Pacherie, E. (2008). The phenomenology of action: A conceptual framework. *Cognition, 107(1)*, 179-217.
Previc, F.H. (1998). The neuropsychology of 3-D space. *Psychological Bulletin, 124(2)*, 123-164.
Riva, G. (2007). Virtual Reality and Telepresence. *Science, 318*(5854), 1240-1242.
Riva, G. (2008). Enacting Interactivity: The Role of Presence. In F. Morganti, A. Carassa & G. Riva (Eds.), *Enacting Intersubjectivity: A cognitive and social perspective on the study of interactions* (pp. 97-114). Amsterdam: IOS Press: Online: http://www.emergingcommunication.com/volume10.html.
Riva, G. (2009). Is presence a technology issue? Some insights from cognitive sciences *Virtual Reality, 13(3)*, 59-69.
Riva, G. (2012). What is Positive Technology and its impact on CyberPsychology. *Stud Health Technol Inform, 181*, 37-41.
Riva, G., Banos, R. M., Botella, C., Wiederhold, B. K., & Gaggioli, A. (2012). Positive technology: using interactive technologies to promote positive functioning. *Cyberpsychology, behavior and social networking, 15(2)*, 69-77.
Riva, G., Davide, F., & IJsselsteijn, W.A. (Eds.). (2003). *Being There: Concepts, effects and measurements of user presence in synthetic environments*. Amsterdam: Ios Press.
Riva, G., & Mantovani, F. (2012). From the body to the tools and back: a general framework for presence in mediated interactions. *Interacting with Computers, 24(4)*, 203-210.
Riva, G., Waterworth, J.A., & Waterworth, E.L. (2004). The Layers of Presence: a bio-cultural approach to understanding presence in natural and mediated environments. *Cyberpsychology & Behavior, 7(4)*, 405-419.
Riva, G., Waterworth, J.A., Waterworth, E.L., & Mantovani, F. (2011). From intention to action: The role of presence. *New Ideas in Psychology, 29(1)*, 24-37.
Rizzolatti, G., Fadiga, L., Gallese, V., & Fogassi, L. (1996). Premotor cortex and the recognition of motor actions. *Cognitive Brain Research, 3*, 131-141.
Rizzolatti, G., & Sinigaglia, C. (2006). *So quel che fai. Il cervello che agisce e i neuroni specchio.* Milano: Raffaello Cortina.
Rosenblum, L. (2000). Virtual and Augmented Reality 2020. *IEEE Computer Graphics and Applications, 20(1)*, 38-39.

Slater, M., Perez-Marcos, D., Ehrsson, H. H., & Sanchez-Vives, M. V. (2009). Inducing illusory ownership of a virtual body. *Front Neurosci, 3(2),* 214-220.

Slater, M., Spanlang, B., Sanchez-Vives, M. V., & Blanke, O. (2010). First person experience of body transfer in virtual reality. *PLoS One, 5(5),* e10564.

Spagnolli, A., & Gamberini, L. (2002, 9-11 October). *Immersion/Emersion: Presence in hybrid environments.* Paper presented at the Presence 2002: Fifth Annual International Workshop, Porto, Portugal.

Spagnolli, A., & Gamberini, L. (2005). A Place for Presence. Understanding the Human Involvement in Mediated Interactive Environments. *PsychNology Journal, 3(1),* 6-15.

Waterworth, J.A., & Waterworth, E.L. (2006). Presence as a Dimension of Communication: Context of Use and the Person. In G. Riva, M. T. Anguera, B. K. Wiederhold & F. Mantovani (Eds.), *From Communication to Presence: Cognition, Emotions and Culture towards the Ultimate Communicative Experience* (pp. 80-95). Amsterdam: IOS Press.

Waterworth, J.A., Waterworth, E.L., Mantovani, F., & Riva, G. (2010). On Feeling (the) Present: An evolutionary account of the sense of presence in physical and electronically-mediated environments. *Journal of Consciousness Studies, 17(1-2),* 167-178.

Waterworth, J.A., Waterworth, E.L., Mantovani, F., & Riva, G. (2012). Special Issue: Presence and Interaction. *Interacting with Computers, 24(4),* 190-192.

Wilson, M., & Knoblich, G. (2005). The case for motor involvement in perceiving conspecifics. *Psychological Bulletin, 131*(3), 460-473.

Wirth, Werner, Hartmann, Tilo, Bocking, Saskia, Vorderer, Peter, Klimmt, Christoph, Schramm, Holger, Jancke, Petra. (2007). A Process Model of the Formation of Spatial Presence Experiences. *Media Psychology, 9(3),* 493-525.

2 Altered, Expanded and Distributed Embodiment: the Three Stages of Interactive Presence

John A. Waterworth and Eva Lindh Waterworth

Abstract: This conceptual chapter outlines three stages in the development of interactive presence, and outlines some possibilities and challenges raised by each, and by their combination. The first stage, presence via altered embodiment, refers to the way technology allows us to experience the world with modified or enhanced senses. The second stage, via expanded embodiment, refers to technology pushing the envelope of the mental body in which one feels present, out beyond the physical body. Finally, distributed embodiment refers to how the sense of being present in the world can be separated from that of ownership of a particular body, through the development of new approaches to deploying the technologies of virtual realization. We suggest that presence is the yardstick of embodiment from an experiential perspective. If you cannot feel presence, you are not embodied in the world.

Keywords: Embodiment; Perception; Augmented Reality; Virtual Reality; Non-mediation.

2.1 Introduction to Chapter 2: Presence and Three Categories of Embodiment

We define presence as the feeling of being bodily located in a perceived external world. This definition applies to both unmediated and mediated presence. Experienced variations in the strength of this feeling provide vital information to the organism in its struggle for survival (see Waterworth et al., 2010 for more details). A useful definition of presence must have implications for what is not presence (Floridi, 2004) and we have previously termed this "absence", a state of absorption in the internal world of the mind detached from the current perceptual flow (Waterworth & Waterworth 2001, 2003). Our view of presence is thus closely related to embodiment in the external world and to attention. Indeed, we see the possibility to feel present (in the present time, in a present place) as a defining characteristic of embodiment. In the same way, the possibility to experience presence in an external reality mediated by technology is a defining characteristic of embodiment in interactive media.

When we feel present in the physical world, we are naturally embodied as the human beings we are. We have a certain kind of body, acting according to certain perceptual and motor capacities that allow us to move and act in the world. We also have a sense of our own bodies, as part of our self-consciousness, which may be more or less salient at a given time. But experiencing presence is not the same thing as being embodied. When we experience presence our attention is directed towards the world in which we find ourselves. Often we are attending to something else, such as thoughts, memories or plans, and then we do not feel much presence, we are mentally absent from the current world around us.

We are seldom very aware of "the technology" making possible our experience of being in the world unless there is something wrong with it, such as when we feel ill or are injured. Rather, the human bodily "technology" delivers the possibility of an experience of being present as a self, located in a body, and surrounded by a world that is not part of us - but only when we attend to that world.

In the same way, mediated presence is possible only via technology that we are not currently aware of as having that role (Biocca, 1997; IJsselsteijn, 2005), giving us a perceptual "illusion of non-mediation" (Lombard and Ditton, 1997) – which is a popular definition of presence. In that case, our attention may be directed to the present mediated reality in which we have (at least to some extent) the illusion of being physically located. In the cinema, for example, if we are highly aware of the projector, the sound system, the seating, and so on, we are unlikely to feel much sense of presence in the movie we are watching. Instead, the physical world of the theatre will be where we experience being present.

The experience of presence in a computer-mediated environment is also often a function of the possibilities for direct action in that world, in the same way that feeling present in the physical world is grounded in perception and bodily action. Unless we can act in a world (whether physical, virtual, or a mixture of both) we will not feel ourselves to be greatly present in it. When we act in mediated worlds, we may interact through different degrees and forms of embodiment and this has implications for the extent to which we can potentially feel present in the world (Haans & IJsselsteijn, 2012). We suggest that in principle we can understand when and how some technologies become embodied and others do not by examining the strength and nature of our feelings of presence in the world the technology creates or mediates.

The three categories of embodiment we will describe in the rest of the chapter represent progressive stages in the design of interactive presence. They are key concepts for understanding possible ways in which designed interactive experiences affect and will continue to change our experience of the world and of our own bodies in the future. They are stages both in a progressive sense and in terms of their distance from the physical body.

The first approach, presence via altered embodiment, refers to the way technology allows us to experience the world with modified or enhanced senses. If one hears (what would naturally be experienced as) sights and looks at (what would naturally be experienced as) sounds, what becomes of one's sense of being present in the world, of one's bodily relation to it? The second approach, via expanded embodiment, refers to technology pushing the envelope of the mental body in which one feels present, out beyond the physical body. This involves the incorporation of information technology as part of the self, implying a change in the boundary between the self and the non-self (the other) that constitutes the world around one. Finally, distributed embodiment refers to how the sense of being present in the world can be separated from that of ownership of a particular body, through the development of relatively new approaches to deploying the technologies of virtual realization.

In the following sections, each of these three categories of interactive presence is described, followed by a consideration of various possibilities and challenges raised by them, and by their combination.

2.2 Altered Embodiment: Changing Senses, Changing the World

Don Idhe (1990) distinguished between an embodiment relation between a person and a technological artefact and a hermeneutic relation. In the former, the technology becomes embodied – as if part of the user's body – and perception is through the technology, which itself is essentially transparent. In the latter, in contrast, the user must interpret a more abstract representation of the information the technology provides. For us, Ihde's embodiment relation is a clear example of altered embodiment, which is characterized by a situation whereby my viewpoint is located in my physical body as normal, but I have changed perception, so that my sense of presence in the world around my body is potentially altered in some way and the technology mediates a world of which it is not perceived to be a part.

Altered embodiment is often an intended or unintended aspect of interacting with digital technology. Virtual Reality (VR) can, in some circumstances, achieve a kind of "sensory rearrangement" resulting in modified experiences of one's own body (Biocca and Rolland 1998; Castiello et al. 2004; Normand et al. 2011; Riva 1998; Riva et al. 2011). In addition, altered embodiment can be seen as part of a general trend in the way many computer applications are designed: as perceptual tools, rather than cognitive artefacts (Norman, 1993). Waterworth (1997) refers to the potential of "synaesthetic media" – computer applications that provide an experience of information that is usually perceived in one form in a radically different form – to support enhanced creativity through new ways of perceiving information (see also Waterworth, 2003).

When the idea of synaesthetic media is applied to a body functioning normally in the physical world, technology becomes a perceptual transducer producing a radically altered state of embodiment in the world. As an example, imagine how it would feel to have your senses rewired. This is the experience of wearing the Reality Helmet (Waterworth and Fällman, 2003), a wearable computerised system developed with the purpose of providing its users with altered interactive experiences of physical reality. It consists of a custom-made helmet that the user wears, and computational equipment placed in a custom built backpack, which allows a high degree of mobility for its wearer (*Figure 2.1*). The eyes and ears are completely covered, so that users become audio-visually isolated from the environment, while the other senses are not interfered with. A digital video camera and stereo microphones are mounted on the outside of the helmet, while inside there are a pair of small visual displays and

Figure 2.1: The Physical Set-up of the Reality Helmet

headphones. Through computer signal processing, the user's perceptual experience is transformed by providing a real-time visualization of the auditory environment in which the wearer is situated and, likewise, a landscape of sound generated from digital video input. The user sees what she would normally hear, and hears what she would normally see.

Applications such as the Reality Helmet challenge the argument that degree of presence is a simple function of the level of subjective realism (see also Bouchard et al., 2012), at least in the normal sense of the word. A user trying to navigate the physical world while wearing the helmet will feel highly present, because almost all her attention will be directed towards perceptual information – much of which will be provided to her via the helmet and associated technology. Navigation of the world is not easy, because of the novelty of this form of perception. But the technology does effectively become part of the body – an altered body with changed senses applied to the physical world.

In altering the nature of embodiment, the form of the world is also changed. We naturally take for granted that the world has the form we normally perceive it to have, even though we may know that the senses we have are different from the senses other animals have, and that their perceptions of the world will be different from our own. The physical world exists and has real content – this is the actual environment in which organisms strive to survive – but its form is a matter of perception. Evolutionary adaptation results in forms of perception for particular types of organism (people, bats, cockroaches) that have tended to help them survive over many generations. Through the technical mediation that characterises altered embodiment, we can now choose other forms – of perception and therefore of the world – that may help us to function in the rapidly changing mediated world we humans now inhabit.

The Reality Helmet usefully exemplifies the notion of presence through altered embodiment and is unusual, possibly unique in the way two major senses are 'reversed' to completely alter how external reality is perceived. But there are many other examples of the related idea of sensory substitution (e.g., Bach-y-Rita & Kercel, 2003 is a well-known example), most commonly developed as assistive technology for those with some sensory disability such as blindness. "The vOICe" (The vOICe, 2012) is a recent system providing "augmented reality for the totally blind". Its main functionality is to convert video camera images into sound to enable the blind to navigate the world (and other information) by hearing instead of seeing.

Altered embodiment is the first stage of interactive presence. When our embodiment is altered and we feel present in the physical world that surrounds the body, our perceptions of that world are radically changed. At the same time, when this is achieved to a high degree, we experience a highly effective perceptual illusion of non-mediation, even though the world is dramatically changed for us relative to our everyday experience.

2.3 Expanded Embodiment: Embodiment without a Body?

Some degree of expanded embodiment accompanies mediated presence as the term is commonly understood (Bracken & Skalski, 2010). This is most clear in a VR environment where the actual physical surroundings are shielded from the user as far as possible – to avoid distraction away from the virtual world. These distractions have been termed "breaks in presence" (Slater & Steed, 2000) but are actually shifts of presence from the virtual world to in the physical world.

As with our sense of presence in the physical world, a first-person perspective is often a key ingredient in evoking strong presence in media. This is the norm in 'classical' virtual reality, where we view the mediated world as if embodied there ourselves (to some degree) with normal senses and with a first person perspective on things. We move our physical head and the virtual view changes accordingly; we move our physical arms and hands and we see a representation of these body parts depicted as if they were co-located with the internal image we have of our physical body.

Expanded embodiment brings with it the possibility for presence in a mediated world, experienced as a more or less convincing perceptual "illusion of non-mediation" (Lombard & Ditton 1997). This might be a fictional world, such as an immersive VR game, or the convincing experience of being in another physical place – the original goal of telepresence (Minsky, 1980). Presence mediated in this way is the feeling of being embodied in a non-physically-present external world, in the realization of which technology plays an active and direct role. The more the technology disappears from a person's attention and becomes experientially part of the self, the higher the level of presence through expanded embodiment. When this kind of VR realisation is technically done well, there is no conflict between the mediated reality and the user's body schema or body image.

We will not discuss this variety of mediated presence further here, which is not the main focus of this chapter and is the topic of several chapters in this volume (see especially Chapter 1 by Riva and Mantovani). The reader is also referred to our earlier publications on this topic, in particular Waterworth & Waterworth (2001), Riva et al. (2004), and Waterworth et al. (2010). In the rest of this section, we take the opportunity to discuss other candidates for realising presence through a different form of expanded embodiment.

As already stated, we consider mediated presence to be basically an interactive perceptual illusion (Waterworth & Waterworth, 2003; Waterworth et al. 2010). It involves more than just perception and action, since high levels of presence cannot be maintained without intellectual and/or emotional engagement, but perception of an apparently real interactive environment surrounding the self is its core. Perception as a process results in hypotheses about what things exist in the immediate environment and what is happening (Gregory 1997), experienced as those things and events. Virtual reality, especially high quality and fully immersive VR with rich interactivity, fools the brain into perceiving that the body is somewhere it physically is not. This is why VR can have such powerful effects on the perceiver (Waterworth et al. 2010).

But high quality VR is expensive and cumbersome and requires that the person who is the perceiver to have normal abilities to act in the world, making it unusable by people who cannot move their bodies in normal ways – such as paraplegics. This latter consideration has helped to drive a line of research and development aimed at achieving direct brain-computer interaction (BCI), whereby a user can interact with a virtual world without moving body parts. Instead, brain activity is captured and interpreted by the computer to carry out intended actions in virtual space. BCI has been successful (e.g., Leeb et al. 2007), but the level of presence achieved is relatively low, as indicated by the significant effort of carrying out actions in the world. A degree of expanded embodiment is achieved however, and motivated users can learn to produce reliably recognised patterns of electrical activity in their brains, sufficient to carry out their intended actions successfully (Hochberg et al. 2006).

In the other direction, computer-brain interaction (CBI) seeks to sidestep perception by presenting a virtual world directly to the brain, by stimulating it with magnetic fields - a technique known as Transcranial Magnetic Stimulation (TMS). The theory is that if this is done in the right way at the correct locations, the necessary electrical activity can be induced in the brain corresponding to the required perceptions of the virtual world. TMS has also been used in psychotherapy in the treatment of neurological and psychiatric disorders, such as depression and auditory hallucinations, but the evidence for its effectiveness is weak (Slotema et al. 2010). Interestingly, TMS has become notorious because of its ability to induce a feeling of the presence of another being in the vicinity of the observer (Persinger et al. 2010). Sometimes this is experienced as a divine presence, sometimes a malevolent one, and sometimes as distortions and extensions of the observer's body, while in some studies, an absence of reliable effect has been reported (e.g., Larsson et al. 2005).

In summary, feelings of embodiment can be produced through BCI and CBI, without engaging the bodily systems of action and perception. But these are relatively weak via BCI, because of the effort of action in the virtual world. With CBI, presence effects can be experienced, but may be highly variable or non-existent. In the some cases at least, they produce effects resembling our third step in interactive presence, distributed embodiment.

2.4 Distributed Embodiment: That's Me Over There!

According to Metzinger (2006) there are three distinguishable aspects of human embodiment in the world. Like all animals, we are a body with certain physical characteristics and so have what Metzinger terms first-order embodiment. And like all but the simplest animals, we also have associated and integrated perceptual and motor systems that allow our bodies to function effectively in the world, often without the need for attention or even conscious supervision. This 'body schema' comprises Metzinger's second-order embodiment. The third order of embodiment is the 'body image', the mental representation we have of our own bodies and which, it is said, few animals possess.

The sense of what is self and what is not is actually quite flexible, and may be altered to extend beyond the reality of the biological body (e.g., Normand et al. 2009). Some technology can change the boundary of the body, by becoming perceptually part of the self – the blind man's stick is the classic example from phenomenology (Merleau-Ponty 1962) – when it is incorporated into the body schema. When this happens, it is as if the technology were functionally part of the body. When using the technology, it is as if the world starts where the tool ends. The technology is effectively part of the body during use, not of the world in which the body acts.

When we are aware of being in that external world and are not aware of the technology mediating our experience, this produces a feeling of presence through a perceptual "illusion of non-mediation" (Lombard and Ditton, 1997). Haans & IJsselsteijn (2012) consider third-order embodiment to be necessary for presence, but this is only the case when there is a conflict between the mediated view of the body and the body image of the perceiver. When this happens, the relevant mediating body extension becomes an object in the world rather than an integral part of the self. In contrast, in classic perceptual effects such as 'the rubber hand illusion' (Botvinick & Cohen 1998), the mediated body part (the rubber hand) is integrated with the viewer's body image, to dramatic effect. This and similar effects have been reproduced successfully in virtual reality and mixed reality situations (IJsselsteijn et al. 2006: Holmes N., & C. Spence. 2007, Slater et al. 2008).

Distributed embodiment goes beyond these cases, by separating the observer from the observed body. By this, we do not refer to the possibility merely to observe oneself as a controllable avatar in a virtual world, even though the characteristics of a represented avatar may have a significant effect on self-perception and behaviour (e.g., the Proteus Effect; Yee & Bailenson, 2007). An avatar may differ completely from one's own appearance, and even from the way one's actions are mapped onto the bodily responses of the avatar (for detailed coverage of this topic see see Chapter 5 in this volume, by Won et al.).

What we call distributed embodiment is experientially very similar to naturally occurring out-of-the-body experiences (Blackmore, 1984). In these we may feel present, while at the same time observing our bodies from a "disembodied" viewpoint (see *Figure 2.2*). These are relatively rare in nature, and poorly understood, so that they often connote something supernatural or mystical. The idea of distributed embodiment is stranger and harder to grasp than the other steps in interactive presence that we have discussed, because it is a contradictory state arising from conditions that – as far as the perceiving organism is concerned – should not be possible.

It is already possible to produce the feeling of being in a virtual body that is also experienced as remotely located, separated from our own body (see also Chapter 4 for a broader discussion). Simple technology has been used in this way to produce something similar to out-of the-body experiences for several years (e.g., Ehrsson 2007; Lenggenhager et al. 2007, Petkova and Ehrsson 2008). This is achieved by combining

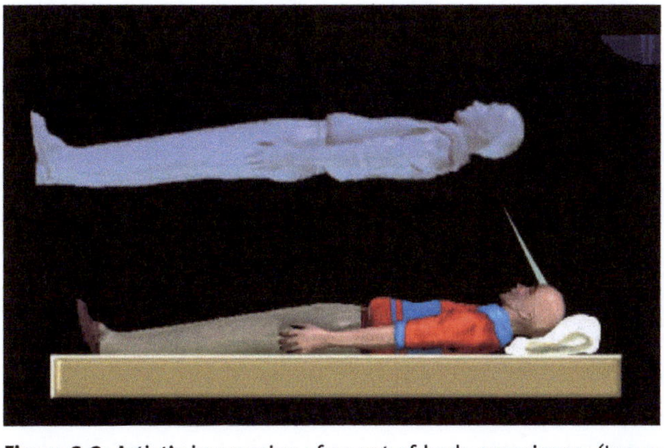

Figure 2.2: Artist's impression of an out-of-body experience. (Image in the public domain)

tactile and visual stimulation of the observer with corresponding and synchronised displays of the observed body apparently experiencing matching stimulation. As Petkova and Ehrsson report:

Manipulation of the visual perspective, in combination with the receipt of correlated multi-sensory information from the body was sufficient to trigger the illusion that another person's body or an artificial body was one's own. This effect was so strong that people could experience being in another person's body when facing their own body and shaking hands with it. Our results are of fundamental importance because they identify the perceptual processes that produce the feeling of ownership of one's body. (Petkova and Ehrsson 2008, from the abstract)

In these experiments, observers perceive representations of themselves from an external viewpoint while simultaneously experiencing presence as the observed person. The distant body may look like one's normal body, or like someone else. If the latter, the observer would feel present in that person's body, an effect that has already been confirmed through physiologic responses indicating appropriate emotional changes in the observer (see New Scientist 2010; Slater et al. 2010). Ehrsson & Petkova (2008) suggest that it can be difficult to distinguish actual body transference from more cognitive identification with a representation of their body. But this is a familiar problem (for example in interpreting presence questionnaire responses). In principle, comparison of measures of presence taken on multiple dimensions would enable the two to be distinguished.

2.5 Our Future Embodiment(s): Challenges and Possibilities

Many existing computing applications can be viewed as synaesthetic media; they are too numerous and too familiar to be reviewed in detail here. Obvious examples include programs that take an input – such as a stream of music – and turn it into an output in another form – such as a dynamic visual display of the amplitude of various frequency bands. The point is that almost any computer-produced visualization, sonification, haptic or other display that presents information through a realization form other than the original can be conceived of as a synaesthetic medium. But most of these do not provide altered embodiment, because the experience is not integrated with that of the surrounding environment.

Whenever computer-based information is blended with the perception of the surrounding physical world, as in augmented reality this may become integrated into a new form of altered embodiment. But that requires that the augmentation of the physical with the virtual be carried out in such a way that the user has the potential to feel present. Given the clear popularity of mobility and social connectivity, it seems that presence will increasingly be experienced through attention to an external world in which the physical and the virtual are somehow blended (see also Benyon, 2012; Hoshi, Öberg and Nyberg, 2011). This trend is presaged by developments such as Google Glass (2013). For this to work in practice, a major challenge is to make media devices sensitive to the situational context of their use, and the state of their users. Presence levels could in principle then be dynamically adjustable to maintain optimal functioning in an unfolding blended reality stream. If this can be achieved, then true Ambient Intelligence (see, e.g., MIT Project Oxygen) might become a reality irrespective of personal location.

The design space of sensory transformations with technology is huge, which provides enormous potential but is also highly challenging for designers. We can see that altered embodiment opens up a new way of being in a world, and of experiencing presence. Indeed, it changes not only the body but also the perceived form of the physical world in which the body is located. In designing altered embodiment, the possibilities are almost endless - but we do not yet know much about what will work best for which purpose, or about possible longer term effects on the perceiver.

Many convincing demonstrations of expanded embodiment already exist, for example in psychotherapy, entertainment, training, and mental and physical rehabilitation. The power of expanded embodiment as produced by well-designed immersive VR applications is already well know, and several of these are treated in detail elsewhere in this volume.

New design possibilities are opened up when already successful approaches to eliciting expanded embodiment are combined with the huge, but relatively untapped, potential of altered embodiment. For example, the most promising potentials for BCI are perhaps in blends of the physical world and the virtual.

Currently available and emerging technologies, especially gaming and teleconferencing systems based on cheap technology (such as Microsoft's Kinect interface for the Xbox gaming platform) can be adapted to locate and track several individual bodies, voices, and faces in a three-dimensional physical space. A robot or avatar could, for example, be programmed to mirror the movements and facial expressions of the person. When combined with synchronised dual sensory stimulation, this opens up a wide range of possible applications - including co-presence systems for teleconferencing, entertainment applications such as games or movies, physiotherapy and sports training, and empathy training. An understanding of how and to what extent we can experience real presence in other bodies will be enormously important in these and other fields.

Design challenges of distributed embodiment include specifying the means of being in other bodies, of switching between bodies, and the characteristics of those bodies – which could include human (self or not, lifelike or not), robotic, animal (Nagel, 1974), or even inanimate objects (Misselhorn, 2009). It is likely that not all these possibilities will be effective in practice. What displays would be needed for the effect to work, and be useful in which situations? It is known that synchronised visual and tactile stimulation is important. What of senses such as proprioception and audition? What types of sensors work best and in which situations? What motor possibilities are needed?

Distributed embodiment can be accomplished in virtual reality, but it can also – at least in principle – be implemented in the blended reality of the physical and the virtual that is increasingly our everyday habitat. Cameras and other sensors, mobile and large scale displays, physically close and distant people will interact through context-sensitive applications producing – as appropriate – altered, expanded and distributed embodiment.

2.6 Conclusion to Chapter 2

The notion of altered embodiment – that we can change our sensory and perceptual capacities in the physical, through the use of mediating information technology – is not unfamiliar to us. Take the example of regularly wearing corrective spectacles as an obvious example. But some of the possible applications and potential uses may be less familiar. Similarly, we are not unfamiliar with what we are calling expanded embodiment. Every interactive game player is used to having their attention transported to another place, as if their bodies were extended into the fictional game space. Similarly, we can readily understand that the controller of an American drone flying into foreign airspace has the experience of being in that place to some extent, and not where his or her physical body is actually located. Distributed embodiment is a stranger concept, since few people have experienced out-of-the-body experiences and, until recently, this was not recognised as a possibility for technological exploitation.

The idea of distributed cognition (Perry 2003) is familiar, along with a variety of related views about how information technologies are assimilated into the way we make sense of and function in the world (e.g., Clark 2003, Dourish 2001, Hutchins 1996, Kaptelinin & Nardi 2006,). However, not all technology that we use for cognitive support becomes integrated with the self; the measurement of experienced presence allows us to distinguish when this happens and when it does not. If the technology is integrated with the self, we attend to and feel present in an external mediated reality in which the mediated nature of the world is invisible. The technology effectively becomes part of the body - we are embodied through the technology. As we have seen this can happen in a variety of ways. If the technology is not integrated with the self, using the technology involves a transfer of attention away from the mediated world and we feel absent from it. These feelings translate into measurable presence phenomena.

I may feel myself to be present here, in a state of altered embodiment; there, through expanded embodiment, and – potentially at least – as someone else there, via distributed embodiment. When I feel present here, in my usual body-centric mode of first-person observation of the world around me, I can alter my experience of the world in a wide variety of ways by technological means. This may be simply a matter of improved vision or hearing, or it could be more analogous to the effects of taking a psychotropic drug – a radically altered perception of the physical world of time and space surrounding my body. When I am said to be present there, this refers to my perception of a world around me that is not the physical world in which my body is actually located. I am virtually and experientially located there (Riva et al. 2002) not here. When I am someone else there, I experience presence there and yet also observe myself as another body. This is a new and puzzling form of interactive presence, with as yet unclear potential for the future of mediated embodiment.

Although three approaches to designing interactive presence have been described in this conceptual chapter, characterising three different forms of embodiment, they are not discrete categories. Perhaps most promising and most challenging is the design of new forms of embodiment in reality blends of the physical and virtual. Such blends are of unimaginable variety, but must be designed to meet the needs of actual people with needs and purposes in the social, shared and physical world in which we still all live and will die. Presence is the yardstick of embodiment from an experiential perspective. If you cannot feel presence, you are not embodied in the world.

References

Bach-y-Rita, P., & Kercel, S. W. (2003). "Sensory substitution and the human-machine interface.". *Trends in Cognitive Neuroscience*, 7(12), 541-546.

Benyon, D (2012). Presence in Blended Spaces. *Interacting with Computers*, 24(4), 219-226.

Blackmore, S. (1984). A psychological theory of the out-of-body experience. *Journal of Parapsychology*. 48, 201-218.

Bouchard, S, Dumoulin, S, Talbot, J, et al. (2012). Manipulating subjective realism and its impact on presence: Preliminary results on feasibility and neuroanatomical correlates. *Interacting with Computers*, 24(4), 227-236.

Biocca, F. (1997). The cyborg's dilemma: Progressive embodiment in virtual environments. *Journal of Computer-Mediated Communications*, 3(2).

Biocca, F. A., & Rolland, J. P. (1998). Virtual eyes can rearrange your body: Adaptation to visual displacement in see-through, head-mounted displays. *Presence*, 7, 262– 277.

Botvinick, M., & Cohen, J. (1998). Rubber hands 'feel' touch that the eye sees. *Nature*, 391, 756.

Bracken, C. & Skalski, P. (2010) (Eds.) *Immersed in Media: Telepresence in Everyday Life*. New York: Routledge.

Castiello, U., Lusher, D., Burton, C., et al. (2004). Improving left hemispatial neglect using virtual reality. *Neurology*, 62, 1958-1962.

Clark, A. (2003). *Natural Born Cyborgs: Minds, Technologies, and the Future of Human Intelligence*. Oxford: Oxford University Press.

Dourish, P. (2001). *Where the Action Is: The Foundations of Embodied Interaction*. Cambridge, MA: MIT Press.

Ehrsson, H. H. (2007). The Experimental Induction of Out-of-Body Experiences. *Science* 317 (5841), 1048.

Ehrsson, H. H., & Petkova, V. I. (2008). E-letter response to: H. H. Ehrsson (2007). The experimental induction of out-of-body experiences, *Science*, 317, 1048.

Floridi, L. (2004). Exploring the informational nature of presence. Opening invited keynote address at *7th Annual International Workshop on Presence*. Polytechnic University of Valencia, Spain, 13-15 October 2004.

Google Glass (2013). http://www.google.com/glass/start/. Accessed November 7, 2013.
Gregory, R. L. 1997. *Eye and Brain*. 5th edition. Oxford: Oxford University Press.
Haans, A., & IJsselsteijn, W. A. (2012). Embodiment and telepresence: Toward a comprehensive theoretical framework. *Interacting with Computers*, 24(4), 211-218.
Hochberg, L. R., Serruya, M. D., Friehs, G. M. et al. (2006). Neuronal Ensemble Control of Prosthetic Devices by a Human with Tetraplegia. *Nature* 442 (7099),164–171.
Holmes N., & C. Spence (2007). Dissociating Body Image and Body Schema with Rubber Hands. *Behavioral and Brain Sciences* 30, 211–212.
Hoshi, K., & Waterworth, J. A. (2009). Tangible Presence in Blended Reality Space, PRESENCE 2009. *Proceedings of the 12th Annual International Workshop on Presence*. November 11-13, Los Angeles, CA, USA.
Hoshi, K., Öberg, F. & Nyberg, A. (2011) Designing blended reality space: conceptual foundations and applications,
Proceedings of BCS-HCI '11: the 25th BCS Conference on Human-Computer Interaction, 217-226.
Hutchins, E. (1996). *Cognition in the Wild*. Cambridge, MA: Bradford Books, MIT Press.
Ihde, D. (1990). *Technology and the lifeworld—From garden to earth*. Bloomington and Indianapolis: Indiana University Press.
IJsselsteijn, W. A. (2005). Towards a neuropsychological basis of presence. *Annual Review of CyberTherapy and Telemedicine*, 3, 25-30.
IJsselsteijn, W.A., de Kort, Y.A.W., & Haans, A. (2006). Is this my hand I see before me? The Rubber Hand Illusion in Reality, Virtual Reality, and Mixed Reality. *Presence: Teleoperators and Virtual Environments* 15, 455-464.
Kaptelinin, V., & Nardi, B. (2006). *Acting with Technology: Activity Theory and Interaction Design*. Cambridge, MA: MIT Press.
Larsson, M., D. Larhammarb, M. Fredrikson, P. et al. (2005). Reply to M. A. Persinger and S. A. Koren's Response to Granqvist et al. Sensed Presence and Mystical Experiences Are Predicted by Suggestibility, Not by the Application Of Transcranial Weak Magnetic Fields. *Neuroscience Letters* 380 (3), 348–350.
Leeb, R., D. Friedman, G. R. Müller-Putz, R. et al. (2007). Self-Paced (Asynchronous) BCI Control of a Wheelchair in Virtual Environments: A Case Study with a Tetraplegic. *Computational Intelligence and Neuroscience*, 20 (April 2007): Article 7.
Lenggenhager, B., Tadi, T., Metzinger, T. et al. (2007). Video Ergo Sum: Manipulating Bodily Self-Consciousness. *Science* 317 (5841), 1096–1099.
Lombard, M., & Ditton, T. (1997). At the Heart of It All: The Concept of Presence. *Journal of Computer Mediated-Communication* 3(2).
Merleau-Ponty, M. (1962). *The Phenomenology of perception*. Translated by Colin Smith. London: Routledge and Keegan Paul.
Metzinger, T. (2006). Reply to Gallagher: Different conceptions of embodiment, *Psyche* 12(4).
Minsky, M. (1980). Telepresence. *Omni Magazine*, June 1980.
Misselhorn, C. (2009). Empathy with Inanimate Objects and the Uncanny Valley. *Minds and Machines* 19 (3), 345–359.
MIT Project Oxygen. Computer Science and Artificial Intelligence Laboratory. http://www.oxygen.lcs.mit.edu/. Accessed 7 November 2013.
Nagel, T. (1974). What Is It Like to Be a Bat? *Philosophical Review* 83(4), 435–450.
New Scientist (2010). The Real Avatar: Body Transfer Turns Men into Girls. May 13. http://www.newscientist.com/article/dn18896-the-real-avatar-body-transfer-turns-men-into-girls.html. Accessed June 27, 2013.
Norman, D. A. (1993). *Things that Make Us Smart*. Reading, Mass: Addison-Wesley.
Normand, J.-M., Giannopoulos, E. Spanlang, E. B et al. (2011). Multisensory Stimulation Can Induce an Illusion of Larger Belly Size in Immersive Virtual Reality. *PLoS ONE* 6(1): e16128.

Perry, M. (2003). Distributed Cognition. In J. M. Carroll, (Ed.) *HCI Models, Theories, and Frameworks: Toward an Interdisciplinary Science*, (193–223). San Francisco, CA: Morgan Kaufmann.

Persinger, M. A.,. Saroka, K., Koren, S. A. et al. (2010). The Electromagnetic Induction of Mystical and Altered States within the Laboratory. *Journal of Consciousness Exploration & Research* 1(7), 808–830.

Petkova V.I. & Ehrsson H. H. (2008). If I Were You: Perceptual Illusion of Body Swapping. *PLoS ONE* 3(12): e3832.

Riva G. (1998). Modifications of body-image induced by virtual reality. *Perceptual & Motor Skills*, 86(1), 163-70.

Riva, G. (2007). Virtual Reality and Telepresence. *Science, 318*(5854), 1240-1242.

Riva G., Davide, F & IJsselsteijn, W.I. (2002). *Being There: Concepts, Effects and Measurements of User Presence in Synthetic Environments*. Amsterdam: IOS Press.

Riva, G., Waterworth, J. A. and Waterworth, E. L. (2004). The Layers of Presence: a bio-cultural approach to understanding presence in natural and mediated environments. *Cyberpsychology and Behavior*, 7(4), 402-416.

Riva, G., Waterworth, J. A., Waterworth, E. L. et al. (2011). From Intention to Action: The Role of Presence. *New Ideas in Psychology* 29(1), 24–37.

Slater, M. & Steed, A.J. (2000). A virtual presence counter, *Presence: Teleoperators and Virtual Environments*, 9(5), 413–434.

Slater M., Perez-Marcos, D. Ehrsson, H. H. et al. (2008). Towards a Digital Body: The Virtual Arm Illusion. *Frontiers in Human Neuroscience*. 2, Article 6, 1-8.

Slater, M., Spanlang, B. Sanchez-Vives, M. V. et al. (2010). First Person Experience of Body Transfer in Virtual Reality. *PLoS ONE* 5(5): e10564.

Slotema, C. W.,. Blom, J. D., Hoek, H. W. et al. (2010). Should We Expand the Toolbox of Psychiatric Treatment Methods to Include Repetitive Transcranial Magnetic Stimulation (rTMS)? *Journal of Clinical Psychiatry* 71(7), 873–884.

The vOICe (2014). http://www.seeingwithsound.com. Accessed 30 January 2014.

Waterworth, E. L. & Waterworth J. A. (2001). Focus, Locus and Sensus: the 3 Dimensions of Virtual Experience. *Cyberpsychology and Behavior*, 4(2), 203-214.

Waterworth, J. A. (1997). Creativity and Sensation: The Case for Synaesthetic Media. *Leonardo*, 30(4), 327-330.

Waterworth, J. A. (2003). Virtual Realisation: Supporting Creative Outcomes in Medicine and Music. *Psychnology*, 1(4), 410-427.

Waterworth, J. A. and Fällman, D .(2003). The Reality Helmet: Transforming the Experience of Being-in-the-World. *Proceedings of HCI 2003: Designing for Society*, Bath, UK, Volume 2, 191-194.

Waterworth, J. A .& Waterworth, E. L. (2003). The Core of Presence: Presence as Perceptual Illusion. *Presence-Connect*, 3(3), posted 24-07-2003.

Waterworth, J. A., Waterworth E. L., Mantovani, F. et al. (2010). On feeling (the) present: an evolutionary account of the sense of presence in physical and electronically-mediated environments. *Journal of Consciousness Studies*, 17(1-2), 167-189.

Yee, N. & Bailenson, J.N. (2007). The Proteus Effect: Self transformations in virtual reality. *Human Communication Research*, 33, 271-290.

3 Measuring Presence in the Simulating Brain

Daniel Sjölie

Abstract: A description of the brain as an organ for simulating its environment can inform and illuminate a discussion about brain measurements in connection with the sense of presence. Developing theories of how mental simulations and continuous predictions underlie brain function have implications for how presence can, or cannot, be associated with brain measurements. Here, the simulating brain is accepted as a working hypothesis. The resulting implications are discussed and briefly related to how brain measurements have been used to investigate presence in previous studies.

Keywords: Presence; Brain Measurements; The Simulating Brain; fMRI; Predictions.

3.1 Introduction to Chapter 3

The subjective nature of the sense of presence makes it difficult to relate it to objective measurements. One tempting possibility is to target the neural functions underlying subjective experiences by measuring brain activity using methods such as *fMRI* (functional Magnetic Resonance Imaging). The technology and expertise necessary for using such methods has become relatively common over the last decade, and a few studies have been conducted to measure what happens in the brain in connection to a varying sense of presence. However, how such measurements should be interpreted, and how they should be related back to presence in theory and practice, remains an open question. For example, explanations that focus on specific brain areas are not conclusive since most areas of the brain have been shown to be involved in many different cognitive functions and brain function is heavily influenced by context.

3.2 Background

The range of methods used to measure presence has evolved over the years, from pure subjective measures using questionnaires, to more objective measures based on behaviour or physiology (Insko, 2003) and, more recently, including brain measurements (Baumgartner et al., 2008; Clemente, Rodríguez, Rey, & Alcañiz, 2012; Kober & Neuper, 2012). Interested readers are encouraged to look up the references above, for a more complete overview of the background of presence measurements. The rest of this chapter focuses on how brain measurements might be used to measure presence (and associated challenges) based on a theoretical perspective on the brain summarized as "the simulating brain".

There are many different definitions of presence that may be related to brain function with varying ease. Several definitions relate directly to subjective experiences that are essentially hidden. Two common definitions of presence, as the "sense of being there" or as the "perceptual illusion of non-mediation" (Insko, 2003), both come down to what is actually sensed or perceived "inside of the users mind." That is, to how percepts (sensory input) and information flows through and is processed in the user's brain.

The relation between brain function and definitions such as the ability to "do there" (successful intentional interaction) or responding to stimuli from a virtual environment (VE) "as if they were real" may be less obvious, but the connection has been established explicitly and repeatedly (Jäncke, Cheetham, & Baumgartner, 2009; Sanchez-Vives & Slater, 2005).

This chapter aims to avoid an explicit definition of presence (see Chapters 1 and 2 for a wider discussion about this topic), but important aspects of presence in the simulating brain are summarized in Section 4.

3.3 The Simulating Brain

The idea that the brain is essentially about predicting the future is becoming increasingly popular (Clark, 2013; Friston, 2009b, 2010; Hawkins, 2005; Schacter, Addis, & Buckner, 2007). The basic function of the brain is, it is suggested, to use information from the past to make predictions about what is likely to happen in the future. The concept of mental simulations is helpful to focus on these predictions as running, continuously updating expectations. In much the same way as remembering the past seems to involve "a constructive process of piecing together bits and pieces" (Schacter et al., 2007, p. 659), partial simulations based on previous experience are continuously pieced together to simulate future states and guide action.

Partial simulations are stored in brain areas related to the corresponding modalities, providing a basis for higher-level aspects of simulations. For example, the higher-level concept of "colour" is related to simulations of seeing colour, stored in the areas of the brain related to the actual perception of colour; and the concept of "up" is related to simulations of looking up, stored in motor areas. Cognition is further described as having a hierarchical structure where concepts and phenomena at higher levels are grounded in lower levels. High-level predictions correspond to contexts for low-level predictions. For example, a high-level expectation of walking on a flat surface triggers lower-level predictions of your foot hitting the ground at a certain moment. Higher-level contexts only need to change when predictions fail at lower levels, highlighting the importance of prediction errors and feedback in the brain. As long as the foot hits the ground as predicted one does not need to reconsider the walking context. Simulations pieced together throughout a hierarchy, based on current percepts (bottom-up) and current context (top-down), enable efficient interaction by continually preparing for what is likely to happen next.

Particularly interesting for this chapter is how this framework suggests that the brain essentially contains a model of reality, and that brain activity in large part corresponds to experiences that are unexpected or surprising; that is, experiences that were not correctly predicted. Poor predictions can be caused either by an incomplete knowledge of the phenomenon, or by fundamental unpredictability. If the stimuli are fundamentally predictable however, the brain is excellent at detecting and adapting to these stimuli, integrating them into mental simulations and expectations. This effect can be recognized in many well-known phenomena, such as repetition suppression, habituation, and odd-ball paradigms, commonly employed as reliable effects in cognitive neuroscience studies.

The proponents of these theories are not shy about their potential. Karl Friston writes that "one can see easily how constructs like memory, attention, value, reinforcement and salience might disclose their simple relationships within this framework" (Friston, 2009b, p. 293), and in a somewhat more nuanced target paper Andy Clark writes that "what is on offer is a multilevel account of some of the deepest natural principles underlying learning and inference, and one that may be capable of bringing perception, action, and attention under a single umbrella" (Clark, 2013, p. 20).

It may be illustrative to reflect on why humans perceive some things as more "real" than others. To quote Hawkins, "predictability is the very definition of reality" (Hawkins, 2005, p. 128). Consider the opposite of reality: the unreal. If something is unreal it means that it does not fit into one's current understanding of the world, it is inconsistent with the patterns one has learned to recognize, and there is no basis for making predictions about this phenomenon, or running matching simulations. Depending upon how large the deviation from the familiar is, this may lead to confusion, and/or adaptation of the models for what is familiar: that is, learning.

Many aspects of the theories presented above are still debated. Including enough arguments to convince sceptics is outside the scope of this chapter. For an introduction to the discussion surrounding these theories the recent target paper by Andy Clark is recommended (Clark, 2013).

3.4 Presence in the Simulating Brain

The simulating brain suggests possible explanations of phenomena generally associated with presence. The basic reasoning is based on a view of the human brain as continually running a simulation of the surrounding environment, trying to match and anticipate the future as well as possible. Such simulations have reached the brain through experience with reality, through prediction errors that force refinements of the dynamic models. The (hypothesized) fact that these mental simulations originate in (interaction with) the real environment leads to an expectation of similarities between actual reality and the simulation in the brain, both in behaviour and in structure. When the world the brain currently inhabits is a computer-generated virtual reality, this perspective constitutes the foundation for an interpretation of brain function and brain measurements as tightly related to phenomena in and aspects of this virtual reality.

Within the simulating brain, information that reaches any higher levels of the brain is related to internal expectations of the brain to an extremely high degree, rather than being anything like direct information from the external environment. One way to think of such expectations is as mental simulations that together create a subjective mental reality. This subjective mental reality may be more or less influenced by the current external environment, but it does run on its own, as "a generative model of the world it inhabits" (Friston, 2010, p. 135), to a large degree. Since most areas of the brain primarily operate in relation to the rest of the brain, it is reasonable to say that the brain is present in the subjective mental reality that is simulated in the brain. Within this perspective, the degree of presence in a certain environment may be considered to be the degree of synchronization between this environment and your (simulated) subjective mental reality (Sjölie, 2012). In an office: to what degrees are you currently simulating surrounding desks, chairs, pens, etc.?

One implication of this perspective on presence is that brain activity associated with a high level of presence should depend strongly on the specifics of the current environment and task. Conversely, a low level of presence should be related to a mismatch between the actual brain activity and the brain activity required to simulate the environment. If being present in an environment means that your brain is simulating aspects of that environment, then your brain activity should reflect this, and being present in different environments should lead to corresponding differences in the patterns of brain activity. In the case of reduced or disrupted presence in relation to a specific environment, the "alternate environment," representing reduced presence, may be another actual environment, a state of general confusion, or some form of daydreaming.

The simulating brain may be easily related to many previous accounts of presence, such as the importance of avoiding "breaks in presence" (Slater, 2002), the ability to use familiar representations to "do there" (Jäncke et al., 2009), the successful transformation of intentions into actions, or the perceptual illusion of non-mediation (Giuseppe Riva, Waterworth, Waterworth, & Mantovani, 2011). For example, *breaks in presence* (BIPs) correspond to events that destroy the sense of presence through events that go against the expectations that underlie the acceptance of a VE as real, such as hearing a chair move in a forest VE. In relation to the simulating brain, BIPs are prediction errors that are big enough to rise through the hierarchy of predictions and finally invalidate the prediction that one is in a context that can be treated as a real place.

The importance of expectations and their violation for achieving and maintaining presence has been explicitly emphasized several times, for example, in terms of simulations in the brain (Giuseppe Riva et al., 2011; Sjölie, 2012), or the importance of being able to rely on expectations and existing motor schemas to be able to "do there" (Jäncke et al., 2009; Sanchez-Vives & Slater, 2005).

Two key aspects of the conception of presence presented above are:

1. Presence is a general function of cognition, related to your familiarity with and attention to your current environment. It is not specifically related to immersive VR, although VR provides unique opportunities to manipulate and explore all aspects of presence.
2. The brain activity related to presence, and differences in the level of presence, in any specific environment, is tightly related to the actual environment and the current task.

These points should primarily be understood as a delimitation of the conception of presence discussed here, rather than a claim on what presence should be generally.

3.5 Measuring What, How?

The rest of this chapter delves into what one can expect to be able to measure when it comes to presence in the simulating brain. How may measurements be gathered, and how might previous results be integrated? The present section focuses on methodological issues and theoretical background, while the next section delves into previous studies.

Ensuring reliability and validity when estimating presence using brain measurements can be challenging. The primary problem for validity is that there is no obvious or generally agreed upon ground truth to compare measurements against. According to common conceptions of presence, the ideal would be to be able to ask the user a question like "where are you?" while they are immersed and engaged within a VE. In general, this is not possible without disrupting the very experience (of presence) that we wish to measure, although some studies suggest that this disruption may be manageable (Kober & Neuper, 2012). Behavioural and physiological measurements are interesting alternatives that may be recorded during VR interaction (Insko, 2003). Such measurements are related to presence indirectly, for example, by assuming that increased arousal corresponds to increased presence. However, such assumptions are debatable and any practical measure quickly becomes very dependent on specific conceptions of presence. Questionnaires may focus on factors assumed to be related to the sense of presence, such as the sense of control, or variations of whether the environment is experienced as a place (Insko, 2003). Given how tightly measurements are tied to theory in general, new potential measurements should be considered based on whether they are theoretically defendable, rather than on compatibility with previous measures of presence.

The complexity and context sensitivity of human brain function provide challenges to both reliability and validity. Brain measurements are often presented in terms of which areas of the brain “light up.” This is particularly common in fMRI studies, where the most common data analysis looks at each point in the brain separately, checking whether the local “activity” is significantly different between some conditions. Interpretation of such activations is usually related to what previous research tells us about the functional role of specific brain areas (functional segregation) (Friston, 2009a). However, such interpretations must be tempered by the fact that activation in any specific brain area can be caused by many different combinations of excitation and inhibition from other brain areas, essentially representing different contexts (Jäncke et al., 2009; Logothetis, 2008). These issues are well known in the brain imaging community in general, but addressing these issues fully requires sophisticated studies that are still relatively rare, and reporting in the popular press is often flawed. The basic message to readers not familiar with brain imaging is: avoid interpretations on the form “the function X is located at position Y in the brain”. Brain areas do tend to play specific roles and data about brain area activations is valuable, but interpretations need to acknowledge the importance of context.

Unravelling how local brain activity depends on interactions with the rest of the brain usually requires additional analysis. One approach is to investigate connectivity between specific brain areas explicitly (Baumgartner et al., 2008). Another increasingly popular approach is to compare measured brain activity with models, with explicit expectations (Friston, 2009a). Theoretical frameworks such as the simulating brain provide a valuable basis and starting point for the construction of such models for presence in the brain.

If we accept the simulating brain as a working hypothesis: can we expect some areas of the brain to always be associated with increased presence? As suggested above, in a perfect VE, with perfect presence, presence-related brain activity should be dictated by the particular task and context. However, no such perfect environment exists today, and it is debatable if presence is ever perfect for any length of time. Thus, we are primarily dealing with degrees of imperfect presence.

Brain measurements related to imperfect presence should be related to aspects of the current environment and task that fail to synchronize properly with the simulated subjective mental reality. In particular, brain areas that correspond to a (higher-level) context or (lower-level) detail predictions related to a problematic phenomenon can be expected to be activated in an attempt to resolve the prediction error. For example, a troublesome virtual fork may trigger re-evaluation of both lower-level “physical fork handling” simulations and higher-level “eating with a fork” simulations.

Keeping in mind how brain areas correspond to aspects of simulations within a hierarchy may be helpful to get an initial sense of how measured local brain activity fits into the larger context and affects the total sense of presence. For example, significant disruptions in presence should correspond to large prediction errors that rise through the hierarchy, leading to increased activity in more frontal brain regions. Also, brain areas that are consistently implicated in relation to varying presence should be interpreted as corresponding to aspects of the simulated mental reality that are particularly important for the creation and maintenance of a general sense of presence.

One common approach is to compare brain measurements related to different conditions designed to elicit varying levels of presence. Subjective reports of presence may be used to verify a significant difference in reported presence between conditions (Baumgartner et al., 2008; Clemente et al., 2012), but variability in how subjects report presence and biases like the recency effect are an issue, in particular since brain imaging studies often have a relatively small number of subjects. Asserting that measured responses are related to changes in subjective presence more generally, rather than related to specifics of the employed conditions, is also a primary challenge.

The latter problem may be addressed either with variability in the conditions, leaving differences in presence as the primary explanatory variable, or by trying to keep the conditions as similar as possible and still elicit different sensations of presence. Bouchard et al. (2012) demonstrated the second approach by using different narratives to produce differences in presence while keeping the VE itself constant across conditions. Such methods provide a level of confidence that measured activity is related to differences in presence, but it is still unclear how the results depend on particulars of the context.

Another approach is to focus on what happens when presence changes. That is, focusing more on transitory events or short time periods where the sense of presence changes. The great challenge here is that it is difficult to get reliable information on the subjective experience of presence over time without seriously impacting the experience we want to investigate. As remarked above, if we were to ask the subject about their degree of presence at regular intervals this would be very likely to affect their sense of presence. One may design the experiment to introduce events that are expected to lead to differences in experienced presence, for example, by violating expectations and (potentially) triggering BIPs. However, this approach has the same vulnerabilities as the comparison of conditions above, potentially drowning effects of changing presence in effects related to particulars of the designed events.

An alternative to using designed changes to affect presence is to try to piece together when subjects experienced changes in presence through some combination of behavioural data and post-scan reports. Spiers and Maguire have used such a setup in several studies, for example, to investigate the neural correlates of spontaneous mentalizing (Spiers & Maguire, 2006).

3.6 Previous Studies

There are many brain imaging studies with results that can be related to presence, but only a small number that investigate presence explicitly. This chapter cannot begin to give a complete review of relevant studies, but the selection below should provide an introduction to the kind of studies conducted.

VR and brain imaging have been used together in a number of studies over the last decades. A recent review by Maguire (2012) provides a general overview of research using a combination of VR and fMRI (VRfMRI). Early VRfMRI studies by Hoffman et al. (2003) and Lee et al. (2004) include a discussion of presence, but neither present any brain measurements directly related to presence.

Baumgartner et al. (2008) conducted the most comprehensive fMRI study on presence to date. Their study is based on the comparison of two conditions designed to elicit high and low presence, respectively. Both conditions were presented as non-interactive roller-coaster rides in a 3d-environment, with a flat track in the low-presence condition and spectacular slopes and loops in the high-presence condition. Post-scan questionnaires were used to relate differences in reported presence to differences in brain activation, across subjects. Restricting initial analysis to the prefrontal cortex based on an a priori hypothesis, activity in bilateral dorsolateral prefrontal cortex (DLPFC, a "high-level control" area) was reported as negatively correlated with the sense of presence. Subjects who reported a smaller increase in presence between conditions showed a greater BOLD (blood-oxygen-level-dependent) increase in DLPFC. Using connectivity analysis, DLPFC activity was further related to down-regulation of the egocentric dorsal visual processing stream (including parietal areas) and up-regulation of the medial prefrontal cortex (MPFC).

The results from the study by Baumgartner et al. are further discussed in a paper by Jäncke et al. (2009). Among other things, it is acknowledged that the identified network of brain areas is not exclusively related to modulation of presence, since the areas in question are involved in many other psychological functions. However, the DLPFC is suggested to play a central role in regulating (among other things) the sense of presence, as it serves as an "executive control". The simulating brain suggests an essentially compatible but conceptually different explanation. The DLPFC corresponds to a higher position in the hierarchy of simulations and predictions in the brain. From a bottom-up perspective any failure of lower-level predictions, such as internalized simulations of spatial interaction, is expected to give rise to prediction errors that must be dealt with further up, for example, in the DLPFC. From a top-down perspective, when a situation is familiar and simulations are synchronized with external phenomena, predictions can be pushed down through the hierarchy relatively effortlessly. In essence, lower-level areas can successfully run simulations based on (among other things) predictions from DLPFC and need not bother the DLPFC further. An association between reduced activity in DLPFC and increased presence fits well with both these perspectives.

An interesting alternative to the comparison of different environments has been presented by Bouchard et al. (2012). Their study used narratives to convince some subjects that an immersive VE was real, while others were immersed in the same VE without believing that it was real. Believing that the VE was real was correlated with an increased sense of presence and increased activation in bilateral parahippocampal cortex.

As remarked above, if presence requires a close match between simulations in the brain and phenomena in the interaction environment, brain measurements related to varying presence should be related to important aspects of the environment and task in question. Indeed, in the study by Baumgartner et al. (2008) increased presence while riding a roller-coaster was related to visual and spatial brain regions. Similarly, in the study by Bouchard, increased presence related to believing oneself to be in a real room was related to activations in parahippocampal cortex, a brain region known to be involved in spatial/location processing.

It should be noted that none of the studies above allowed the user to interact with the environment. A recent study by Clemente et al. (2013) compares conditions in a manner similar to Baumgartner et al., but also includes an interactive condition. While this study has a lower number of subjects, making it somewhat harder to interpret with confidence, the primary findings are in line with Baumgartner et al. and other brain imaging studies comparing similar conditions, implicating DLPFC and spatial brain regions, among others.

fMRI may be the brain imaging method with the greatest promise for understanding brain measurements related to presence generally, but other methods may be more suitable for practical measurements. For example, EEG (electroencephalography) can be much cheaper and easier to use, with far fewer restrictions on possible interactions and scenarios. In one recent study, Kober et al. used EEG to compare a highly immersive VR-system with a less immersive VR-system (Kober, Kurzmann, & Neuper, 2012). Both conditions were interactive, differing primarily in visual field and use of stereoscopy. A comparison across subjects, with different groups for each condition, showed that an increased sense of presence in the highly immersive condition was accompanied by EEG measures signifying increased parietal activation, particularly compared to frontal brain areas. These results seem to agree with Baumgartner et al. in implicating parietal and frontal areas in the modulation of presence. It is interesting that the difference between the conditions is relatively small in this study, but given the poor spatial resolution of EEG some caution may be prudent. Additional studies conducted using commercially available and affordable EEG headset (Emotiv EPOC) (Clemente et al., 2012), or transcranial Doppler (TCD) (Rey, Parkhutik, Tembl, & Alcañiz, 2011) exemplify additional work towards practical brain measurements.

Kober and Neuper illustrate the conceptual overlap between behavioural, physiological and brain measurements in a recent study using EEG to measure brain activity triggered by sounds not related to VR (Kober & Neuper, 2012). The response to the external sounds was measured and related to reports of experienced presence. In principle, this type of response could have been detectable with behavioural or physiological measurements, but by using EEG one may be able to detect smaller, hidden, responses, making it possible to use less intrusive triggers (the sounds) and reduce unwanted impact on presence.

3.7 Conclusion to Chapter 3

As with brain imaging in general, "the conceptual challenge ahead may not lie in finessing the techniques at our disposal but informing the models used to explain data" (Friston, 2009a, p. 402). A theoretical understanding of presence in the simulating brain suggests rich explanations that provide a basis for the construction of such models. Previous studies relating brain measurements to the sense of presence provide valuable data for the initial comparison of models as well as for the continued generation of models and hypotheses.

While results based on comparisons of different environments may be influenced by the particular contexts, they provide important pieces to the puzzle. To improve the general understanding of the relation between brain measurements and the sense of presence, additional research investigating a varied set of environments and contexts would be very valuable. Moreover, established associations to brain activity, for example, in the DLPFC and parietal regions, may be further evaluated in relation to practical measurements in contexts and environments matching the corresponding studies. In either case the perspective provided by the simulating brain may be helpful in teasing out and explaining how differences in environments and contexts may impact presence and its neural correlates.

References

Baumgartner, T., Speck, D., Wettstein, D., Masnari, O., Beeli, G., & Jäncke, L. (2008). Feeling Present in Arousing Virtual Reality Worlds: Prefrontal Brain Regions Differentially Orchestrate Presence Experience in Adults and Children. *Frontiers in Human Neuroscience*, *2*(8).

Bouchard, S., Dumoulin, S., Talbot, J., Ledoux, A.-A., Phillips, J., Monthuy-Blanc, J., ... Renaud, P. (2012). Manipulating subjective realism and its impact on presence: Preliminary results on feasibility and neuroanatomical correlates. *Interacting with Computers*, *24*(4), 227–236.

Clark, A. (2013). Whatever next? Predictive brains, situated agents, and the future of cognitive science. *Behavioral and Brain Sciences*, *36*(03), 181–204.

Clemente, M., Rey, B., Rodríguez-Pujadas, A., Barros-Loscertales, A., Baños, R. M., Botella, C., Ávila, C. (2013). An fMRI Study to Analyze Neural Correlates of Presence during Virtual Reality Experiences. *Interacting with Computers*, In Press.

Clemente, M., Rodríguez, A., Rey, B., & Alcañiz, M. (2012). Measuring presence during the navigation in a virtual environment using EEG. *Studies in Health Technology and Informatics*, *191*, 136–140.

Friston, K. (2009a). Modalities, Modes, and Models in Functional Neuroimaging. *Science*, *326*(5951), 399–403.

Friston, K. (2009b). The free-energy principle: a rough guide to the brain? *Trends in Cognitive Sciences*, *13*(7), 293–301.

Friston, K. (2010). The free-energy principle: a unified brain theory? *Nat Rev Neurosci*, *11*(2), 127–138.

Hawkins, J. (2005). *On Intelligence*. Owl Books.

Hoffman, H. G., Richards, T., Coda, B., Richards, A., & Sharar, S. R. (2003). The illusion of presence in immersive virtual reality during an fMRI brain scan. *Cyberpsychology & Behavior: The Impact of the Internet, Multimedia and Virtual Reality on Behavior and Society*, *6*(2), 127–31.

Insko, B. E. (2003). Measuring Presence: Subjective, Behavioral and Physiological Methods. In G. Riva, F. Davide, & W. A. IJsselsteijn (Eds.), *Being There: Concepts, effects and measurement of user presence in synthetic environments*. Amsterdam, The Netherlands: Ios Press.
Jäncke, L., Cheetham, M., & Baumgartner, T. (2009). Virtual reality and the role of the prefrontal cortex in adults and children. *Frontiers in Neuroscience*, *3*(1).
Kober, S. E., Kurzmann, J., & Neuper, C. (2012). Cortical correlate of spatial presence in 2D and 3D interactive virtual reality: An EEG study. *International Journal of Psychophysiology*, *83*(3), 365–374.
Kober, S. E., & Neuper, C. (2012). Using auditory event-related EEG potentials to assess presence in virtual reality. *International Journal of Human-Computer Studies*, *70*(9), 577–587.
Lee, S., Kim, G. J., & Lee, J. (2004). Observing effects of attention on presence with fMRI. In *Proceedings of the ACM symposium on Virtual reality software and technology* (pp. 73–80). Hong Kong: ACM.
Logothetis, N. K. (2008). What we can do and what we cannot do with fMRI. *Nature*, *453*(7197), 869–878.
Maguire, E. A. (2012). Studying the freely-behaving brain with fMRI. *NeuroImage*, *62*(2), 1170–1176.
Rey, B., Parkhutik, V., Tembl, J., & Alcañiz, M. (2011). Breaks in Presence in Virtual Environments: An Analysis of Blood Flow Velocity Responses. *Presence: Teleoperators and Virtual Environments*, *20*(3), 273–286.
Riva, Giuseppe, Waterworth, J. A., Waterworth, E. L., & Mantovani, F. (2011). From intention to action: The role of presence. *New Ideas in Psychology*, *29*(1), 24–37.
Sanchez-Vives, M. V., & Slater, M. (2005). From presence to consciousness through virtual reality. *Nature Reviews. Neuroscience*, *6*(4), 332–9.
Schacter, D. L., Addis, D. R., & Buckner, R. L. (2007). Remembering the past to imagine the future: the prospective brain. *Nat Rev Neurosci*, *8*(9), 657–661.
Sjölie, D. (2012). Presence and general principles of brain function. *Interacting with Computers*, *24*(4), 193–202.
Slater, M. (2002). Presence and the sixth sense. *Presence: Teleoperators & Virtual Environments*, *11*(4), 435–439.
Spiers, H. J., & Maguire, E. A. (2006). Spontaneous mentalizing during an interactive real world task: An fMRI study. *Neuropsychologia*, *44*(10), 1674–1682.

4 A Framework for Interactivity and Presence in Novel Bodies

Andrea Stevenson Won, Antal Haans, Wijnand A. IJsselsteijn, and Jeremy N. Bailenson

Abstract: Researchers are beginning to explore the consequences of interacting with virtual worlds using non-human bodies. As virtual environments become more advanced, it is possible for participants to interact with their environments in increasingly sophisticated ways. Using trackers, users can control multiple avatar limbs in order to manipulate objects, move through space, and otherwise act in the virtual world. These avatar bodies need not conform to the normal human configuration, either in their appearance or in the way the tracked movements of the user are rendered to control the movements of the avatar. In this chapter we use the framework developed by Haans and IJsselsteijn to investigate the experience of presence in cases of nonhuman avatars or avatars that otherwise differ in ability or control schema from the user's own body; for example, avatars with more than two arms. We focus on cases where participants inhabit avatars in which the veridical mapping between tracking and rendering is disrupted.

Keywords: Homuncular Flexibility; Body Schema; Body Morphology, Body Image.

4.1 Introduction to Chapter 4

Media changes our behavior in the real world, and the way we understand media is based on our evolved responses to real world stimuli (Nass and Reeves, 1996). But what happens when our mediated experiences have no real world analogue- when we are experiencing life as a cow being raised for beef, or manipulating our environment with eight claws instead of two arms? How will we understand how to navigate in a body that is so dissimilar from the human, and how will our behavior be altered after such an experience?

One vision of virtual reality, in particular, looks to experiencing the impossible rather than duplicating the physical world. As Sutherland (1965) states in his classic "The Ultimate Reality", "There is no reason why the objects displayed by a computer have to follow the ordinary rules of physical reality with which we are familiar." (p. 507). Classic virtual reality simulators were designed to allow users to experience environments, such as flight simulators, which were not physically available for reasons of expense or danger. As virtual systems advanced, it became possible for participants to interact with— and be represented within— these virtual environments in increasingly sophisticated ways. While it has become possible to customize avatars so that they resemble their controller, it is also possible to create avatars that are very different from their users' own bodies.

Social science research in virtual reality has leveraged this ability to alter the appearance avatars in order to give participants virtual self-representations which diverge from their real life appearance; changing gender, race, height, and level of attractiveness, among other qualities. Changing the appearance of a participant's avatar can lead to changes in the participant's behavior. This so-called "Proteus effect" has been demonstrated in a number of different experiments (Yee and Bailenson, 2006). In one experiment, participants who inhabited an avatar pre-rated as more than average attractiveness acted more socially and selected more attractive potential dating partners in a post-experiment task than participants who inhabited less attractive avatars. In another experiment, participants who inhabited a taller avatar acted more assertively post task. While this Proteus effect indicates that people adapt to and are affected by their avatars in a relatively short period of time, those avatars all conformed to the basic human template, and were controlled, to the extent that their gestures were incorporated, by tracking the natural movements of the participant and rendering them as accurately as possible in virtual reality.

However, it is also possible for people to inhabit and control nonhuman avatars, which may not follow the template of a primate walking on two legs and manipulating objects with his or her hands (Lanier, 2006; Kilteni, Normand, Sanchez-Vives & Slater, 2012; Steptoe, Steed, & Slater, 2013). This alters not only the relationship between how a participant appears in real life and how they appear in virtual reality, but also the relationship between a participant's tracked and rendered gestures. Potentially, then, people can experience presence in environments and in bodies that have never before been inhabited by humans in the physical world. However, they will understand these experiences based on their experiences with their human bodies, and the effects of these mediated experiences may resonate in the physical world as well.

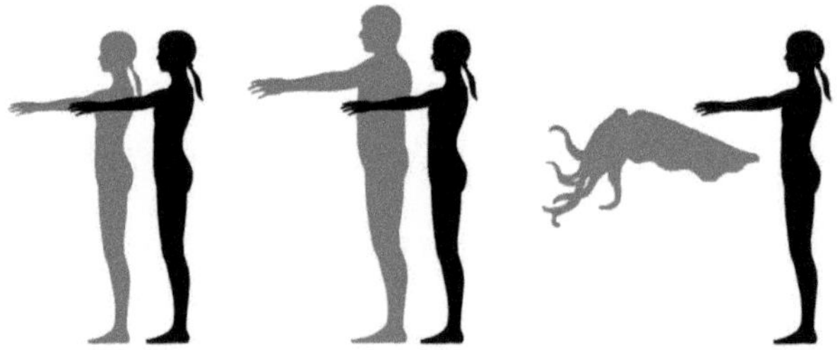

Figure 4.1: The leftmost figure shows a one-to-one relationship between the user (black silhouette) and her avatar (gray silhouette). The middle figure shows the Proteus effect, where the user controls an avatar that differs from her physical appearance, but the tracking/rendering relationship remains one-to-one, such that when the user raises her arm, her male avatar's arm is also raised. The rightmost figure shows a user controlling a non-human (cephalopod) avatar, where the rendered movement of the novel avatar cannot directly relate to the tracked movements of the user

The investigation of presence has often been considered in the context of technological advances in media, although as Steuer (1992) points out in his discussion of virtual reality, it cannot be solely defined by hardware. Immersive virtual reality is a medium which makes the perceptual mediation of our sensory experiences very evident (Loomis, 1992). Thus, virtual reality has been a natural arena of research on the nature of presencel, and is a logical medium in which to investigate presence in novel avatar bodies.

Presence is slippery to define and quantify. While some authors have linked presence to the affordances available from a given system, such as immersiveness and interactivity, others have defined it as the absence of awareness of technology, or the "perceptual illusion of non-mediation" (Lombard & Ditton, 1997). One useful way to consider presence in the context of inhabiting an avatar is to follow Lee (2004) and break presence into three categories; environmental or spatial presence, social presence, and self-presence. We will focus primarily on self-presence when considering novel bodies. Self-presence may include the experience of not just being located in the virtual, but having a sense of ownership over it as well; feeling as if the virtual body is indeed your own (cf., Cole, Sacks, & Waterman, 2000).

Self-presence has been further explicated (Riva, Waterworth, Waterworth, & Mantovani, 2011; Ratan, 2012; Chapter 1 in this book) by being divided into three categories based on Damasio's theory of the self (1999). These categories, which are proto self-presence, core self-presence, and extended self-presence, relate to different areas of research on self-representation with avatars. Extended self-presence may be considered more related to an individual's identity, including the social construct of his or her personality, while core and proto self-presence appear to be more closely linked to the body as it affects and is affected by the surrounding environment. The way the body is understood in this context has to do with the sensation it receives from the environment, and the ability it has to act purposefully upon that environment. This leads to an understanding of presence as dependent on embodiment, where the latter is defined in Heideggerian terms as being an active participant in the world (also Zahorik & Jenison, 1998). As Riva defines it, "presence is the intuitive perception of successfully transforming intentions into action (enaction)."

Understanding embodiment thus appears crucial for understanding presence, and in particular "presence" in atypical virtual bodies (see also Biocca, 1997; IJsselsteijn, 2004; Slater & Usoh, 1994). Biocca, for example, argued that the body itself is not much different from the typical components of a virtual reality system: Both mediate the communication between the mind and the physical world. Indeed, as Loomis (1993) argued, any satisfactory theory of presence should be grounded in the understanding of ordinary sensorimotor processes. Thus, to explain how it is possible that people may learn to control a virtual body so different from their own, and may even come to consciously experience it as their own body, we must first have an understanding of how we are embodied in our natural bodies. One such theoretical framework was recently proposed by Haans and IJsselsteijn (2012).

Based on the works of natural philosophers such as Metzinger (2003, 2006) and Gallagher (1986, 2005), Haans and IJsselsteijn (2012) describe the three different levels of human embodiment: morphology, a body schema, and a body image. In this theoretical framework, the body schema and image instigate a perceptual illusion of non-mediation; not with respect to media technology but to our own biological bodies. The body schema renders the workings of the body transparent to its owner; for example, allowing an individual to walk without having to pay attention to each individual muscle. Similarly, the body image is effectively a transparent self-model (Metzinger, 2009) which allows humans to make sense of the world as distinct from themselves, connecting past, presence and future, and allowing for the learning of refined bodily actions and offline simulations thereof. Both the body schema and image are highly flexible in accommodating technological tools as respectively functional and phenomenological extension of the body; allowing the same transparency in the use of tools as in using our natural bodies.

In the next sections we will use Haans and IJsselsteijn's framework for embodiment to interrogate the concept of presence in novel bodies. First we will examine the design, or morphology, of novel bodies. Next we will discuss tool use, and how this may relate to both embodiment broadly and the process of controlling avatar bodies. We will then examine the phenomenon of body transfer/body ownership, and how this relates to what changes in body image may be achievable when embodying novel avatars. Finally, we will look at the consequences of embodying novel avatars within the framework of embodied cognition.

4.1.1 Extending Human Morphology In Novel Ways

Morphology refers to the number, kind, and location of limbs, muscles, and sensory receptors. Our human morphology largely determines and constrains our action possibilities and perceptual experiences. For example, we lack the capacities for active flight or navigation by means of echolocation which are more typical of the bat morphology. Tools, including media technologies, may be used to extend the possibilities of our natural morphology, or to repair it in case of an accident. But what if, instead of simply extending our morphology, a person could become some*thing* else- a bat perhaps or an animal so far removed from the human that it does not even have the same kind of skeleton— an invertebrate, like a lobster?

Altering the physical appearance of the avatar, and changing how physical movements control it, using ipsimodal remapping, is only one aspect of potential novel avatar morphology changes. *Sensory substitution*, a remapping between two different sensory modalities, also provides the opportunity for novel avatar experiences. For example, visual information may be rendered as tactile stimuli; a technique used in the physical world in order to provide visually impaired people with information about their environment beyond the limits of touch (Bach-y-Rita & W Kercel, 2003).

Para-synthetic expression is another way of altering the morphology of an avatar body, by tracking input from the user which he or she may not be consciously aware of (such as psychological arousal, heart rate, or brain activity) and then rendering it so that it is easily observed (Janssen, Bailenson, IJsselsteijn & Westerink, 2010). Further examples of novel remappings are described by Waterworth and Waterworth (Chapter 2, this volume).

However, mapping a new avatar body or sensory receptor onto our existing morphology is only the first step in establishing a sense of presence in that body. In order to control and interpret such a new mapping in a fluent and time efficient manner, the body schema should adapt to the new virtual body and / or the media technology that is used to map it into our existing one.

4.2 Body Schema and Extending the Body Functionality with Tools

Following Gallagher (1986), who defined the body schema "as the unconscious performance of the body" (p. 548), Haans and IJsselsteijn (2012) propose a definition of the body schema as a dynamic distributed network of procedures aimed at guiding behavior. One important aspect of the body schema is that these procedures can largely operate outside of our conscious awareness; for example, being involved in distance estimation, action selection, muscle activation, keeping balance and other abilities that allow us to control our bodies in a fluent manner. In other words, having a body schema allows us to use the various parts of our complex morphology as a coherent functional unity. A second important aspect of the body schema is that it is highly adaptive, not only in accommodating the natural growth of the body, but in incorporating technological artifacts as functional extensions of the body.

4.2.1 Tool Use

One avenue of research on tool use has examined whether and how tools may be incorporated into the body schema--or alternatively phrased (see also Chapter 1, this volume): whether and how the network of body schema procedures adapts to the use of a tool. One example is Berti and Frassinetti's (2000) research on a patient (P.P) suffering from left-sided near space neglect. When a line was presented in far space, she performed equally well on a line bisection task as healthy controls. However, when pointing to the perceived midpoint of the line using a stick rather than a laser pointer, her near space neglect suddenly shifted into far space. This suggests that the brain remaps the space around the body to accommodate for the expansion of our reaching space when using a stick as a tool. Other research suggests that representations of the arm, as part of the dynamic body schema, are similarly adaptive and may become elongated when using tools that increase our reaching space. Cardinali and colleagues

(2009),for example, asked blindfolded participants to indicate various positions on their right arm with their other hand before and after using a grabber. Their results show an increase in distance between the indicated position of fingertips and the elbow as a result of tool use.

While the nature of the changes imposed by tool use remains subject to debate (e.g., Holmes, 2012), the ability of users to alter their behavior in order to interact with the environment through the medium of some tool is relevant to adaptation to novel avatar bodies. As described in Riva & Mantovani (2012 ; Chapter 1, this volume), the way people learn to manipulate an environment using tools shapes both their understanding of space and their sense of presence therein. As Haans and IJsselsteijn (2012) point out, adapting to the sensory feedback provided by tools is directly analogous to adapting to the feedback provided by immersive media technologies, and thus by inference, when interacting with a simulated environment by means of a virtual body. Thus when controlling an avatar, as with tool use, the user has the opportunity to actually enact movements that are not possible in real life with the unassisted human body.

Observers are not able to intuitively understand anatomically impossible movements by avatars when observing them from the third person perspective (Borroni, Gorini, Riva, Bouchard & Cerri, 2011). However, allowing users to create these impossible movements from a first person perspective in a way that imitates the mediation offered by normal sensory input raises very interesting questions of how they may incorporate such movements into the body schema, as some aspects of body schema development appear to be affected by experience and agency.

It is this potential flexibility of the body schema that led Jaron Lanier to choose the term "homuncular flexibility" to describe users' adaptability to novel bodies in virtual reality. The name reflects Lanier's proposal that the "homunculi" of the somatosensory and motor cortices- the portions of the brain described by Penfield and Boldrey (1937) that roughly map areas of bodily sensation and motor control- can be altered based on sensory input such as that provided by virtual reality. "Flexibility" refers to the idea that controlling an avatar body from the first person perspective without using a tool- that is, by using body movements alone and not manipulating a secondary object— is a very special example of tool use.

When considering presence in novel bodies, tool use probably provides the best analogy to consider how a feeling of presence may be created. With homuncular flexibility, presence is the expected result of learning to control an avatar body through the degrees of freedom available in the user's physical body without requiring that the avatar match the user, either in appearance or in the method of control. However, to feel present in this atypical avatar, the workings of that new body, and thus the way in which it is mapped upon the original one, should become transparent to its user. Within the framework of Haans and IJsselsteijn (2012) this requires that the body schema can adapt to include the components of the new body.

Presence in an avatar, however, means more than being present in the location of the avatar. It may also involve the experience that the avatar body is indeed your own; self-presence rather than spatial presence. This involves not just incorporation in the body schema, but in the body image as well.

4.3 Body Image and the Transfer of Body Ownership to Novel Bodies

In the framework by Haans and IJsselsteijn (2012), the body image is a product of consciousness. According to Edelman (2003; 2006) consciousness is the result of neural processes that allow for a large amount of refined discriminations and perceptual categorizations ranging from, for example, the "redness" of red to the unitary perceptual scene, emotions, and memories alike. The body image, as defined by Haans and IJsselsteijn, consists of those discriminations that pertain to the individual's own body (i.e., to those objects that the central nervous system has categorized as being a part of the physical body). In contrast to the body schema, the body image requires a notion of the body as owned by the user (see Gallagher, 1986).

This sense of body ownership may at times be transferred to tools as well, including the arms of a virtual avatar or teleoperation robot. Such incorporations into the body image are conceptually different from body schema incorporations: Body schema incorporations allow for proficient use of tools (i.e., as functional extensions of our morphology), but do not require a transfer of body ownership toward that tool (i.e., a phenomenological extension in which the tool becomes part of our bodily selves). The extent to which virtual avatars that do not correspond to the natural human body can be incorporated into the body image remains to be discovered.

4.3.1 Body Transfer and Body Ownership

While body transfer has been studied in and out of virtual reality, it began as investigations in the real world. In the rubber hand illusion, first demonstrated by Botvinick and Cohen (1998), participants are seated in front of a table on which an obviously fake rubber hand is placed in approximately the orientation of their real hand. Their own real hand is placed out of sight, either under the table or behind a screen. Subsequently both hands are simultaneously and synchronously stroked with a soft brush. After a few minutes, many participants report a sense of body ownership over the fake hand, and when the rubber hand is suddenly struck with a rubber mallet, many react violently, as if their own hand had been struck (Armel & Ramachandran, 2003). This work has been extended in virtual reality. IJsselsteijn, de Kort and Haans (2006) replicated the rubber hand illusion in physical, virtual and mixed reality, demonstrating similar effects although the strength of the subjective illusion differed (see also Slater, Perez-Marcos, Ehrsson, & Sanchez, 2008).

Research on the rubber-hand illusion has revealed that body ownership results from establishing so-called body specific sensorimotor contingencies (Botvinick, 2004). The clapping of one's hands, whether self-initiated or not, consists of correlated multisensory impressions. Some of these patterns of sensorimotor contingencies are exclusively associated with the body, and hence self-specifying: When the visual image of clapping hands is accompanied immediately by a tactile sensation in the hands, then by inference it must be your hands that do the clapping. In the rubber hand illusion, some of these body specific contingencies are mapped onto the fake hand. At the same time, the incorporation of the fake hand into the body image appears to be modulated top-down by an internal model of what the human body is like: Objects that differ morphologically from the human body are less easily incorporated (e.g., Haans, IJsselsteijn, & de Kort, 2008; de Vignemont, Tsakiris, & Haggard, 2006; Tsakiris & Haggard, 2005).

The rubber hand illusion has been extended by, among others, Petkova and Ehrsson (2008), who investigated whole body transfer, including establishing a sense of ownership in a mannequin body, and switching the gender of the body from the participants' own gender. In addition, work on "body transfer" in virtual reality further supports the idea that people can be brought to identify with avatars that differ in appearance and gender (Slater, Spanlang, Sanchez-Vives & Blanke, 2010). Such experiments show results similar to the Proteus effects shown by first-person perspective in a mirror condition. Consistent with the rubber hand illusion research, Petkova and Ehrsson demonstrate that the body had to be human-like in order for body ownership to transfer. However, some work has been done than indicates that disruption of the normal human template does not preclude this effect. For example, Schaefer, Flor, Heinze and Rotte (2007) created a sense of ownership in a very long arm by simultaneous touch, and Kilteni, Normand, Sanchez-Vives and Slater, (2012) duplicated this phenomenon in a virtual environment.

In the experiment by Kilteni et al (2012) participants were able to transfer ownership to an extremely long virtual arm extending up to three to four times the length of the participant's own; showing thus little of the top-down modulation consistently found in the rubber hand illusion literature (cf. Armel and Ramachandran, 2013). The authors argue that this top-down modulation may perhaps be countered by increasing the richness of the multisensory stimulation, which in their experiment involved not just establishing visuotactile contingencies, but visuomotor, and tactilemotor contingencies as well. Recent evidence on the rubber-hand illusion supports this claim by demonstrating that increasing the amount of information in the visuotactile stimulation (e.g., tapping versus stroking the fingers) makes it easier for people to experience the illusion (Haans, Kaiser, Bouwhuis, & IJsselsteijn, 2012).

Body transfer or body ownership emphasizes the role of simultaneous, synchronous multisensory input over taking action in a virtual environment. While much of the experimental work has examined variations of the normal human template, the potential exists for body transfer to occur in bodies that stretch the definition of the normal.

Creating a sense of ownership over novel bodies not only requires the establishment of new body-specific sensorimotor contingencies, but the morphological discrepancies between the novel body and its human counterpart are more extensive as well. Developing a sense of ownership over a novel body may be more difficult than establishing it over a human-like body or body part. Rich multisensory stimulation may help to successfully transfer ownership to a novel body--realizing of course that action allows for richer sensorimotor interactions then exclusively passive stimulation. Also, such ownership transferal may not come instantaneously. While the original definition of homuncular flexibility specifically referred to the alteration of a map of the body over the very short term (the minutes in which a person could inhabit an avatar in virtual reality) considerable time and practice with using a novel morphology may be required before such a morphology may be incorporated in the body schema and image. At the same time, we should not forget the possibility that the plasticity of our human embodiment may have limits, for example because of congenital factors (for a discussion, see Price, 2006).

4.4 Embodied Cognition and Virtual Environments

Embodied cognition proposes that people understand the world through their bodies. In other words, not only does the mind guide and prompt the body to action, but the actions the body takes and the resulting experiences, shape how a person comes to understand not only his- or herself, but the surrounding environment (Wilson, 2002; Anderson, 2003). For example, most people are right-handed and can complete tasks more easily using their dominant hand. Embodied cognition researchers propose that right-handed people thus develop a preference for the right side of their world, such that objects that are placed on the right side of a person's body are viewed more positively than those on the left (thus the etymology of the word "sinister" which means, to the left (Casasanto & Chrysikou, 2011).

Embodied cognition is a particularly useful concept when considering presence in a non-human avatar because it takes into account the effects that such an avatar may have on the user's ability to understand and manipulate the virtual environment. If people inhabit an environment in a body with different affordances, that experience may affect their understanding of both that environment, and possibly that of the physical world to which they return.

Some work on embodied cognition does imply that this influence can be changed rather rapidly, as in an experiment by Casasanto and Chrysikou (2011) where right-handed people were temporarily handicapped by wearing a ski glove on their right hand, such that their left hand was temporarily more able than their right. Participants then showed the same association as natural left-handed people in assigning "good" objects to the left and "bad" objects to the right. Clark (2007) similarly emphasizes the role of activity when he describes the body as a "suite of potentials for action" in which tools can augment and extend the body. This concept reinforces the idea that the extent to which a user may interact with the virtual world using a novel body may alter the extent to which said user feels truly present in that body and that world.

Research in embodied cognition would thus imply that relatively short interventions affecting an individual's ability to take action in the environment will result in changes in how that individual perceives that environment and how present they feel. Altering the appearance and functionality of an avatar may also lead to changes in how the virtual environment is perceived. When a person operates an avatar with multiple, elongated limbs, far may become near. If a person's legs become much more fluent than his or her arms, perhaps the positive valence for higher objects may reverse. However, many of the associations that an adult holds for his or her body have been in existence since birth and augmented by experience. The extent to which these long-standing associations may be altered by a brief experience in an avatar body remains to be seen.

4.5 Conclusion to Chapter 4

As virtual reality has developed, the worlds and experiences available therein have continued to diverge from the real. In addition, the ability of users to interact with virtual environments and effect changes in these virtual worlds has been augmented as technology improves. More naturalistic gestures expand the situations in which users may or may not experience a sense of presence. In addition, methods of tracking human gestures that are much less obtrusive will probably continue to proliferate. Current efforts to use interfaces that do not require the user to wear any markers or hold any devices (for example, the Microsoft Kinect) point the way to a future in which movements can be captured in an everyday environment and be used to drive mediated interactions.

Investigating avatar design can provide concrete evidence for ways of improving user interfaces. Aspects of design decisions that are often made intuitively can have effects on users' understanding of their bodies and their interactions with their environment. In addition, virtual reality offers the opportunity to change the world and the body, and examine the resulting effects on the self, in ways that are not possible in real life. This allows us to manipulate embodiment to change outcomes, attitudes, and learning.

Virtual reality allows us to see explicitly the affordances of our mediated bodies. However, our abilities are being changed by current technologies in both virtual reality and real life, as we see devices proliferate that provide increased memory, ability to access group knowledge instantly, etc. This illustrates Biocca's "cyborg's dilemma” (Biocca, 1992) as we consider how extending our sense of embodiment, by augmenting the mediated ways in which we may control our environment, may be changing our fundamental sense of our selves.

References

Anderson, M. L. (2003). Embodied Cognition: A Field Guide. *Artificial Intelligence, 149,* 91-130.

Armel, K. C. & Ramachandran, V. S. (2003). Projecting sensations to external objects: Evidence from skin conductance response. *Proceedings of the Royal Society of London B, 270,* 1499-1506.

Bach-y-Rita, P., & W Kercel, S. (2003). Sensory substitution and the human–machine interface. *Trends in cognitive sciences, 7*(12), 541-546.

Berti, A., & Frassinetti, F. (2000). When far becomes near: re-mapping of space by tool use.

Biocca, F. (1999). The cyborg’s dilemma: Progressive embodiment in virtual environments. *Human Factors in Information Technology, 13,* 113-144.

Borroni, P., Gorini, A., Riva, G., Bouchard, S., & Cerri, G. (2011). Mirroring avatars: dissociation of action and intention in human motor resonance. *European Journal of Neuroscience, 34*(4), 662-669.

Botvinick, M., & Cohen, J. (1998). Rubber hands’ “feel” touch that eyes see. *Nature, 391*(6669), 756-756.

Botvinick, M. (2004). Probing the neural basis of body ownership. *Science, 305,* 782-783.

Carlson, T. A., Alvarez, G., Wu, D. A., & Verstraten, F. A. (2010). Rapid assimilation of external objects into the body schema. *Psychological Science, 21*(7), 1000-1005.

Cardinali, L., Frassinetti, F., Brozzoli, C., Urquizar, C., Roy, A. C., & Farnè, A. (2009). Tool-use induces morphological updating of the body schema. *Current Biology, 19*(12), 478-479

Casasanto, D., & Chrysikou, E. G. (2011). When left is “right” motor fluency shapes abstract concepts. *Psychological Science, 22*(4), 419-422.

Clark, A. (2007). Re-inventing ourselves: The plasticity of embodiment, sensing, and mind. *Journal of Medicine and Philosophy, 32*(3), 263-282.

Cole, J., Sacks, O., & Waterman, I. (2000). On the immunity principle: A view from a robot. *Trends in Cognitive Science, 4,* 167.

Damasio, A. (1999). The feeling of what happens: body, emotion and the making of consciousness. San Diego: Harcourt Brace.

de Vignemont, F., Tsakiris, M., & Haggard, P. (2006). Body mereology. In G. Knoblich, I. M. Thornton, M. Grosjean, & M. Shiffrar (Eds.), *Human body perception from the inside out* (pp. 147–170). New York: Oxford University Press.

Edelman, G. M. (2003). Naturalizing consciousness: A theoretical framework. *Proceedings of the Natural Academy of Sciences of the United States of America, 100,* 5520-5524.

Edelman, G. M. (2006). *Second nature: Brain science and human knowledge.* New Haven, CT: Yale University Press.

Ehrsson, H. H. (2007). The experimental induction of out-of-body experiences. *Science, 317,* 1048–1048.

Gallagher, S. (1986). Body image and body schema: A conceptual clarification. *Journal of Mind and Behavior, 7,* 541-554.

Gallagher, S. (2005). Dynamic models of body schematic processes. In H. de Preester, V. Knockaert (Eds.), *Body image and body schema* (pp. 233-250.). Amsterdam: John Benjamins.

Haans, A., & IJsselsteijn, W. A. (2012). Embodiment and telepresence: Toward a comprehensive theoretical framework. *Interacting with Computers, 24*(4), 211-218.

Haans, A., & IJsselsteijn, W. A., & de Kort, Y. A. W. (2008). The effect of similarities in skin texture and hand shape on perceived ownership of a fake limb. *Body Image: An International Journal of Research*, *5*, 389-394.

Haans, A., Kaiser, F.G., Bouwhuis, D.G. & IJsselsteijn, W.A. (2012). Individual differences in the rubber-hand illusion: Predicting self-reports of people's personal experiences. *Acta Psychologica, 141,* 169-177.

Holmes, N. P. (2012). Does tool use extend peripersonal space? A review and re-analysis. *Experimental brain research, 218*(2), 273-282.

IJsselsteijn, W. A. (2005). Towards a neuropsychological basis of presence, *Annual Review of CyberTherapy and Telemedicine, 3,* 25-30.

IJsselstein, W. A., de Kort, Y. A., & Haans, A. 2006. Is this my hand I see before me? The rubber hand illusion in reality, virtual reality and mixed reality. *Presence, 15*: 455–464.

Janssen, J.H., Bailenson J.N., IJsselsteijn, W.A., & Westerink, J.H.D.M. (2010). Intimate heartbeats: Opportunities for affective communication technology. *IEEE Transactions on Affective Computing, 1*(2), 72-80.

Kilteni, K., Normand, J-M., Sanchez-Vives, M. V., & Slater, M. (2012). Extending Body Space in Immersive Virtual Reality: A Very Long Arm Illusion. *PLoS ONE 7*(7): e40867.

Lanier, J. (2006). Homuncular Flexibility, http://www.edge.org/response-detail/11182print.html - lanier. Edge Foundation, Inc. Accessed February 3, 2014.

Lee, K. M. (2004). Presence, explicated. *Communication theory, 14*(1), 27-50.

Lombard, M., & Ditton, T. (1997). At the heart of it all: The concept of presence. *Journal of Computer Mediated Communication, 3*(2), 0-0.

Longo, M. R., & Lourenco, S. F. (2006). On the nature of near space: Effects of tool use and the transition to far space. *Neuropsychologia, 44*(6), 977-981.

Loomis, J. M. (1992). Distal attribution and presence. Presence: Teleoperators and Virtual Environments, 1(1), 113-119.

Loomis, J. M. (1993). Understanding synthetic experience must begin with the analysis of ordinary perceptual experience. In *Proceedings of the IEEE Symposium on Research Frontiers in Virtual Reality* (pp. 54-57). Los Alamos, CA: IEEE Press.

Maselli, A., & Slater, M. (2013). The building blocks of the full body ownership illusion. Frontiers in human neuroscience, 7 (83), 1-20.

Metzinger, T. (2003). Being no one: The self-model theory of subjectivity. Cambridge, MA: MIT press.

Metzinger, T. (2006). *Reply to Gallagher: Different conceptions of embodiment.* Psyche 12(4), 1-7.

Metzinger, T. (2009). *The ego tunnel: The Science of the mind and the myth of the self.* New York: Basic Books.

Nass, C., & Reeves, B. (1996). The Media Equation: How People Treat Computers, Televisions, and New Media as Real People and Places. Stanford, Calif.: CSLI Publications ; New York: Cambridge University Press.

Penfield, W., Boldrey, E. (1937) Somatic motor and sensory representation in the cerebral cortex of man as studied by electrical stimulation. *Brain, 60,* 389–443.

Petkova, V. I., & Ehrsson, H. H. (2008). If I were you: perceptual illusion of body swapping. *PloS one, 3*(12): e3832.

Price, E. H. (2006). A critical review of congenital phantom limb cases and a developmental theory for the basis of body image. *Consciousness and Cognition*, *15*(2), 310-322.

Ratan, R. A. (2012). Self-presence, explicated: Body, emotion, and identity extension into the virtual self. In R. Luppicini (Ed.), Handbook of Research on Technoself. New York, NY: IGI Global.

Riva, G., & Mantovani, F. (2012). From the body to the tools and back: a general framework for presence in mediated interactions. *Interacting with Computers, 24*(4), 203-210. doi: doi: 10.1016/j.intcom.2012.04.007

Riva, G., Waterworth, J. A., Waterworth, E. L., & Mantovani, F. (2011). From intention to action: The role of presence. *New Ideas in Psychology, 29*(1), 24-37.

Schaefer, M., Flor, H., Heinze, H. J., & Rotte, M. (2007). Morphing the body: illusory feeling of an elongated arm affects somatosensory homunculus. *Neuroimage, 36*(3), 700-705.

Slater M., Perez-Marcos D., Ehrsson H.H., Sanchez-Vives M.V. (2008) Towards a digital body: The virtual arm illusion. *Frontiers in Human Neuroscience, 2*(6), 1-8.

Slater, M., Spanlang, B., Sanchez-Vives, M. V., & Blanke, O. (2010). First person experience of body transfer in virtual reality. *PloS one, 5*(5): e10564.Slater, M. & Usoh, M. (1994). Body centred interaction in immersive virtual environments, in: N. Magnenat Thalmann, D. Thalmann (Eds.), *Artificial life and virtual reality* (pp. 125-148). Chichester, UK: John Wiley.

Steptoe, W., Steed, A., & Slater, M. (2013). Human Tails: Ownership and Control of Extended Humanoid Avatars. *Visualization and Computer Graphics, IEEE*

Transactions on, 19(4), 583-590.Steuer, J. (1992). Defining virtual reality: Dimensions determining telepresence. *Journal of communication, 42(4)*, 73-93.

Sutherland, I. E. (1965). The ultimate display. Multimedia: From Wagner to virtual reality. *Proceedings of the IFIP Congress*, 506-508.

Tsakiris, M., & Haggard, P. (2005). The rubber hand illusion revisited: Visuotactile integration and self-attribution. Journal of Experimental Psychology. *Human Perception and Performance, 31,* 80–91.

Wilson, M. (2002). Six views of embodied cognition. *Psychonomic bulletin & review, 9*(4), 625-636.

Yee, N., & Bailenson, J. (2007). The Proteus effect: The effect of transformed self-representation on behavior. *Human communication research, 33*(3), 271-290.

Zahorik, P., & Jenison, R.L. Presence as being-in-the-world. *Presence-Teleoperations and Virtual Environments, 7,* 78-89.

5 Presence and Hyperpresence: Implications for Community Awareness

John M. Carroll, Patrick C. Shih, Blaine Hoffman, Jing Wang, and Kyungsik Han

Abstract: A prominent issue in community informatics is community awareness: the awareness of community members of activity in their community. Community awareness helps community members understand and appreciate their community, motivates them to participate and reciprocate, and evokes feelings of empathy, intimacy and solidarity. In this chapter we analyze community awareness technologies as helping community members feel more present to others and feel that others are more present to them. We draw upon several design investigations of supporting community awareness through aggregation of RSS feeds and Tweets, digital cultural heritage, volunteer efforts, and fieldwork understanding community awareness designs in the *LiveStrong* health community.

Keywords: Social Presence; Social Presence Technologies; Hyperpresence; Community Awareness.

5.1 Introduction to Chapter 5

Social presence is the feeling of being engaged with, and connected to others, the phenomenal sense of being together (see also Chapter 1, this volume). Conceptions of social presence derive from Goffman's (1959, 1963) analysis of co-presence as persons being embodied in the same place, mutually visible to and aware of one another, and socially available to one another. For Goffman, co-presence is grounded in the here-and-now physicality of the interaction situation, in one's social perception of others, and in one's awareness of being reciprocally perceived by similar others. It is the foundation for social interaction.

As a contemporary technical term, "social presence" was first used by Short, Williams & Christie (1976) to analyze social interactions mediated by telecommunications channels. This early work emphasized the (surprising) extent to which an experience of social presence could be evoked through technology-mediated human interactions, all the more surprising given the fairly low-bandwidth interactions relative to contemporary networking capabilities. Short et al. (1976) suggested further that mediated social presence is not a simple contrast of present versus absent, but rather a quality with nuances of kind and degree, potentially modulated by relationships among participants, by the salience of a given participant in a given interaction, as well as by attitudes towards the technological mediation, in their case, the telecommunications channel.

Contemporary networking infrastructures enable a great variety of what Biocca, Harms and Burgoon (2003) call *social presence technologies*, giving high-bandwidth teleconferencing, collaborative work environments, mobile and wireless interactions, speech interfaces, and 3D social virtual environments as examples. Various social presence technologies enable a wide range of social presence phenomena, such as the experience of remote interaction mediated by avatars (Bailenson et al. 2008). Biocca et al. also emphasize that we do not have a comprehensive theory of social presence, as they describe it, "of how differences in technological connection, representation, and mediated access affect, distort, or enhance the perception (mental model) of others' intentional, cognitive, and affective states and behavior resulting from those perceptions." (Biocca et al., 2003, p. 473).

In this chapter, we focus on place-based and community technologies that amplify sense of presence in the embodied world, and on particular ways that such technologies may amplified social presence. In order to assess and analyze the role and effects of social presence in any situation, we must understand how technology-mediated interaction reveals important characteristics that shape and influence the perception of social presence. We report a design research investigation of social presence for interactions among persons living in a placed community. Community members are often co-present, in Goffman's sense, as they move about in local public space. However, their interactions can also be mediated, through interactions with local information and services. We coin the term *hyperpresence* to refer to social presence heightened beyond what is (normally) possible face to face, on analogy to the term *hyperlocal news*, news about a locale created by people at or in that locale for the use of people at or in that locale (Farhi, 1991).

We illustrate hyperpresence through several design inquiries. *CiVicinity* is a platform that utilizes community feeds such as news, events, and discussions to make people more aware and feel more present in their community. Smartphone applications such as *Lost State College*, *Local News Chatter*, and *Mobile Timebanking* add the dimension of mobility to hyperpresence, and allow community members to more easily contribute to a continuing discourse of community topics. We describe our studies of an online virtual community: *LiveStrong.com*, and how various designs afford the sense of social presence in a virtual community. In each of these, the capabilities of the technology support feelings of hyperpresence that would not arise otherwise.

5.2 Hyperpresence in Local Communities

In our work with community partners and groups, our research group has established a community-driven portal site for the surrounding area. Typically, the information generated by and within a given community originates from a number of sparse sources, each generating seemingly little information over time. Many of these sources might employ feeds (e.g., RSS, ATOM, iCalendar), a technology that enables updates and information to be automatically pushed to subscribers, as opposed to requiring readers to discover and check a web site manually.

Built upon the foundation of previous prototypes, CiVicinity is a web-based community portal that employs Web 2.0 assets to deliver up-to-date community information and news closely associated with community places and members. CiVicinity populates its news page and its events calendar with data from community-owned feeds. It also incorporates location-sensitive, event-based features and expands upon the idea to pair maps and coordinate data across the whole site. The site serves as a centralized aggregate of community information, reducing the effort required for any individual to access and peruse the information. Each news feed entry on CiVicinity provides a link to the original source, enabling readers to easily navigate to the blog, news site, organization's web page, and so on. Categories identify the type of feed source, making it easier for readers to seek specific types of stories and to filter the feeds by interest. On the events calendar page, we parse iCalendar feeds from community sources to list events in a calendar view. As with the news feeds, the description of these events includes the name of the source organization. Since news and calendar feeds sometimes provide geocode data, we pair news and calendar information with a map visualization, provide a view that sorts lists and items by distance from the user, and provide directions to events and addresses. CiVinicity is integrated with social networking sites such as Facebook, Twitter, and email using the respective APIs provided by these platforms. Any news story or event that catches a reader's interest can be shared. Our prior prototypes were deployed in support of specific meta-events, such as a local arts festival and holiday activities on New Year's Eve, focusing on various activities and locations within the community.

Using CiVicinity, individuals can all be on the same page about the relevant *where* of information. For example, the explicit use of map visualizations enhances awareness of community events and their relevance to planning social interactions and shaping an understanding of the community itself (Hoffman et al, 2012). The aggregated community information portal creates a virtual space that augments the physical spaces of the community to create a more complete community place. As a result, CiVicinity is part of the process of creating and maintaining social presence rather than a separate arena of presence itself. Furthermore, the use of CiVicinity can convey presence regardless of synchronous use or concurrent physical co-location. The commenting and interactions associated on the site, such as reading historical information about a place while also visiting that place or viewing the comments left by others about community news and events, help to affirm the feeling of others' presence within the community. Exploring community places and community-generated discussion is not reliant upon individuals meeting up in person. CiVicinity's online existence and digital nature afford interactions not possible in face-to-face

Figure 5.1: Screenshot of the CiVicinity Events page

settings. The timing of an individual's travels throughout town no longer dictate whom he or she might bump into, just as strangers in the same crowd that might never interact could find themselves engaged with others using the site. CiVicinity makes individuals and events more available to the community.

With CiVicinity, individuals are more present in their community due to removing restrictions of space and time. Civicinity presents a more complete and clear overview of the community via maps that show where interactions are, or will be, and enables community members to share in knowing who is involved. CiVicinity is meant to raise community awareness among community members. By highlighting what is being discussed and what is happening within a community and delivering that information directly to individuals, their overall understanding of the community increases. Being accessible at any time and explicitly keeping location and position at the forefront of interactions increases the understanding of technology's ability to enhance and supplement activity. Together, these two characteristics foster an easier acceptance and comfort of the frame of interaction across the community via technology. Technology-mediated interaction that aggregates community information, geolocation, and social media is embraced by CiVicinity to enhance the construction of hyperpresence.

5.3 Hyperpresence in Mobile Technologies

Expanding on enhancing hyperpresence in the same geographical communities with traditional Web 2.0 technologies, our research group has been investigating how mobile platforms would make people more aware of and ease participation in various local community news, events, or activities. Although a great amount of concern with social isolation due to the Internet and mobile device does exist, many recent studies have indicated that technology use contributes to having more social connection, interaction, and participation (Hampton et. al, 2009). Similarly, by analyzing national survey data of internet usage and friendship, Wang and Wellman demonstrate that technologies blurred boundaries between online and offline and people who use the Internet and mobile technology still interact with others on a regular basis and the number of friends itself even increased because of the popularity and penetration of social media (Wang & Wellman, 2010).

A growing number of people adopt and use mobile devices in their daily lives and start to leverage its unique opportunities, such as personalization, portability and ubiquitous connectivity, to facilitate and reinforce their social interactions and connections with other people (Carroll & Rosson, 2009). Local residents' presence within a geographical community can be mediated by the use of their mobile devices, which would lead to the construction of a social presence in which one's activities and actions become more visible to their community as well as other community members. To articulate the notion of hyperpresence and social interaction mediated by mobile technology in a local community context, we have been extensively working on three projects that leverage the capabilities of smartphones to support local heritage (Lost State College), local news and events (Local News Chatter), and local volunteer efforts (Mobile Timebanking). Each project has a designated smartphone app that enables enhanced community awareness, participation, and engagement and social connection and interaction, and thereby one's sense of social presence.

Lost State College (LSC) is a smartphone app to make local cultural heritage more visible and available to community members, aiming to capture and share the collective memories of a town's history (Han et al., 2014). The meaning of LSC implies preservation efforts of local history; otherwise it will be "lost" in the future. LSC utilizes a geo-coded dataset of a number of historic downtown landmarks provided by a Borough of State College. For each location, LSC provides a name, address, a set of official historical and current photos, a text description, and a pre-recorded audio description for each landmark. Along with these official content, LSC also provides four additional interfaces (named *Social Features*) for social interactions in which people can add their personal reflections on and stories to the landmarks by augmenting visits, likes, comments, or photos on their mobile device.

Our user study with local residents indicates that participants both utilized official and social information when appreciating the landmarks through LSC. In particular, by adding their own or accessing others' photos, comments, likes, and visits, social

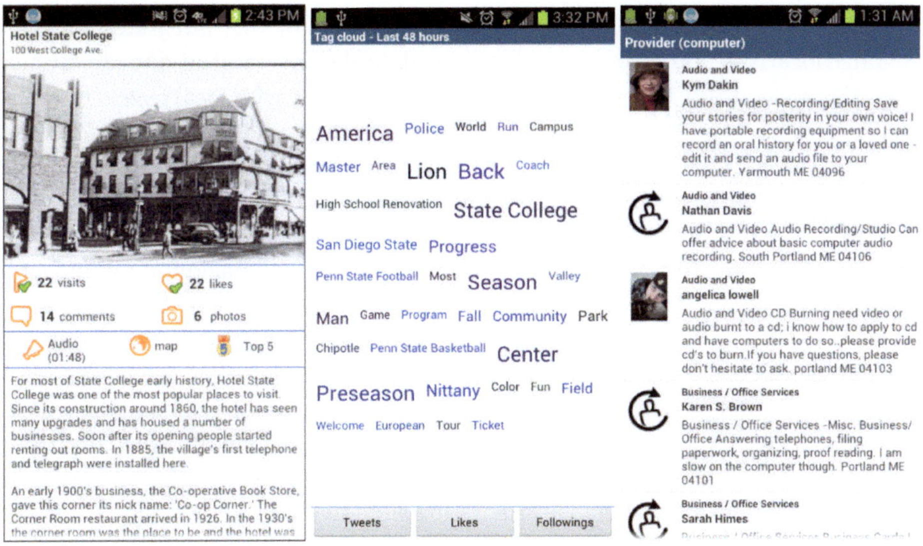

(a) (b) (c)

Figure 5.2: Screenshots of (a) Lost State College, (b) Local News Chatter, and (c) Mobile Timebanking

features allowed participants to not only increase their awareness of local landmarks and history but also reconstruct landmarks into more dynamic and socially meaningful places to themselves and their community. LSC enabled participants to realize that the place where they live has its own long and rich history as well as giving them heartfelt appreciation for the people and families who built up the town over many generations. Some participants mentioned,

> "I really didn't know buildings have some stories and history. Giving more different perspectives to my community" (Han et al., 2014: Participant 20) and "I have learned a lot about this community, like it used to be a bank, theatre, and it got burned, etc. I think it is a learning experience" (Han et al., 2014: Participant 28).

They also mentioned that they felt more identity and belonging to a community after completing the tour.

> "I love to know about the story of each building. Knowing a little bit more makes me feel even more like 'townie' " (Han et al., 2014: Participant 30).

Using and interacting with the app suggests that local residents' use of mobile technology evoked different perspectives and feelings of social presence not present otherwise. Local landmarks that merely existed as part of the environment and subconsciously acknowledged as people walked by every day became focal points of interaction and historical meaning.

Local News Chatter (LNC) is the local new aggregator that integrates socially-generated local tweets and formal local news feeds to elicit new and unique community value (Han et al., 2013). Users would see local stories along with local tweets relevant to those stories. Since local news and tweets are publicly available data, no additional effort from the users is required in creating this content. Rather, existing content is leveraged through keyword analysis that organizes stories with relevant tweets. When users see the tweets about stories that are interesting or relevant to their lives, they can follow up with the other community members who made the tweets. As a result, community members benefit from better community awareness of local issues and personal perspectives and can share their interests and concerns without any content creation cost. LNC utilizes relevant local topics reported in the newspapers and existing Twitter comments of local residents about these topics to provide a local discussion space. LNC makes its users more aware of the community knowledge and sentiment about local topics and enhances the social presence of other members in the community who will otherwise remain invisible to the users, thereby achieving hyperpresence.

Based on the user study with local residents, we found that participants appreciated accessing a rich amount of local news information from the formal news and the social media. They in particular liked reading tweets from other community members, because it broadens their insights on local community topics.

> "Pointed me to news stories or insights about the local area which I might not know (and therefore be interested in) otherwise" (Han et al., 2014: Participant 22) and "Yes, I enjoyed the festival tremendously. It's good to realize that almost everyone feels the same way" (Han et al., 2014: Participant 18).

This also affected their participation and engagement in local news information.

> "I could see people's interests and eager for support the apartment residents [who suffered from a fire]. People retweeted the way how to donate, the motivation of fire, and so forth. [...] I was very interested in how to help and what I can do to help them" (Han et al., 2014: Participant 29).

Many participants expressed that they wanted to engage more in news activities by creating personal thoughts or opinions, retweeting existing ones, or following other users to receive their updated news in the future.

Lastly, Mobile Timebanking is the extension of conventional timebanking, which uses time as a form of currency to encourage service exchanges among timebank members in the same community (Bellotti et al., 2013; Carroll, 2013). For example, one resident might be a competent handyman, while another plays guitar. Each can provide community service doing what he or she can do for other members and receives time credits that can be exchanged for services from other members, such as gardening. Since timebanking requires interpersonal communications and interactions, much research on timebanking has shown that it strengthens interpersonal trust, social connection and the sense of community attachment (Collom et al., 2012). With this goal in mind, our design research of leveraging mobile technology in a timebank context attempts to take advantages of the affordances of smartphones, such as facilitating access to communications and transaction management activities. The Mobile Timebanking app supports not only the basic timebanking functionalities of posting, accessing tasks, giving time credits, and accessing task history and user's profile details but also those that are suited to the use of smartphones, such as having a map view that shows both user and task locations and notifying users of any incoming text messages from other users or status updates of the tasks in near-real time.

Our user study with local residents reveals how hyperpresence of local volunteer efforts is mediated by mobile technology. We found that participants were surprised by the fact that there was a lot of tasks posted by others and were pleased to discover that many people were willing to provide help in the community. The local volunteer interactions and activities was made more visible to other people, the local volunteers were made more accessible by the mobile platform because their offers were easily shared and accessed by their mobile device, and people were able to respond to urgent requests more easily with the app. Mobile Timebanking shows a potential of fostering community altruistic exchanges and creating social connections by using one's skills or resources to help others.

Overall, mobile computing enables the use of hyperlocal information, wherein users' location can be capitalized upon and used to tailor the collection and delivery of community knowledge and social communication. Our investigations through Lost State College, Local News Chatter, and Mobile Timebanking show that information delivered over mobile platforms can enhance the experience in-situ, extending the interaction beyond the tangible and crossing spans of time to connect individuals. As a result, the technology transcends a role of connecting remote or disparate individuals to serve as a platform that extends the notion of place beyond the physical spaces upon which a community is built, and generates a notion of hyperpresence in the community not tied to physical interaction alone.

5.4 Hyperpresence in Online Virtual Communities

As Web 2.0, social media, and other communication technologies become more widely adopted, more and more people are collaborating, communicating, and meeting with friends and even strangers in a purely virtual environment with no physical face-to-face interactions. In order to understand how social presence takes place in virtual communities with no physical, face-to-face interactions, we conducted an empirical study of LiveStrong.com, an online health community, and how technological affordances help enable social presence in a virtual community platform.

LiveStrong.com is a platform that supports several health conditions but is primarily known for its online weight management community and its calorie-tracking tool with data sharing capability. It was launched in 2008 and had over four million registered users as of 2011. The community supports member interactions in its blog-style groups. Members can create custom groups that are either open to public or private to group members. Many active and popular groups have thousands of members. For example, the 100+ Pounds to Lose Group has more than 4,000 members. Group spaces are organized in a blog format: they are segmented by dates with members' posts and corresponding comments constituting each segment. Anyone can post open-texts to a public group without membership; by joining a group, one's tracking data will be aggregated with the data of other group members. The MyPlate calorie tracker allows users to log their food and fitness activities manually. Users can select their daily or weekly weight management goal to be losing, gaining, or maintaining a specific amount of weight. MyPlate also enables users to customize their ultimate weight and daily nutrient goals. Weight progress is visualized in a line chart as well as in a highlighted note, such as, *"I've lost <amount of pounds> lbs!"*. Individual users' daily tracking data of calorie goals, calories consumed, logs of food intake and calories of each food item and its nutrient breakdown, calories burned, logs of fitness activities, and net calories consumed can be presented and shared in two ways. One is called *Food Diary*, an integral record that consists of tracked food and fitness information and allows comments from other members. Users can configure which items of the tracked data are to be shown in the diaries and who can access their diaries (i.e., public, friends only, private, and selected individuals). The other is an aggregate view of group members' daily tracked data, which summarizes parts of the individuals' data. Both total and average values of these measurements from members who have tracked their activities on that day are shown in a table, which can also be expanded to display data at the individual level. Groups can choose whether to enable this visualization feature in their group space.

Presence of LiveStrong.com users is mediated by both the community spaces and the tracking technology. As the core benefit of online health communities, the presence—the sense of availability—of a large support network was cited as the one of the critical criteria participants employed to decide which LiveStrong.com group to join. Such presence is mainly indicated by regular posting from group members. In contrast to face-to-face support groups, these online groups do not emphasize real-time responses to people's frustration, anxiety, or concerns. Moreover, people do not expect support from a specific person, accepting it from anyone as long as it is positive and constructive. What matters is the sense that someone will be there within a certain period of time when an individual needs support. Every member benefits from others' presence; at the same time, their presence contributes to other members' weight management processes. The following example illustrates how participating in LiveStrong.com with others who share similar experiences generates a sense of presence among the community members.

> "I like this group because I feel there is a fellowship amongst us who have lost a lot of weight or who are in the process of it. There is nothing better than having someone who has been there along for the ride" (Wang et al., 2014: Participant 9).

Aside from creating the perceived social presence of a large support network, LiveStrong.com, like other online health communities, also mediates such presence by grouping people with similar experiences and attributes. Different from physically presenting oneself, which is often enabled by co-location or rich media (e.g., video, virtual modeling), LiveStrong.com heightens a dimension of individual identity, making it salient and easy to relate to for people. The majority of participants mentioned the importance of such similarities: peers sharing similar health-related experiences were especially competent to offer empathy and pertinent informational support, keeping them engaged in the community.

> "I initially joined the 5'2" group because there are constraints for a short person working out that tall people don't get. However, I quickly veered away from this group because while the group members meet the 5'2" or less criteria, this community is comprised mostly of women in their 20's who have no idea what it's like to be short and old and trying to get and stay fit and healthy. 8-)... The [Getting Fit and Fabulous Over 40] group is not constrained by a specific height, but they are all people (primarily women) in their 40's or thereabouts who share their experiences..." (Wang et al., 2014: Participant 1).

The tracking data generated by individuals, either narratives (e.g., amount of weight loss per week shared in group discussions) or structured daily activities (e.g., food diaries), create opportunities of new ways of self-presentation in the community. It is hardly possible for peers to maintain awareness of one's every food intake and exercise. It is also difficult for them to generate a holistic view of one's overall progress towards his/her calorie goals as well as weight goals. The tracking tool enables all the information to be captured and accessed at various levels of detail beyond individual's own cognitive capabilities. This provides the basis for peers to exchange social support with each other.

> "I met all of these 'friends' in various groups that I was active in before. We can 'visit' each others diaries, read what they wrote and make comments. We often:
> ---Encourage a friend if they're down.
> ---Compliment them on having a nice "plate" of tracked food.
> ---Comment specifically on what they wrote and the things they said.
> ---Ask questions about what they wrote, or the food they tracked.
> In my 'circle', there are between 3-10 ladies who "run around" visiting each other's diaries and posting nice comments. If someone posts a comment to your diary, it's only courteous to return the favor and share the love. It creates a kind of reciprocal community" (Wang et al., 2014: Participant 3).

At LiveStrong.com, aggregating group tracking data of calorie goals and intake was intended to create interdependence and accountability among group members;

however, such a design failed to achieve this purpose because many users did not regularly log into the system or completely recorded their activities. Instead, participants found the mutual awareness of weight loss progress—the amount of weight lost—during weekly weigh-in activities effective in sustaining their motivations to achieve their goals.

> "I fed on the Monday weigh-ins and Tuesday summaries, and took great delight as I progressed up the 'weight list' ladder" (Wang et al., 2014: Participant 7).

Constraining one's presence by not disclosing one's own tracking data, on the contrary, was perceived as detrimental to goal achievement.

> "I notice that those who complain the most about not being able to get results often don't make their food diaries public and that leads me to believe that they're not honest with themselves or others. If you're eating right and exercising enough, you WILL lose the weight!" (Wang et al., 2014: Participant 4).

Although members in a virtual community encounter certain challenges that do not apply to geographical communities, such as sharing a common reference of tangible objects that exhibited prior shared understandings, technologies such as activity trackers and awareness feeds allow members to receive social support and be up-to-date about other members' progress. Hyperpresence is enhanced even without physical and face-to-face interactions.

5.5 Conclusion to Chapter 5

Social presence is the quality and degree of mutual visibility and social availability (Goffman, 1959; 1963; Short et al. 1976). It can be evoked in mediated interactions even when they are relatively brief and instrumental (telecommunications, remote collaborative work, e-commerce and online help, and 3D social virtual environments; Biocca et al., 2003).

We analyzed social presence in community contexts that involve technology mediation; we argued that community awareness technologies help community members feel more present to others, and feel that others are more present to them, than they might feel interacting only face-to-face. These technologies can help community members to be aware of more (that is, a greater number and diversity of community news, events, places, opinions), but also more aware (that is, more deeply aware of what others are doing and achieving, what they care about and tweet about, how they manage challenges). We coined the term hyperpresence to describe such situations.

Social presence is important to communities. High mutual visibility and social availability enable the key beliefs, behaviors, and emotions that constitute community membership, identity and belonging, participation and reciprocity, empathy, intimacy and support. Contemporary community is in some jeopardy (Putnam, 2000). Supporting hyperpresence more effectively could be an important direction for community informatics.

References

Bailenson, J. N., Yee, N., Blascovich, J., & Guadagno, R. E. (2008). Transformed social interaction in mediated interpersonal communication. In E. Konijn, M. Tanis, S. Utz & A. Linden (Eds.), *Mediated interpersonal communication*, Mahwah, NJ: Lawrence Erlbaum Associates, 77-99.

Bellotti, V., Carroll, J. M., & Han, K. (2013). Random acts of kindness: The intelligent and context-aware future of reciprocal altruism and community collaboration. *Proceedings of IEEE CTS 2013: International Conference on Collaboration Technologies and Systems* (San Diego, CA, May 20-24). IEEE, 1-12.

Biocca, F., Harms, C., & Burgoon, J. K. (2003). Towards a more robust theory and measure of social presence: Review and suggested criteria. *Presence: Teleoperators and Virtual Environments,* 12 (5), 456-480.

Carroll, J.M. (2013). Co-production scenarios for mobile time banking. In Y. Dittrich et al. (Eds.). *Proceedings of IS-EUD 2013: Fourth International Symposium on End-User Development* (Copenhagen, Denmark, June 10-13). Lecture Notes in Computer Science, LNCS 7897. Heidelberg: Springer, 137-152.

Carroll, J. M. & Rosson, M. B. (2009). Theorizing mobility in community contexts. *Journal of Human Computer Studies*, 66(12), 944-962.

Collom, E. Lasker, J., & Kyriacou, C. (2012). *Equal Time, Equal Value: Community Currencies and Time Banking in the US*. Ashgate Publishing, Ltd.

Farhi, P. (1991, March 11). Taking Local Coverage to the Limit: 24-Hour Cable News, *Washington Post,* Financial Section, 25.

Goffman, E. (1959). *The presentation of self in everyday life.* Garden City, NY: Anchor.

Goffman, E. (1963). Beha*vior in public places: Notes on the social organization of gatherings.* New York: The Free Press.

Hampton, K., Sessions, L., Her, E. J., & Rainie, L. (2009, November). Social Isolation and New Technology: How the internet and mobile phones impact Americans' social networks, *Pew Internet Project.*

Han, K., Shih, P. C., & Carroll, J. M. (2013). Aggregating community information to explore social connections. *When The City Meets The Citizen Workshop, ICWSM 2013: 7th International AAAI Conference On Weblogs And Social Media* (July 8-11, Boston MA).

Han, K., Shih, P. C., Rosson, M. B., & Carroll, J. M. (2014). Enhancing Community Awareness of and Participation in Local Heritage with a Mobile Application. *Proceedings of the 17th ACM Conference on Computer Supported Cooperative Work & Social Computing* (Baltimore, MD, Feb 15-19). New York, ACM Press, 2014.

Hoffman, B., Robinson, H., Han, K., & Carroll, J. M. (2012). "CiVicinity events: pairing geolocation tools with a community calendar". *Proceedings of the 3rd International Conference on Computing for Geospatial Research and Applications* (COM.Geo '12). ACM, New York, NY, USA.

Putnam, R. (2000). *Bowling Alone: The Collapse and Revival of American Community*, New York: Simon & Schuster.

Short, J., Williams, E., & Christie, B. (1976). *The social psychology of telecommunications.* London: John Wiley and Sons.

Wang, J., Shih, P. C., and Carroll, J. M. (2014). *Life after Weight Loss: Challenges and Opportunities in Designing for Weight Management Communities*. Manuscript submitted for publication.

Wang, H. & Wellman, B. (2010). Social Connectivity in America: Changes in Adult Friendship Network Size From 2002 to 2007. *Journal of American Behavioral Scientist*, 53 (8), 1148-1169.

6 Measuring Social Presence in Team-Based Digital Games

Matthew Hudson and Paul Cairns

Abstract: Increasingly, digital games offer sophisticated multiplayer experiences with teams of players able to play against "the computer" in raids or against each other in a variety of team matches. Social presence is therefore an important part of the gaming experience. However, existing measures of social presence in games lack the sophistication to deal with these more diverse gaming situations. This paper describes the development of a new questionnaire to measure the complex nature of social presence in digital games. The resulting questionnaire consists of 39 items with two main modules addressing competitive and collaborative components of social play.

Keywords: Social Presence; Questionnaire Development; Digital Games; Competitive & Cooperative Game Play; Gaming experience.

6.1 Introduction to Chapter 6

Computer games are increasingly offering multiplayer experiences. Whereas most games will have an individual player version, often this is but a lesser sibling to the much bigger online experience that the game can offer. It is becoming clear that this social aspect of digital games is an important part of understanding the totality of the gaming experience (de Kort et al, 2007; Cairns et al. 2013). However, measuring subjective concepts such as social presence in these complex multi-user virtual environments is tricky. In order to see the effect of social presence on the gaming experience (or any experience of digitally-mediated interaction), it is important to be able to know what social presence people are experiencing. This is typically done through measuring social presence in some way, often through questionnaires. However, previous research into the measurement of social presence is heavily influenced by the field of study from which it comes, and the underlying theory of social presence the researchers have. This has led to the majority of measures being unsuitable for measuring social presence within prevalent forms of social gaming, such as the collaborative and competitive environments found in current online First Person Shooter (FPS) games. This chapter therefore documents the process of establishing our own measure on social presence based on a number of user studies.

Biocca, Harms, and Burgoon (2003) state that social presence is the sense of being together with another. Social presence is about the social connections one makes to entities within a virtual environment, and the level of social presence one feels in a virtual environment depends upon the strength of these connections (see also Chapters 1 and 5, this volume). Schouten (2011) argues that social presence is a concept built around the evidence of other humans within a virtual environment, with even simple cues such as the score of other players in a computer game being enough to increase social presence. Alexander, Brunyé, Sidman, and Weil (2005) support this view by stating that in an interactive multi-user environment "greater interaction and presence of others will lead to higher engagement of the individual with the game and the group".

Our research set out to explore social presence in online team-based games, primarily online FPS games which contain both cooperative and competitive game play, as two or more teams consisting of multiple players compete. These games were chosen over more explicitly social games such as *Second Life*, *World of Warcraft* or other *massive multiplayer online role playing game* (MMORPG) type games to highlight the phenomenon of social presence in less obvious multi-user virtual environments. In an MMORPG, one of the primary reason for logging on is for the social interaction and the feeling of sharing the virtual world with other players, this is the essence of an online role playing game. The Daedalus project, a substantial study of MMORPG players, states that there are many different motivations to play these games, socializing, the accumulation of wealth and tangible power, exploring and being part of a fantasy world, and so on (Yee, 2007, 2009). Yet all these motivations are quintessentially social. It would be therefore quite unremarkable to discover a high level social presence felt by the players of these games.

Previous studies have suggested that as well as competitiveness and challenge, social reasons such as the possibility of cooperation and communication are strong motivators for people to play online FPS games (Jansz and Tanis, 2007, Frostling-Henningsson, 2009). However, while social gaming has been extensively studied, there are few methods for quantifying the level of social presence felt in these team-based online games, which are some of the most popular games available today, with FPS games like *Battlefield 3* gaining a reported 3 million pre-sales and *Multiplayer Online Battle Arena* (MOBA) games such as *League of Legends* having a reported 32 million players per month (Lyons, 2012).

6.1.1 Measuring Social Presence

There have been many tools and methods developed for measuring social presence in virtual environments. In a review of various measures of social presence in an online learning context, Kreijns, Kirschner, Jochems, and Van Buuren (2011) cite a number of potential tools, including a 'Group Atmosphere Scale'(Fiedler, 1962, 1967), a 'Work-Group Cohesiveness Index'(Price and Muller, 1986), and 'Social Presence Scales and Indicators' (Gunawardena, 1995, Gunawardena and Zittle, 1997).

De Kort, IJsselsteijn, and Poels (2007) developed a measure for social presence in games, based on the 'Networked Minds Measure of Social Presence' (Biocca and Harms,

2002). While the Networked Minds Measure has a strong theoretical underpinning, the questionnaire was primarily designed for teleconferencing, and so is completely unsuitable for games, especially team-based games. While the 'Social Presence in Gaming Questionnaire' (SPGQ) (de Kort et al., 2007) can be used to measure social presence in some circumstances (Cairns, Cox, Daya, Martin, and Perryman, 2013), the questionnaire is unsuitable for team-based games for a number of reasons. The SPGQ appears to be designed for use with only competitive games, including items which refer to 'revenge' and 'schadenfreude', which are not expected components of social presence in cooperative games. In the SPGQ, there is also no distinction between who the other players are in relation to the respondent. This is easily remedied if the respondent is playing one other person who is an opponent in the game, but it is difficult to make the SPGQ suitable for team-based games. In this situation, when there are both opponents and teammates sharing the virtual environment the SPGQ items would either have to be doubled up, asking about both opponents and teammates, or generalized to refer to simply 'others'. Neither of these solutions are favourable; doubling up would significantly increase the length of the questionnaire and thus increasing the likelihood that participants would become bored and fail to complete the questionnaire accurately (Cairns and Cox, 2008). Generalizing the questions on the other hand would create answers which would not clearly refer to any other entity, providing results that would at best be hard to interpret, and at worst so generic as to be meaningless. This makes the SPGQ unfit for studies involving collaborative and competitive team-based scenarios.

In addition to taking inspiration from the Biocca and Harms (2002) questionnaire, the SPGQ was developed using data gathered via a focus group study (Poels, de Kort, and Ijsselsteijn, 2007). The focus group study consisted of 16 participants, half of which were undergraduate students described as infrequent gamers. The first concern with the methodology is the question of whether the participants were an adequate sample of social gamers, and how the sampling has biased the development of the SPGQ. Second is the general weakness of the focus group methodology, for example in focus groups disproportionate attention can be given to some members of the group, groups can be dominated by a single individual, and so on (Lazar, Feng, and Hochheiser, 2010). So what alternatives are there to the SPGQ?

In a comprehensive review of presence measures, van Baren and IJsselsteijn (2004) set out the details of 28 current presence questionnaires, some original, some developed by combining older telepresence questionnaires, and only 6 of which contained social presence elements. These six questionnaires were the Lombard et al. (2000) Questionnaire, the Nowak and Biocca (2003) Questionnaire, the Schroeder et al. (2001) Questionnaire, the Bailenson, Blascovich, Beall, and, Loomis (2001) Questionnaire, and the 'Temple Presence Inventory' (TPI) (Lombard, Ditton, and, Weinstein, 2009). However once again none of these tools are relevant to team-based games. The Lombard et al. (2000) Questionnaire measured physical and social presence and was developed and tested based solely on previous literature. The study which sought to test the author's theory of presence was based upon film media, and therefore cannot be considered entirely valid for testing digital gaming. The Temple Presence Inventory (Lombard et al., 2009) was created by combining elements from previous questionnaires such as the Lombard et al. (2000) Questionnaire above, and elements created from studies by the authors. It was developed and tested by exposing participants to 'dramatic television programs' and film. The questions reflect the influence of the chosen media and would be unsuitable for interactive virtual environments such as computer games. For example the TPI included such items as "During the media experience how well were you able to observe the facial expressions of the people you saw/heard?" which, while potentially relevant to non-interactive media, is largely irrelevant to games, particularly team-based online games.

The Nowak and Biocca (2003) Questionnaire was designed to measure presence, however in this questionnaire the term social presence was used to mean social realism and was measured using questions such as "To what extent was this like a face-to-face meeting?", which is irrelevant to social connections in digital games. The Schroeder et al. (2001) Questionnaire focused mainly on the feeling of being physically present with another, rather than feelings of social presence. For example the question "To what extent did you have a sense of being in the same room as your partner?" aims to measure co-presence, but seems to actually be measuring physical presence. The Bailenson et al. (2001) Questionnaire aimed to measure purely social presence and asked five direct and focused questions which would likely be effective in measuring social presence in general virtual environment settings such as virtual meetings, etc. However, the measure lacks the competitive/cooperative elements, which are important to video games and team-based training in virtual environments.

In the Van Baren and IJsselsteijn (2004) report, questionnaires appeared to be the most prevalent method of measuring presence and there are good practical reasons for this, namely, that, where valid, they are quick to use, easy to administer and able to be administered in large numbers. Other methods have been used such as 'Autoconfirmation' (Retaux, 2003) through retrospective video protocols, Content Analysis of transcripts of online text-based interaction (Rourke, Anderson, Garrison, and Archer, 1999), Ethnographic Observation of users of teleremote technology (McGreevy, 1992), and Focus Group explorations (Freeman and Avons, 2000). But these methods are better for small scale studies leading to more qualitative insights and even then may have issues of validity as indicators of social presence. In particular, regardless of whatever data is gathered, there is the need to relate this, through self-reporting, to the subjective experience of the individuals. Questionnaires perhaps simply make this aspect explicit.

In summary then, questionnaires promise to be a useful instrument in researching social presence in digital games appropriate to this early stage of research in this area. However, there is no suitable questionnaire for social presence in team-based online games. The general social presence questionnaires are unsuitable due to the media used in their development and the subsequent lack of references to interactivity, while the only questionnaire designed to be used with games was unsuitable for cooperative game play. It is this gap that the current questionnaire is intended to address.

6.2 Overview of the Questionnaire Development

There are many approaches and techniques that can be applied in the development of questionnaires. And although there is some debate about the correct methods to use in the context of human-computer interaction (see for instance Vol. 25(4) of *Interacting with Computers*), there are nonetheless some established techniques that are widely accepted. We follow the process set out by Kline (2000) where the most reliable techniques are clearly laid out. Kline's (2000) methodology consists of creating an item pool and using item analysis of the responses to questionnaires to reduce the pool to an effective set of items that will constitute the instrument. Factor analysis is then used to validate the questionnaire.

An initial pool of items for our questionnaire was created around a group of concepts which arose from the literature and research conducted into social presence in cooperative and competitive environments (Hudson and Cairns, in press). The research consisted of 5 social presence studies: two online user surveys; a cooperative *Tetris* based experiment; analysis of found user data; and a user experience study using the games *Unreal Tournament* and *Puji*. From this work the concepts that emerged as elements of social presence in team-based games were:

1. Awareness of other consciousness.
2. Theory of Mind (Ratcliffe, 2007), that is, the player is able to theorise about what other players are thinking.
3. Team identity.
4. Motivation to play.
5. Social action and the awareness of the social significance of action within a shared environment.
6. Task and social 'joint commitments' (Clark, 2006).

From the list of concepts above an initial pool of 116 items was created and structured into groups with common themes to aid data analysis. These 116 items were then given to 12 experienced gamers who attempted to respond to all items after having played the team-based online game *Darkest Hour: Europe '44-'45*. Their feedback led to the removal of 36 items because the items were perceived as redundant or meaningless in the context of the playing experience. The remaining 80 items formed the preliminary version of what we termed the 'Competitive and Cooperative Presence in Gaming' questionnaire, CCPIG (pronounced sea-pig), the CCPIG v0.5 (*Table 6.1*).

Three further surveys were used to refine from 80 items in the CCPIGv0.5 to 39 in the final version (CCPIGv1.1). From the first two surveys centred on specific games, item analysis was used to remove items found to be unsuitable, redundant or irrelevant, leaving a focused set of items and a more succinct measure. *Table 6.1* shows that while much of the original core structure remains similar from the first to the final version of the CCPIG, the extraneous sections and modules have been removed or merged.

In the final CCPIGv1.1, Section 1 is designed to measure what we term 'competitive social presence', the social presence felt towards one's opponents in a digital game. Module 1.1 measures competitive involvement, the percieved interplay between the respondent and their opponents, and the extent to which a respondent felt they used their Theory of Mind. Module 1.2 measures competitive engagement, and the sensations of competitive play with another human. Section 2 is designed to measure what we term 'cooperative social presence', the social presence felt towards team-mates in cooperative digital games. This section functions as a single component, and a number of concepts cut across the section, including Theory of Mind, and social 'joint commitments' (Clark, 2006). However while this section functions as one component we feel the modules in this section can highlight the various elements of cooperative social presence at work. Module 2.1 measures the extent to which a

Table 6.1: The structural changes from CCPIGv0.5 to CCPIGv1.1

CCPIGv0.5 (80 Items)	CCPIGv1.1 (39 Items)
Section 1: General Social Engagement (9 Items)	
Section 2: Competitive social presence	Section 1: Competitive (14 Items)
Module 2.1: Behavioural and Cognitive Involvement (9 Items)	Module 1.1: Awareness (6 Items)
Module 2.2: Competitive Engagement (9 Items)	Module 1.2: Engagement (8 Items)
Module 2.3: Competitive Sensation (4 Items)	
Module 2.4: Competitive Motivation (3 Items)	
Section 3: Cooperative social presence	Section 2: Cooperative (25 Items)
Module 3.1: Team Identification (5 Items)	Module 2.1: Team Identification (5 Items)
Module 3.2: Team Security (5 Items)	
Module 3.3: Cooperative Motivation (11 Items)	
Module 3.4: Social Action (6 Items)	Module 2.2: Social Action (8 Items)
Module 3.5: Social Commitments (7 Items)	Module 2.3: Motivation (6 Items)
Module 3.6: Team-mate Value (3 Items)	Module 2.4: Team Value (6 Items)
Section 4: Team-based Confirmation (5 Items)	
Section 5: Task (3 Items)	

respondent feels as though they were part of a cooperative team. Module 2.2 aims to measure the level of interplay respondents felt between themselves and their team. Module 2.3 measures the extent to which being part of a team motivated a respondent to play, and Module 2.4 measures how much value the respondent placed on their team-mates, and how cohesive their team felt. A full list of the items and a guide to scoring the CCPIGv1.1 can be found in the Appendix.

The next three sections give details of the survey studies that were used to progress from the CCPIGv0.5 to the CCPIGv1.1. First, though, it is worth making some general points about how items were assessed statistically and the method for collecting data in all the validation studies.

6.2.1 Statistical Criteria

Cronbach α and the measures of sampling adequacy (MSA) and Kaiser-Meyer-Olkin (KMO) scores were the primary statistics used to check the statistical reliability of the questionnaire and its subscales. These indicate the degree to which the items as a whole provide a consistent statistical structure and also how individual items relate to all the other items. Following the guideline thresholds common in the literature (Kline, 2000; Everitt, 1993; Nakazawa, 2007) KMO and Cronbach α scores of over 0.6 were desirable indicators of statistically reliable items. The correlations between items in modules were also used to identify items which did not fit with their module and if so, if they correlated with any other modules. Examples of very high levels of correlation were also used to identify items which were perhaps too similar and therefore redundant, especially if the two items were similarly worded.

6.2.2 Data

The data for the item analysis and PCA was gathered using online user surveys, for which respondents were recruited using calls for participants on game community forums. Game communities were chosen based on a number of factors. First the games around which the communities were based were all team-based online games, which while differing in genre, setting, play style and graphical style, shared the core element of two collaborating teams competing with each other. Another important factor in the specific game communities chosen for these online surveys was the presence of an active forum on which community members could be recruited as participants. When creating the online questionnaire the items were mixed together rather than being structured in their original groups. This was to reduce the risk of participants flatlining their responses (Cairns and Cox, 2008), or producing the “right” answers (social desirability bias (Nederhof, 1985))

6.3 Trial 1: Chivalry

The initial 80-item of CCPIG (v0.5) was trialled with players of the game *Chivalry: Medieval Warfare* (for concision referred to henceforth as *Chivalry*), a team-based online first person melée game, much like an online FPS, but with a focus on medieval-esque combat. It was deliberately chosen to contrast with the games used in the previous item analysis by the experienced gamers. Forty-eight respondents were recruited from the community forums to play the game and fill out an online version of the questionnaire.

The primary aim of Trial 1 was to refine and reduce the questionnaire items to form a shorter but still reliable instrument. The item data produced by the respondents, together with their open feedback, was used to analyse and trim the questionnaire. To begin with the largest single cuts were the removal of two whole modules, removing 9 items in total, the 'General Social Engagement' module and the 'Cooperative Confirmation'modules. These modules were deemed unsatisfactory from a statistical point of view, as well as conceptually unnecessary as they did not directly address

Table 6.2: The structural changes from CCPIGv0.5 to the post-Trial 1 CCPIGv0.6

CCPIGv0.5 (80 Items)	**CCPIGv0.6 (47 Items)**
Section 1: General Social Engagement (9 Items)	
Section 2: Competitive social presence	Section 1: Competitive (15 Items)
Module 2.1: Behavioural and Cognitive Involvement (9 Items)	Module 1.1: Competitive Behavioural Involvement (3 Items)
Module 2.2: Competitive Engagement (9 Items)	Module 1.2: Engagement (5 Items)
Module 2.3: Competitive Sensation (4 Items)	Module 1.3: Theory of Mind(3 Items)
Module 2.4: Competitive Motivation (3 Items)	Module 1.4: Competitive Sensation (4 Items)
Section 3: Cooperative social presence	Section 2: Cooperative (27 Items)
Module 3.1: Team Identification (5 Items)	Module 2.1: Team Awareness (5 Items)
Module 3.2: Team Security (5 Items)	Module 2.2: Team Security (4 Items)
Module 3.3: Cooperative Motivation (11 Items)	Module 2.3: Cooperative Motivation (6 Items)
Module 3.4: Social Action (6 Items)	Module 2.4: Social Action & Communication (5 Items)
Module 3.5: Social Commitments (7 Items)	Module 2.5: Social Commitments & Team-mate Value (7 Items)
Module 3.6: Team-mate Value (3 Items)	
Section 4: Team-based Confirmation (5 Items)	
Section 5: Task (3 Items)	

the specific experiences of competitive or cooperative social presence. These sections were therefore prey to being subjective opinions rather than subjective measures of the gaming experience.

A further 29 items were either removed or merged with other similar items. Most modules had one or two items which could be removed, either based on the statistical results, user feedback, or by identifying redundancy. This process of statistical testing and conceptual scrutinization both reduced the items of the questionnaire and led to its restructuring. Though much shorter, the questionnaire had greater focus through addressing only issues relating to competitive and cooperative engagement with others.

6.4 Trial 2: Natural Selection 2

The second trial used CCPIGv0.6 to continue the item analysis and achieve the 100 participant minimum that Kline recommends for item analysis. While Trial 1 had worked to heavily reduce the questionnaire, this survey was intended to ensure that the questionnaire retained statistical coherence in a different context. Using the same online questionnaire method as Trial 1, data was gathered from 56 respondents from the *Natural Selection 2* (NS2) online gaming community. This game was chosen in particular because it provides a more complex mix of roles and tasks throughout the two teams than *Chivalry*. NS2 is an asymmetrical team-based online FPS game, in which two teams vie for control of a map. This game has the rather uncommon feature that the two competing teams are functionally completely different, one being a team of humans with guns, while the other is made up of melee-based aliens. Both teams are controlled by a commander who plays the game more like a traditional real-time strategy (RTS), buying upgrades for his forces, instructing them, and so on. NS2 was therefore highly suited to providing a different context in which to trial the CCPIG.

Throughout Trial 2, while the competitive section achieved reasonable KMO and Cronbach's α scores, it was clear that the individual modules were not reflecting this collective success (see *Table 6.2*). It was concluded that modules 1.1 & 1.4 (Sensation, Ego & Behavioural Involvement) were far too short to stand alone as individual modules after the cuts of Trial 1. As modules 1.1 & 1.2 were conceptually similar, both referring to actions and reactions, these were merged, and this new merged module showed high levels of internal consistency and sampling adequacy (see *Table 6.3*).

When taken as a whole the cooperative section had good sampling adequacy and a strong Cronbach's α (*Table 6.3*). Only module 2.4 was modified at this stage, removing one item, due to the statistical measures not achieving the commonly accepted thresholds. In Trial 2 the cooperative section also suffered from similar issues as the competitive, with some of the reduced modules not performing well. Modules 2.2 and 2.5 were somewhat less successful than the other cooperative modules, and

Table 6.3: The structural and statistical changes from CCPIGv0.6 to CCPIGv1

CCPIGv0.6					CCPIGv1			
Section	**Module**	**Items**	**Alpha**	**KMO**	**Module**	**Items**	**Alpha**	**KMO**
Competitive		15	0.88	0.76		14	0.88	0.76
	1.1.	3	0.69	0.54	1.1 + 1.2	8	0.83	0.83
	1.2.	5	0.69	0.73				
	1.3.	3	0.65	0.61	1.3 + 1.4	6	0.81	0.77
	1.4.	4	0.68	0.56				
Cooperative		27	0.95	0.81		26	0.95	0.80
	2.1.	5	0.74	0.77		5		
	2.2.	4	0.60	0.61	2.2 + 2.5	9	0.83	0.75
	2.3.	6	0.81	0.75		6		
	2.4.	7	0.86	0.81	2.4	6	0.87	0.86
	2.5.	5	0.78	0.66				

because the modules were conceptually similar (both dealing primarily with team interaction) it was decided to attempt to reorganise the items by merging the modules. This larger module produced a far higher Cronbach α, produced more consistently high MSA scores, and a higher KMO.

This survey did not substantially reduce the number of items in the questionnaire but did lead to a restructuring to bring greater conceptual and statistical coherence. The fact that many items were retained though having been used in response to data gathered from an entirely different sort of team game is encouraging, suggesting that the items were tapping into robust concepts that were relevant to a variety of team-based games.

6.5 Principal Component Analysis

Principal Component Analysis (PCA) is a common method to validate questionnaires. It is used to find the overall relationships between the items of the questionnaire and in particular which items meaningfully group into subscales or components. It is a purely statistical approach that does not assume a prior component structure but rather that the components emerge as a consequence of iteratively conducting the analysis and interpreting the components generated. Following typical practices (Kline, 2000), we used PCA with the oblique rotation method, direct oblimin. Thus the final components are able to correlate and this can be an indication of the overall coherence of the questionnaire.

6.5.1 Data Gathering

Two hundred and thirty eight participants were recruited through posts on several online game community forums to provide a large sample collected over a wide range of games. The games chosen were:
- *Team Fortress 2* (TF2) (57 respondents), a typical FPS game with teams of between 2 and 12 players.
- *Darkest Hour: Europe '44-'45* (102 respondents), a "combined arms" FPS with teams of up to 35 players.
- *Mount & Blade* (50 respondents), a 3rd person medieval/renaissance era game in which players take part in pitched battles, skirmishes and sieges on servers which can hold over 100 players.
- *King Arthur's Gold* (KAG) (18 respondents), a 2D fantasy/medieval setting team-based deathmatch game which features dynamic environments for up to 32 players.
- *Planetside 2* (6 respondents), an MMOFPS (massively multiplayer online first person shooter) in which the players share a server with thousands of others.
- *Dota 2* (5 respondents), a multiplayer online battle arena (MOBA) with teams of up to 5 players.

6.5.2 Analysis

The overall dataset was first checked for overall suitability for PCA. The KMO test of sampling adequacy for the whole dataset was 0.92 and the Bartlett test of sphericity was highly significant, $\chi 2 = 4451.5$, $p < 0.001$, both indicating that the overall dataset was suitable for further analysis. The MSA for individual items was also examined and these showed that each item was also suitable for inclusion in the analysis.

In the first analysis, the scree plot of the eigenvalues (that is before rotation) was used to see the overall factor structure of the questionnaire. From *Figure 6.1*, it is clear that there is an "elbow" in the eigenvalues at 3 to 4 factors. We might have expected two clear factors, one for collaboration and one for competition in social presence but if those components also have strong factor structure then this seems a reasonable number of overall factors. The presence of a single factor with a very high eigenvalue is typical of a questionnaire with reasonable coherence and with most of the questions positively worded (Kline, 2000), which is the case in the CCPIG. The first two factors accounted for 40% of the variance and the first three for 45%. The rotated two-factor structure was analysed from the structure matrix (Everitt,

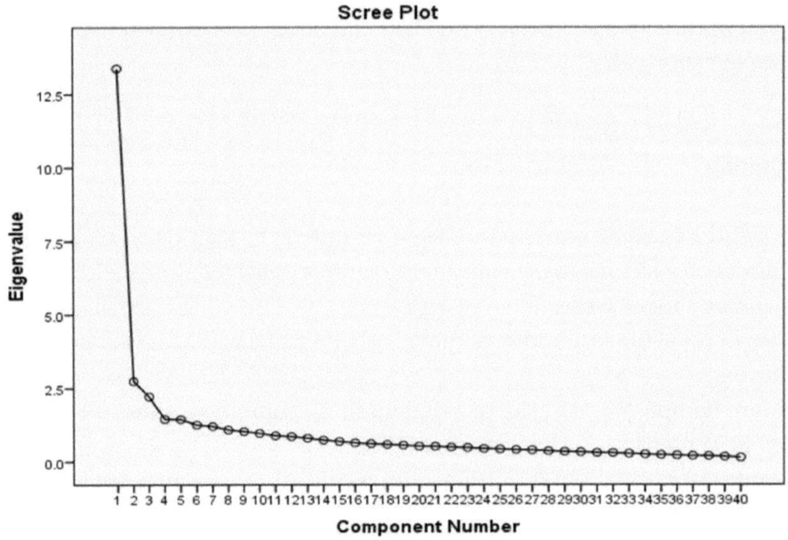

Figure 6.1: The scree plot for the whole questionnaire

1993), and showed two distinct factors consisting primarily of the competition and cooperation modules.

As the competitive and collaborative modules did emerge as stand-alone components of the CCPIG in the overall PCA, they were then analysed separately to see their internal structure. A scree plot for the competitive section showed a breaking point of 2 components, and the structure matrix shows a clear split in components between the two pre-defined modules (*Table 6.4*). However two items in the competitive section did not load as expected, 'My opponents played a significant role in my experience of the game' and 'It seemed as though my opponent was acting with awareness of my actions'. These two items were originally in module 1.1, designed to measure how the interplay between the player and their opponents affected their thoughts and actions, while they load onto module 1.2, designed to measure the competitive feelings of the player. Conceptually these questions are potentially applicable to either module, 'It seemed as though my opponent was acting with awareness of my actions' was created to draw on Theory of Mind. However, the concept of an opponent being aware of one's actions may, in the mind of the participant, be more closely related to the level of challenge an opponent presents. The concept of 'experience' in the item 'My opponents played a significant role in my experience of the game ', may also be conceptually closer to module 1.2. While module 1.1 is phrased in a more reflective way, module 1.2 refers to the sensations of competitive play. The results of the PCA lead to a revaluation of where these items fit conceptually, and it was decided that they would be moved from module 1.1 to module 1.2.

Table 6.4: PCA results with component loading over 0.4 highlighted

Module	Item	Comp. 1	Comp.2
1.1	I acted with my opponent in mind	0.294	0.699
1.1	I reacted to my opponents actions	0.261	0.626
1.1	My opponents played a significant role in my experience of the game	0.400	0.298
1.1	It seemed as though my opponent was acting with awareness of my actions	0.634	0.392
1.1	I knew what my opponent was trying to achieve	0.078	0.697
1.1	I was aware that my opponent might work out my goals	0.442	0.573
1.1	The actions of my opponents affected the way I played	0.418	0.474
1.1	I felt I affected my opponents actions	0.138	0.577
1.2	My opponent was challenging	0.756	0.112
1.2	The game was a battle of skill	0.639	0.123
1.2	The game was a battle of wits	0.534	0.335
1.2	I felt tense while playing my opponent	0.685	0.223
1.2	My opponent created a sense of urgency	0.700	0.121
1.2	The presence of my opponent motivated me	0.555	0.442

The PCA analysis of the cooperative section was less definitive than the competitive. The scree plot for the section suggested between three and five components which suited the presumed four modules quite well. However in general the structure matrix showed a great amount of cross-loading and no convincing 4 component split. In short the cooperative section seemed to consist of 1 single component. While this may not be as predicted, the single component has a lot of coherence, with the majority of the items loading strongly, the cooperative section as a whole having a KMO score of 0.94, and a Cronbach's α of 0.94. However this does not mean that the modules will be abandoned in favour of a single huge section. While the PCA has shown the modules cannot be statistically separated from the overall concept of cooperative social presence, they can show the breakdown of difference aspects of the concept. The subscales in the cooperative section also scored high KMO and Cronbach α which suggests they do work well as subscales to the main section. This single, uni-dimensional component with interpretive sub-scales is similar to that seen in the IEQ (Jennett et al., 2008) and GEngQ (Brockmyer et al., 2009) questionnaires.

6.6 Conclusion to Chapter 6

The development of the CCPIG was born of the aim to explore social presence in the complex social environments that are team-based online games. Unlike previous social presence measures the CCPIG was developed for socially complex virtual environments, and was not designed to be a general measure for social presence across multiple media, but a focused measure for social presence in games. Unlike previous game based measures such as the SPGQ, the CCPIG addresses both competitive and cooperative gameplay, and probes concepts specifically related to team-based games. The development processes show a high degree of coherence between the items of the questionnaire and the separation of competitive and collaborative experiences was evident from the factor analysis.

The CCPIG has been developed to the expected standards of good questionnaires and there are therefore good grounds that this questionnaire will be able to deliver the intended insights into social presence in digital games. Of course there remains much validation work to be done, some of which is already underway. The CCPIGv1.1 and more details about its development and the results of future validation studies will be found online (https://sites.google.com/site/ccpigq/).

References

Alexander, A.L., Brunyé, T., Sidman, J., & Weil, S.A. (2005) From gaming to training: A review of studies on fidelity, immersion, presence, and buy-in and their effects on transfer in pc-based simulations and games. In *The interservice/industry training, simulation, and education conference (I/ITSEC), NTSA, Orlando, Florida.*

Bailenson, J.N., Blascovich, J., Beall, A.C. & Loomis, J.M. (2001) Equilibrium theory revisited: Mutual gaze and personal space in virtual environments. *Presence: Teleoperators & Virtual Environments, 10(6),* 583-598.

Biocca, F. & Harms, C. (2002) Defining and measuring social presence: Contribution to the networked minds theory and measure. *Proceedings of PRESENCE, 2002,* 1-36.

Biocca, F., Harms, C., & Burgoon, J.K. (2003) Towards a more robust theory of social presence: Review and suggested criteria. *Presence, 12(5),* 456-480.

Brockmyer, J.H., Fox, C.M., Curtiss, K.A., McBroom, E., Burkhart, K.M., & Pidruzny, J.N. (2009) The development of the game engagement questionnaire: A measure of engagement in video game-playing. *Journal of Experimental Social Psychology, 45(4),* 624-634.

Cairns, P., & Cox, A.L. (2008) *Research methods for human-computer interaction.* Cambridge University Press, Cambridge.

Cairns, P., Cox, A.L., Daya, M., Martin, H., & Perryman, T. (2013) Who but not where: the effect of social play on immersion in digital games. *International Journal of Human Computer Studies, 71(11),* 1069-1077.

Clark, H. (2006) Social actions, social commitments. In. Enfield, N.J., & Levinson, S.C. (Eds) *Roots of human sociality: Culture, cognition and interaction,* (pp. 126-150) Berg, Oxford.

de Kort, Y., IJsselsteijn, W.A., & Poels, K. (2007) Digital games as social presence technology: Development of the social presence in gaming questionnaire (SPGQ). *Proceedings of PRESENCE 2007: The 10th International Workshop on Presence, 195-203.*

EA (2011) Battlefield 3 launched with record-breaking force. EA.com, http://www.ea.com/news/battlefield-3-launches-with-record-breaking-force. Retrieved Dec.1, 2013.

Everitt, BS. (1993) *Making sense of statistics in psychology: A second-level course*. Oxford University Press, Oxford.

Fiedler, FE. (1962) Leader attitudes, group climate, and group creativity. *Journal of Abnormal and Social Psychology, 65(5)*, 308-318.

Fiedler, F.E. (1967) *A theory of leadership effectiveness*. McGraw-Hill, New York, USA.

Freeman, J., & Avons, S.E. (2000) Focus group exploration of presence through advanced broadcast services. *Proceedings of the SPIE, Human Vision and Electronic Imaging V*, 3959-3976.

Frostling-Henningsson, M. (2009) First-person shooter games as a way of connecting to people: "brothers in blood". *CyberPsychology & Behavior, 12(5)*, 557-562.

Gunawardena, C.N. (1995) Social presence theory and implications for interaction and collaborative learning in computer conferences. *International Journal of Educational Telecommunications, 1(2/3)*, 147-166.

Gunawardena, C.N., & Zittle, F. (1997) Social presence as a predictor of satisfaction within a computer mediated conferencing environment. *American Journal of Distance Education, 11(3)*, 8-26.

Hudson, M., and Cairns, P. (In press) Interrogating social presence in games with experiential vignettes. *Entertainment Computing*.

Hussain, T., Weil, S., Brunyé, T., Sidman, J., Ferguson, W., & Alexander, A. (2008). Eliciting and evaluating teamwork within a multi-player game-based training environment. *Computer games and team and individual learning*, 77-104.

Jansz, J., & Tanis, M. (2007) Appeal of playing online first person shooter games. *CyberPsychology & Behavior, 10(1)*, 133-136.

Jennett, C., Cox, A., Cairns, P., Dhoparee, S., Epps, A., Tijs, T., & Walton, A. (2008) Measuring and defining the experience of immersion in games. *International Journal of Human Computer Studies, 66(9)*, 641-661.

Kline, P. (2000) *A Psychometrics Primer*. Free Association Books, New York.

Kreijns, K., Kirschner, P.A., Jochems, W. & Van Buuren, H. (2011) Measuring perceived social presence in disributed learning groups. *Education and Information Technologies, 16(4)*, 365-381.

Lazar, J., Feng, J.H., & Hochheiser, H. (2010) *Research methods in human-computer interaction*. John Wiley & Sons Ltd., Chichester.

Lombard, M., Ditton, T.B., Crane, D., Davis, B., Gil-Egui, G., Horvath, K., Rossman, J., & Park, S. (2000) Measuring presence: A literature-based approach to the development of a standardized paper-and-pencil instrument. *Third International Workshop on Presence, Delft, The Netherlands.*

Lombard, M., Ditton, T.B., & Weinstein, L. (2009) Measuring presence: The temple presence inventory. In *Proceedings of the 12th Annual International Workshop on Presence.*

Lyons, S. (2012) League of Legends has 32 million monthly active players. Destructoid.com, http://www.destructoid.com/league-of-legends-has-32-million-monthly-active-players-236618.phtml. Retrieved Dec. 1, 2013.

McGreevy, M.W. (1992) The presence of field geologists in mars-like terrain. *Presence: Teleoperators and Virtual Environments, 1(4)*, 375-403.

Nakazawa, M. (2007) R practice: Factor analysis. minato.sip21c.org, http://minato.sip21c.org/swtips/factor-in-R.pdf. Retrieved Sept. 1, 2013.

Nederhof, A.J. (1985) Methods of coping with social desirability bias: A review. *European Journal of Social Psychology, 15(3)*, 263-280.

Nowak, K.L., & Biocca, F. (2003) The effect of the agency and anthropomorphism on users' sense of telepresence, copresence, and social presence in virtual environments. *Presence: Teleoperators & Virtual Environments, 12(5)*, 481-494.

Poels, K., de Kort, Y. & Ijsselsteijn, W. (2007) It is always a lot of fun!: exploring dimensions of digital game experience using focus group methodology. *Proceedings of the 2007 conference on Future Play*, 83-89. ACM.

Price, J.L., & Muller, C.W. (1986) *Handbook of organizational measurement*. Pitman Publishing, Marshfield, MA, USA.

Ratcliffe, M. (2007) *Rethinking Commonsense Psychology*. Palgrave Macmillan, Hampshire/New York.

Retaux, X. (2003) Presence in the environment: theories, methodologies and applications to video games. *PsychNology Journal, 1(3)*, 283-309.

Rourke, L., Anderson, T., Garrison D.R., & Archer, W. (1999) Assessing social presence in asynchronous, text-based computer conferencing. *Journal of Distance Education, 14(3)*, 51-70.

Schouten, D.G.M. (2011) Shared Experience: The influence of the in-game social connection on the player experience in digital gaming. tue.nl, http://alexandria.tue.nl/extra2/afstversl/tm/Schouten%202011.pdf. Retrieved Feb. 25, 2014.

Schroeder, R., Steed, A., Axelsson, A., Heldal, I., Abelin, A., Widestrom, J., Nilsson, A., & Slater, M. (2011) Collaborating in networked immersive spaces: as good as being there together? *Computers & Graphics 25(5)*, 781-788.

Toups, Z. O., Kerne, A., Hamilton, W. A., & Shahzad, N. (2011) Zero-fidelity simulation of fire emergency response: improving team coordination learning. In *Proceedings of the SIGCHI Conference on Human Factors in Computing Systems*, 1959-1968. ACM.

Van Baren, J. & Ijsselsteijn, W. (2004) Measuring presence: A guide to current measurement approaches. *Deliverable of the OmniPres project IST-2001-39237*.

Yee, N. (2007) Motivations of play in online games. *Journal of CyberPsychology and Behavior, 9*, 772-775.

Yee, N. (2009) *Motivations of Play. The Daedalus Project*. http://www.nickyee.com/daedalus/gateway_motivations.html. Retrieved Feb. 25, 2014.

Appendix

CCPIGv1.1P

The items which form the Competitive and Cooperative Presence in Gaming Questionnaire (CCPIG) are listed below. The CCPIG is designed to measure the social presence felt by gamers in competitive and cooperative virtual environments. The version shown here is the 'plural' version of the CCPIG, and is worded to be used in a scenario in which a participant has more than one opponent and team-mate. A version worded for dyads can be found online: sites.google.com/site/ccpigq.

In the items are to be used with 5 point Likert scale and items within sections should be mixed up, not appearing in their original order, nor grouped into their modules. This is essential to aiding validity of the data as it reduces the risk of participants flatlining their responses or producing the "right" answers (social desirability bias).

The CCPIG is split into two sections, Section 1 measures competitive social presence, that is the level of social presence felt by a participant towards their opponent(s). Section 2 measures cooperative social presence, the level of social presence experienced by a participant towards their team-mates. The two sections of the CCPIG measure separate components, therefore it would be possible to use them independently to measure, for example, cooperative social presence in a game which has only cooperative gameplay.

Section 1 is made up of two modules. Module 1.1 measures the extent to which participants feel their thoughts and actions were dependent on their opponent, and the extent to which the participant's theory of mind was at play. Module 1.2 measures how engaging the participant felt their opponent was. Section 2 is made up of 4 modules. Module 2.1 measures how strongly the participant identified with their team and how much they felt a part of something. Module 2.2 measures the level of social actions which supported their team a participant felt was occurring during the game. Module 2.3 measures how motivated a participant was towards helping their team succeed, and Module 2.4 measures how much value a participant placed upon their team.

The CCPIG is scored as follows:

Section 1: Competitive Social Presence

Awareness

I acted with my opponents in mind
I reacted to my opponents' actions
I knew what my opponents were trying to achieve
I was aware that my opponents might work out my goals

The actions of my opponents affected the way I played
I felt I affected my opponents' actions

Engagement

My opponents were challenging
The game was a battle of skill
The game was a battle of wits
I felt tense while playing my opponents
My opponents created a sense of urgency
The presence of my opponents motivated me
My opponents played a significant role in my experience of the game
It seemed as though my opponents were acting with awareness of my actions

Section 2: Cooperative Social Presence

Team Identification

I was aware of my team
I acted with my team-mates in mind
I considered my team-mates' possible plans/thoughts
I felt like I was part of a team
I felt a social connection to my team-mates (camaraderie)

Social Action

I felt my team-mates were looking out for me
I felt I contributed to the team
I felt the team helped me
I felt my actions made a difference to my team-mates
The actions of my team-mates affected my thoughts and actions
My team-mates played a significant role in my experience of the game
My team communicated well
The team had a mutual understanding

Motivation

I put the performance of the team over my personal performance
My actions were determined by the objectives of the team

I wanted my team to value me
Being part of a team motivated me
I felt responsible for achieving the objectives of the team
I did not want my team to think I had let them down

Team Value

I felt my team was committed to working together
I made an effort to work with my team-mates
I felt my team shared a common overall aim
I felt my team shared common short term goals
It was as much about the team as about my own game
My team-mates were useful

7 Recreating Leisure: How Immersive Environments Can Promote Wellbeing

Henry J. Moller, Harjot Bal, Kunal Sudan, and Luke R. Potwarka

Abstract: The connection of virtual reality to holistic healthcare may appear paradoxical on first blush. Yet, a novel paradigm in immersive media technology that seeks to enable an induced state of wellbeing, by creating uplifting states of consciousness rather than generating aversive stimuli or presenting cumbersome tasks for users is now within reach for clinical application. Demand for innovative and patient-centered care to alleviate stress-related and psychosomatic conditions is certainly high in medical and workplace settings. A mental health treatment modality that is effective, safe and free of adverse effects makes up the desirable set of criteria not only from a patient's perspective, but also from the perspective of clinicians who provide healthcare service to patients. As the boundaries between real and virtual, technologically mediated and 'organic' states of consciously experienced presence continue to blur, the need to address this convergence in a therapeutic paradigm is increasingly relevant and warranted. We review the scientific rationale, clinical results and user feedback from patients who have undertaken a standardized course of sensory-based technology-enhanced multimodal meditation to therapeutically address symptoms in a psychosupportive paradigm. Relationships to physiological parameters of human consciousness, rationale to support replicable and evidence-based application in supporting health and wellbeing are reviewed. We highlight the role of 'slow technology' and an inclusive design approach in supporting further development of therapeutics, as well the subjective and experiential nature of the world of inner presence that invite the possibility of further experience design for use in health and wellness. The relevance of leisure states to wellbeing, and specifically the positive experiential learning through inspirational or motivational shifts in consciousness, is described as an important health promotion avenue to pursue on an individual and societal level.

Keywords: Immersive Media; Experience Design; Technology-Enhanced Multimodal Meditation; TEMM; Mindfulness; MBSR; Holistic Health; Consciousness; Leisure; Flow; Health Promotion; Workplace Wellness.

7.1 Introduction to Chapter 7

> "To me, the practice of medicine has no real autonomy: it exists by borrowing and making new application of ideas from other disciplines. Without a constant reinfusion from other scientific domains, the practice of medicine would soon become an outmoded routine" Jean-Marie Charcot (Goetz, 2009).

Meditation is increasingly used by physicians and mental health professionals as a mainstream evidence-based treatment modality and as an adjunctive treatment to other biological or psychological therapies. This is in part based on the desire of many patients to have additional treatment options beyond traditional pharmacotherapy or psychotherapy. Currently, there is increased acceptance of mind-body medicine into mainstream healthcare paradigms. There are many specific styles of meditation practice; the word meditation may carry different meanings in different contexts, and has been applied both in religious/spiritual and healthcare settings. An increasingly popular type of meditation-based psychotherapy has been *Mindfulness-Based Stress Reduction* (MBSR), which allows patients to become more aware of sensations and thoughts that improve or worsen symptoms. Many meditation techniques involve an element of relaxation, which stands quite generally for a release of tension, a return to equilibrium. Relaxation as a mind-body treatment has been studied as a broad-spectrum treatment used to benefit a variety of psychiatric, medical and psychosomatic conditions, ranging from chronic pain to anxiety disorders, insomnia, and hypertension (Wallace & Benson, 1972), and this may in part be related to modulation of EEG (electroencephalography) rhythm (Williams & West, 1975). Presence-enabling experiences may well involve neuromodulation of electrochemical brain systems, and may be enhanced through those neural pathways mediating states of wellbeing such as pleasure or reward.

This paper describes a non-blinded observational clinical evaluation case series for a multimodal sensory-based guided meditation program. The program offers a combination of meditation based on MBSR and audiovisual entrainment with light therapy, a therapeutic technique that aims to satisfy the desirable criteria for available treatment modalities and improve upon the range of existing therapeutic healthcare options. The program can also be administered as an adjunctive psychosupportive therapy, used to enhance the efficacy of other psychotherapeutic or pharmacotherapy strategies.

Given the current relative but growing crisis of confidence in the communication surrounding reliability of reported data relating to the psychological and medical sciences (Pashler & Wagenmakers, 2012), it will be increasingly necessary to adopt new healthcare paradigms that will serve the public's need, and allow for congruence between reported data and lived experience. Informed patients now often seek wellbeing restoration rather than illness treatment as a true healthcare goals (AHHA, 2003); given this fact, the opportunity has arisen for presence-enabling immersive technologies to deliver on the promise of providing credible, safe and effective healthcare solutions. While some applications remain under development in industry and academia in disciplines as diverse as computer science, music and media design, a convergence of these multidisciplinary efforts will push the boundaries towards cutting-edge models of promoting wellbeing, informed by clinical need, available technologies and ethical, reproducible application.

An interesting hypothesis to consider is the role of induced, simulated or "recreated" leisure as being related to the therapeutic effects of meditative states of wellbeing. In fact, immersive environments can be understood within a leisure studies paradigm; scholars are now employing operational definitions of leisure that extend beyond participation in specific types of activities (e.g., bowling, aerobics), settings (e.g., parks, culture/heritage sites) and time (time away from paid employment). In particular, researchers examining the impact of leisure on health and wellbeing have conceptualized leisure as meaningful experiences. (Kleiber et al, 2011; Mannell & Kleiber, 1997). In this way, leisure is perhaps best understood as a state of mind, characterized by notions of intrinsic motivation and perceived freedom (Kleiber et al., 2011). Most leisure episodes, for example, invoke a wide range of feelings and cognitions, the essence of experience. Leisure experiences, whether occurring in settings simulated, virtual, or real, authentic or artificial, have come to be seen as primary aspects of leisure and recreational behaviour (Kleiber et al. 2011).

> *"Many researchers believe that to understand the impact of leisure on health, wellbeing and other domains of daily life, they not only need to be able to assess what people do in and as their leisure but also what they are experiencing while they do it and then how they make sense of, or construe, the experience"* (Kleiber et al., 2011, p. 101).

Indeed, past researchers (e.g., Wessinger & Iso-Ahola, 1984) have argued that the inherent restorative properties, functions, and motivations associated with leisure experiences contribute to its efficacy in reducing stress and subsequent improvements in mental health among individuals. Moreover, leisure may have the capacity to induce an inspired psychological state, promote wellbeing in the form of positive affect and life satisfaction (Thrash et. al, 2010).

7.2 Innovative Research and Industry Applications

Reproducible technology-enhanced meditation sessions are increasingly being incorporated into therapeutic programs to meet the needs of patients seeking mental health care with safe and effective symptomatic relief of stress-related symptoms such as anxiety, insomnia and depression. In parallel to this, the fast pace of technology in work environments, and the impact of this on health is being described (Heusser, 2013). Many of today's patients are unable to readily practice meditation on their own because they find it hard to rehearse mental imagery or meditative affirmations, particularly if suffering from psychiatric illness or trauma that impacts neurocognitive capacity. These patients may lack imaginal capacity for visualization exercises: "*...some patients refuse to engage in the treatment, and others, though they express willingness, are unable to engage their emotions or senses*" (Difede & Hoffman, 2002, p. 529). A further roadblock that might impede the effectiveness of meditation-based relaxation therapies is the consistency and quality of the user's experience, i.e., standardization. Meditation also requires intensive and repetitive practice by patients, who may have difficulty performing their practice autonomously. This has led to a clinical demand for developing standardized meditation techniques that can readily be provided to patients in a safe, effective and reproducible manner.

7.2.1 Related Research Projects at Other Centres

Outside of medical settings, technology-aided relaxation and meditation is also an increasingly popular phenomenon. In addition to offering a more standardized protocol, technology can afford a more complete experience – one that is multimodal and highly responsive. The *Confronting Pain: Redefining Mobility* (CPRM) lab at Simon Fraser University has been actively involved in designing immersive therapeutic experiences simulated by technology (http://www.confrontingpain.com/projects/). The 'Virtual Meditative Walk' program developed by the CPRM lab uses a combination of a projected virtual environment, a unidirectional treadmill, and biofeedback sensors to offer users a relaxation experience tailored to the level of their engagement (Gromala et. al, 2011). Another CPRM project, 'Sonic Cradle', based on the crux of mindfulness meditation offers users a highly responsive audio interface that responds to respiration patterns (Vidyarthi, Riecke, and Gromala, 2012). The lab is also involved with immersive virtual reality approaches to therapy. Similarly, the *Calming Technology* lab at Stanford University, directed by Neema Moraveji, is developing relaxation and meditation-based applications for new technologies (http://www.calmingtechnology.org). 'Breathwear' is a recent project from Moraveji's lab that uses the iPhone to bring to the awareness of the user their breathing patterns throughout the day (Wongsuphasawat, Gamburg, Moraveji, 2012). The project is designed around the concept of calm technology – a practice that involves intentionally creating technologies to operate and communicate in the periphery of a user's attention, in an effort to demand less engagement from the user (Weiser and Brown, 1996).

Health design researcher Patrizia Marti also provides insight into novel projects that demonstrate an appreciation for the human body and an interest in preserving user autonomy in wellbeing practices through the several industrial design projects studied in her book, *Enabling through design: explorations of aesthetic interaction in therapy and care*. (Marti, 2012) From interactive rolling pins that are to be used by patients suffering from dementia and their caretakers in order to foster a sense of empathy to mini-mattresses for babies that send digital signals to a mother's respective belt about the needs of their child, there are multiple projects that have ventured to blend healthcare and innovative design via novel technology explorations.

7.2.2 Related Gaming Applications

Also gaining momentum with employing relaxation, reflective, and meditative elements in technology-simulated experiences is the gaming industry. Video game developer 'thatgamecompany' has garnered critical acclaim for their titles 'flOw', 'Flower', and 'Journey' (Chen, 2012). All games infused virtual landscapes simulating nature in an abstract manner and instead of using text and narrative to provide context, the games were more focused on subtle onscreen movements responsive to user input, encouraging free exploration, followed by moments set up for mental reflection. Co-founder Jenova Chen credits much of his influence to the work of Hungarian psychologist Mihaly Csikszentmihalyi whose psychological construct of presence related to *Flow* was largely implemented in Chen's teams' work to design games that are slower and less adrenaline-driven than recent popular titles (Adu Poku, 2013). The related world of serious games with educational and/or therapeutic potential merits a longer discussion but is related to the use of leisure in fostering productivity and wellbeing on an individual and collective level.

As discussed earlier, it is now increasingly theorized that leisure experiences have a health promoting effect, and particularly around mental wellbeing. Much of this research seems to originate from the proposed discovery of flow states. Researchers (e.g., Csikszentmihalyi, 1975; 1990; Csikszentmihalyi & Kleiber, 1991) have theorized that leisure episodes that result in flow experiences have the potential to contribute to feelings of self-actualization and positive mental states (see also the open access book: "Enabling Positive Change: Flow and Complexity in Daily Experience", De Gruyter Open, 2014). Flow experiences occur when the challenge presented by the activity matches the skills possessed by the individual, which can result in a centering of attention, a loss of consciousness, and an inability to keep track of time (Csikszentmihalyi, 1975). Csikszentmihalyi (1990) describes flow experiences as, *"the best moments of people's lives"* and they occur when *"a person's body and mind is stretched to its limits in a voluntary effort to accomplish something difficult and worthwhile"* (p. 3).

7.3 Clinical Background

7.3.1 About Technology-enhanced Multimodal Meditation (TEMM) and Light and Sound Meditation (LSM)

Technology-Enhanced Multimodal Meditation (TEMM) used in this study is an extension of an established treatment modality known as *Light-and-Sound Meditation* (LSM). LSM is an auto-suggestive relaxation/meditation technique using standardized sounds, music or meditation scenarios delivered through headphones paired with visual stimulation consisting of repetitive flickering of lights delivered via goggles at a frequency of 4-10 Hz using LED while the patient's eyes are closed. The light stimulation typically slows the EEG frequency and enhances the auto-suggestive capacity of the meditation program (Inouye, Sumitsuji and Matsumoto, 1979). Treatment sessions typically involve providing an audiovisual meditation/relaxation session in a supervised clinical setting.

Research and clinical experience dating back to French neuropsychiatrists Pierre Janet, Jean-Marie Charcot and other neuroscientists at the turn of the 20th century has found that for many people LSM triggers a pleasant dissociative state similar to that achieved through deep meditation and/or hypnosis, through entrainment of EEG activity (Janet, 1925; Toman, 1941; Adrian & Matthews, 1934; Walter & Matthews, 1949). LSM has been researched in a number of psychiatric applications, and at this point there is a growing body of evidence documenting its broad-spectrum clinical utility. Clinical researchers have found that repetitive LSM entrainment is effective in facilitating relaxation, meditative, and hypnotic mental states associated with alpha (8-12Hz) or theta (4-8 Hz) activity as well as promoting improvement in numerous mental and physical disorders with a psychosomatic basis (Barlow, 1960; Lane et. al, 1998; Budzynski et. al, 1999; Markland, 1990). There is now an emerging medical and psychological literature demonstrating efficacy and safety of this variant on meditation in a wide variety of psychiatric, psychosomatic and neurological conditions, ranging from anxiety including post-traumatic stress to depression, ADHD, various pain disorders and substance dependence (Cantor & Stevens, 2009; Thomas & Siever, 1989; Patrick, 1996).

LSM has also been described in the literature as "audiovisual entrainment", "light-and-sound neurotherapy", and "light-and-sound stimulation", with most research on mechanism of action focusing on the calming effect of the audiovisual stimulation on psychological and neurological function, as manifested by a relaxation response. As previously described, promotion of theta and alpha EEG activity may facilitate an immersive state of "absence" from externally oriented sensory stimuli into which patients can oscillate with respect to being in a state of externally oriented "presence" (Moller 2006; 2008). Also described as "inner presence" by Finnish neuroscientist and neurophilosopher Antti Revonsuo (2006), this complex consciousness process involves the processing of sensory stimuli and consolidation with previously integrated information, very similar to that described in the psychobiological process of dreaming (Moller & Barbera, 2006). In this model, inner presence experienced through the process of dreaming could be considered the most primordial form of virtual reality, also described as "protoconsciousness" by American psychiatrist and consciousness researcher Allan Hobson (2009).

TEMM improves upon the therapeutic benefits of LSM by incorporating haptic sensory stimulation (gentle massage, heat, vibration) in addition to audiovisual cues, through a specialized chair that the patient rests upon during the meditation process (see *Figure 7.1* below). Furthermore, while basic LSM audiovisual content more typically involves exposure to repetitive binaural sounds or music paired with light therapy, in TEMM the standardized content of the more sophisticated meditation scenarios seek to mimic and on a therapeutic level, reprogram autonomous thought processes. The audio

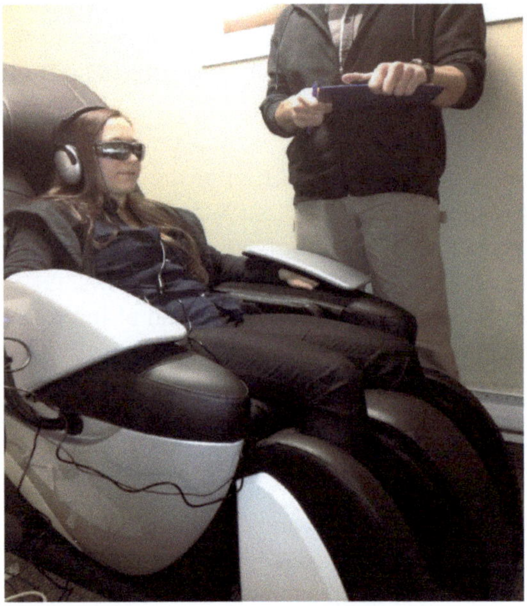

Figure 7.1: TEMM-LSM setup demonstration

component typically involves exposure to a standardized guided meditation invoking a relaxing scenario such as a nature scenario (e.g., walking in a meadow or sitting on a beach) accompanied by repetitive positive affirmations to enhance a participant's self-esteem or psychological outlook. Through the TEMM therapeutic process unhelpful maladaptive cognitive processes can be interrupted and remediated during the multimodal autosuggestive meditation program, resulting in a "reset" state analogous to more invasive psychiatric neurostimulation paradigms such as electroconvulsive therapy (ECT) or repetitive transcranial magnetic stimulation (rTMS), as described by O'Connor et al., 2005 and Lipsman et al, 2014, but without harmful or distressing adverse effects to the patient. Upon completion of TEMM, a desired therapeutic outcome is a state of calm and deep mental and physical relaxation, with a residual awareness of the positive psychotherapeutic content of the meditation session.

7.4 TEMM Clinical Study

We have recently reported the results of a prospective observational pilot study investigating the efficacy and tolerability of technology-enhanced multimodal meditation incorporating LSM in reducing perceived stress and enhancing relaxation and mood in a group of twenty adult patients undergoing medical care for stress-related disorders (Moller & Bal, 2013).

It was hypothesized that a course of technology-enhanced multimodal meditation incorporating LSM would be rated by patients as effective in reducing self-reported stress, while also improving self-rated relaxation and mood, all of which are associated with positive and health-promoting leisure states. Specifically, it was predicted that patients would show improvements in self-ratings of 5-point Likert scale indications of stress, mood and relaxation following completion of the program. It was also anticipated that a broad-spectrum effect would be noted for a variety of stress-related conditions. It is also important to note that due to the nature of the light oscillation that is a part of the TEMM-LSM experience, patients were warned about the theoretical risk of migraines or seizures during the consent process. These theoretical risks were mentioned as cautionary information, even though they have no strong relevance to the TEMM-LSM experience.

7.4.1 Study Design

In this study, following medical screening and evaluation of symptoms and life events, patients were asked to provide self-ratings section on relaxation, stress and mood (using a 5-point Likert scale). Use of psychiatric medication was allowed for those who required so or wanted to continue with medication while participating in the program. Patients with epilepsy, psychotic illness and those who were pregnant were excluded from the study. Study endpoints included the assessment of short-term and long-term efficacy and tolerability of a meditation protocol administered twice weekly for a total of 6 to 21 sessions.

Treatment session duration was typically 30-40 minutes, and treatment plan typically involved one to two sessions weekly for a total of 6 to 20 sessions.

Themes addressed within the meditation sessions included 'dealing with stress', 'relax', 'balancing your moods', 'creative problem solving' and 'overcoming anxiety', chosen by the treating clinician based on clinical impression following initial patient assessment.

Following completion of the course of therapy, patients were invited to complete a feedback form in which they were asked to describe initial symptoms or concerns leading to treatment and overall impression of the treatment. 5-point Likert scales were used to assess:

- Effectiveness of the LSM treatment for initial symptoms or concerns (1 = not at all effective, 2 = somewhat effective, 3 = neutral, 4 = quite effective, 5 = highly effective)
- Adequacy of the duration of sessions (session length: 1 = too short, 2 = somewhat too short, 3 = neutral, 4 = somewhat too long, 5 = too long)
- Adequacy of the number of sessions (treatment plan length: 1 = too few, 2 = somewhat too few, 3 = neutral, 4 = somewhat too many, 5 = very many)

Another set of 5-point Likert scales were also used to allow patients to rate symptom-based self-states before and after the treatment plan, including level of tension, stress and mood state. Lastly, patients were invited to provide open-ended qualitative feedback regarding additional observations and comments. *Table 7.1* outlines patient information and initial qualitative feedback of overall impression of their therapy.

Table 7.1: Patient information and initial qualitative feedback

Gender	# Sessions	Symptoms/Concerns	Overall Impression
F	7	Stress	Very good
F	12	Depression	Slightly helpful
F	21	Stress, anxiety, depression	Calming
M	6	Anxiety, sleep issues	Helpful, leveled out anxiety
F	18	Sleep issues, stress, tension	Improved sleep, calmer and more relaxed
M	8	Stress, sleep issues	Relaxing, calming
M	10	Stress, tension	Impressive
F	10	Insomnia, back pain	Relaxing, improved sleep
F	11	Depression, stress	Relaxing, calming
M	11	Depression, stress	Boost in energy, relaxing
F	15	Brain chatter, stress, sleep issues	Nice way to relax
F	10	Emotionally frozen/blocked, sad	Helpful
F	10	Low energy, depression, stress	Relaxing
M	9	Sleep issues, anxiety	Very helpful for stress reduction, lessens anxiety, relaxing
F	12	Anxiety	Very good, can better understand self
F	13	Anxiety, sleeplessness	Can control anxiety, can sleep without interruption
F	12	Insomnia	Good, very beneficial for stress
F	20	Anxiety, insomnia, stress	Loved it, improved sleep, very beneficial, relaxing
F	15	Anxiety, stress, sleep issues	Worthwhile, helpful
F	8	Stress	Positive

7.4.2 Findings: Data Analysis and Results

This section presents the findings from the patient assessments described in the previous section. Quantitative data across all subjects was calculated into mean values. ANOVA-based statistical analysis was employed to determine significance of difference for repeat measures, before and after assessments of tension, stress and mood. As described above, full demographic information is available in our original publication of the clinical study (Moller & Bal, 2013).

The results shown in *Table 7.2* and *Figure 7.2* indicate that on average the TEMM treatment program was found to be significantly effective in addressing the symptoms and concerns of subjects, with a mean rating of 4.15 points on the 5-point Likert scale. The layout of the treatment was favourably evaluated, with mean ratings for both session and program duration near 3 points on the 5-point Likert scale, known as the neutral point. There was a slight trend towards patients desiring longer individual sessions or longer program duration; one patient received 21 sessions based on a voluntary request for an extra treatment beyond the intended program plan.

The results shown in *Figure 7.3* indicate that on average there was a noticeable decline in perceived levels of tension ($p < 0.001$) and stress ($p < 0.001$), before versus after the program, reported by study subjects. For changes in mood states of patients there was a similarly positive shift ($p = 0.019$).

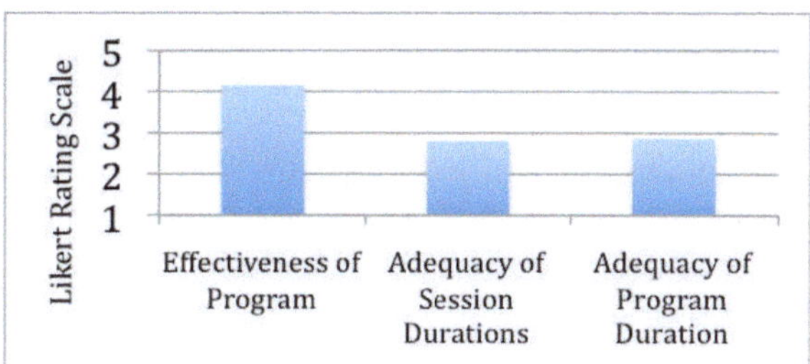

Figure 7.2: Program review assessment: treatment plan

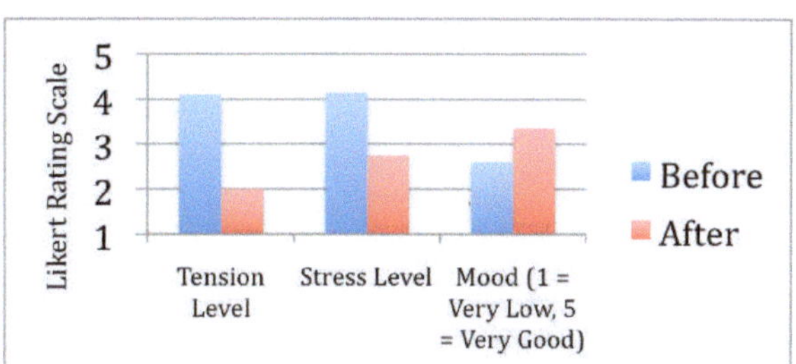

Figure 7.3: Assessment of treatment efficacy: before and after

Table 7.2: Assessment for before and after treatment mean values

	Before	After	Statistical Significance ($p < 0.05$)
Tension Level	4.10	2.00	$p < 0.001$*
Stress Level	4.15	2.75	$p < 0.001$*
Mood	2.60	3.35	$p = 0.019$*

7.4.3 Qualitative Subject Feedback

A summary of the voluntary qualitative feedback received from patients through the additional comments section is shown as follows:

- Over 50% of patients specifically commented on the capacity for TEMM to help them relax and better deal with their stress and anxiety.
- TEMM was consistently reported to have helped initiate an introspective dialogue for a select number of patients — these patients reported more self-awareness of emotions and anxieties and are better able to cope with them outside of the LSM treatment.
- Some patients also articulated on their appreciation of the design of the TEMM-LSM program; using different sensory and psychological elements in combination seems to create a complete and powerful experience.
- Some patients agreed firmly that TEMM has successfully induced actual sleep states but they felt that this would be best to experience before they actually go to bed at night rather than feeling quite sleepy after the session has ended and then having to go on with their day.
- Common feedback from patients to our centre has been that the "thought stopping" and "resetting" after-effects frequently last for multiple hours, while novel insights and residual mind-body wellbeing states often last for up to a week or more.
- It is relevant to note that no adverse effects were reported during this study.

7.5 Discussion

7.5.1 Clinical Study Review: Key Insights

It is emphasized that this study was not intended to be a comparative study to other forms of therapy such as pharmacotherapy or psychotherapy. It was intended to explore the clinical utility of TEMM with an LSM component as an adjunctive therapy for patients and to widen the range of available options for patients. Furthermore, in recognition of the heterogeneous nature of stress-related illness, no specific diagnostic category was chosen; rather patients who self-identified as seeking this stress-reduction therapy suffered from a range of symptoms including disturbance of sleep, mood, anxiety and somatic tension.

This study was also intended to be a usability study. This means that aside from therapeutic benefit, we had a keen interest to understand how a 'user' (i.e., patient) evaluates a program, device or technique – with additional focus on the integration of new technology in health care. Thus, of interest was both evaluation of how effective the technique is, and if there might be ways to improve upon it (such as making sessions shorter/longer or less/more frequent). On these items, mean ratings of patient satisfaction with individual treatment session duration and overall program length at a neutral level (3 points on the 5-point Likert scale), suggested that patients found their treatment regimen 'just right', despite the variation in total number of sessions. This could be seen as analogous to satisfaction ratings with other mental health therapies of variable duration. The standardized format of meditations used might suggest a manual-driven approach of a set number of sessions. However, having the flexibility to 'dose' session frequency and program length based on individual patient need appears to enhance the therapeutic experience for patients. Presence-related engagement with the therapeutic across multiple senses was considered a holistic therapeutic benefit, however, there was some variation in awareness and recollection of the specifics of the guided meditation they had experienced. This is reminiscent of the phenomenology of a vacationer returning from a journey or trip and being able to remember and integrate novel thought patterns and/or behaviours observed and experienced into their daily routine.

7.5.2 Neurophysiology and Eurochemical Aspects to Consider

It is emphasized that this study was not intended to be a comparative study to other forms of therapy such as pharmacotherapy or psychotherapy. It was intended to explore the clinical utility of TEMM with an LSM component as an adjunctive therapy for patients and to widen the range of available options for patients. Furthermore, in recognition of the heterogeneous nature of stress-related illness, no specific diagnostic category was chosen; rather patients who self-identified as seeking this stress-reduction therapy suffered from a range of symptoms including disturbance of sleep, mood, anxiety and somatic tension.

Qualitative patient feedback suggested that TEMM-LSM might be particularly helpful for sleep-related symptoms if used in the afternoon and evening. Based on patient responses and feedback, it might be hypothesized that a more general relaxation response that is also anxiolytic and mood-enhancing underpinned the benefit of this therapy. However, the audiovisual entrainment of EEG state towards 'absence'-like alpha and theta states also implies that TEMM's mechanism of action may occur through a hypnosis-like therapeutic power-nap with psychological therapeutic benefit derived from the autosuggestive auditory meditation themes administered by the therapist. The fact that there was variability in what separate sensory modality aspects of the TEMM-LSM patients found especially therapeutic echoes the intended multimodal psychotherapeutic experience design alluded to as "dream simulation therapy" (Moller & Barbera, 2006), in which subliminal insertion of pleasant immersive "synthetic" media experiences into sleep-like "organic" states of consciousness can be used to enhance mental and spiritual wellbeing.

Relationship of electrophysiology to neurotransmitter regulation is also important to consider, especially in the facilitation of wellbeing and positive affect; key systems include the dopaminergic and serotonergic (5-HT) systems; 5-HT has been linked to happiness and also sleep regulation and dopamine has been shown to be involved in reward response (Meyer & Quenzer, 2005). Studies in animal models have shown the absence or blocking of serotonin to be linked to depression, in a study by Smith and colleagues (2009) the precursor to serotonin, tryptophan, was withheld and showed an increase in sadness as reported by subjects. Dopamine is involved in reward behavior, which is released from the ventral tegmental area (VTA). Also noteworthy are the cognitive deficits, which may include attention deficits related to dopamine deficits. In studies on rats and primates, observations were made on attention loss via lesions or dopaminergic blocking (Nieoullon, 2002). This is suggestive on how the two neurotransmitters may be involved via activation from TEMM-LMS therapy, as patients report greater affective states after a therapy session.

Another transmitter/receptor system to take into consideration is the cannabinnoid system. Two key molecules involved are, δ-9-THC and CBD, the former works on CB1 receptors and the latter on CB2 receptors. CB2 receptors are involved in immunosuppressive/anti-inflammatory response, which could decrease pain, and CB1 receptors, which respond to the psychoactive component. Anandamide, a neurotransmitter produced naturally by the brain has also been isolated in chocolate; the neuroreceptors for anandamide are the same ones to which TJC, the psychoactive ingredient in cannabis binds to (Mechoulam & Fride, 1995). Anandamide in chocolate may therefore contribute to the feeling of wellbeing reported by "chocoholics". Mahler et al (2007) describe a "hotspot for sensory pleasure" via anandamide in the nucleus accumbens, suggesting an enhanced "liking for sweet reward" and sensory pleasure system that one might consider an optimal leisure state. Behavioural responses to CB1 activation include a relaxed, euphoric state and also increased sensitivity to sensory input (Meyer & Quenzer, 2005), this in combination with TEMM may further the state and feeling of wellbeing. Anecdotally, patient response to the combined use of TEMM and cannabinnoid therapies at our centre have shown success in alleviation of various stress-related symptoms such as mood, anxiety and sleep disturbance but it warrants further investigation if the combined usage would be beneficial to augment TEMM therapy.

7.5.3 Physiological Findings and Clinical Outcomes

Although no physiological measures were taken from users due to the application-oriented nature of our recently reported study (Moller & Bal, 2013), we noted previous studies conducted with the brainLight TEMM system in supporting data that is primarily qualitative. A study by Peters and colleagues (2013) evaluated the use of the brainLight system in a workplace wellness study. brainLight sessions were administered during rest breaks as part of a corporate health promotion program. The researchers evaluated users through EEG and HRV (heart rate variability) and noted frontal EEG slowing as well as a reduction in HRV both during and after the sessions. A study on emotion detection and universal access by Stickel et. al, used the brainLight system as a means for inducing relaxation via *Steady State Visual Evoked Potentials* (SSVEP) (Stickel et. al, 2009). While the brainLight system may not have been a central component in this study, EEG and HRV were used to study control users' baseline data upon the induction of a relaxation state. While the researchers remain unclear on the specific effectiveness of brainLight, induced relaxation was in some instances found to be correlated with successful task completion affected by motivation and reward system activation.

7.5.4 Socioeconomic and Societal Benefits

We wish to point out the potential societal benefit of health promotion on a preventative level through TEMM therapy, for example, if more closely linked to workplace health management services. Specifically with difficulty in regularly scheduling predictable vacations or other leisure events, the notion of "bringing leisure into the workplace" may be a promising avenue to pursue for employee wellbeing and productivity. Recalling the earlier comparison made above in this section, the acute as well as residual effects of such simulated or recreated leisure states is able to approximate real experiences, and perhaps even deliver these more efficiently and predictably. Specifically in preventative workplace initiatives involving high levels of leisure state flow to promote wellbeing, immersive environments can have benefits that extend beyond the level of the individual. Driver and Bruns' (1999), for example, suggested the "leisure benefits chain of causality". Their chain of causality attempts to show how improvements in individual-level health (e.g., that result from immersive environments) can have broader societal implications and economic benefits (e.g., reduced health care costs, improved economy from more productive workers). *Figure 7.4* depicts a process whereby recreational relaxation creates economic benefits, first for the individual at the micro-scale, then the employer, and ultimately country's economy at the macro-scale (Crompton, et al., 2005). Thus, the pragmatic benefits of a safe, reliable and effective technology-enhanced meditation program with the ability to promote mental health and enhance productivity must be emphasized, particularly if it can readily be operationalized into a modern workplace setting.

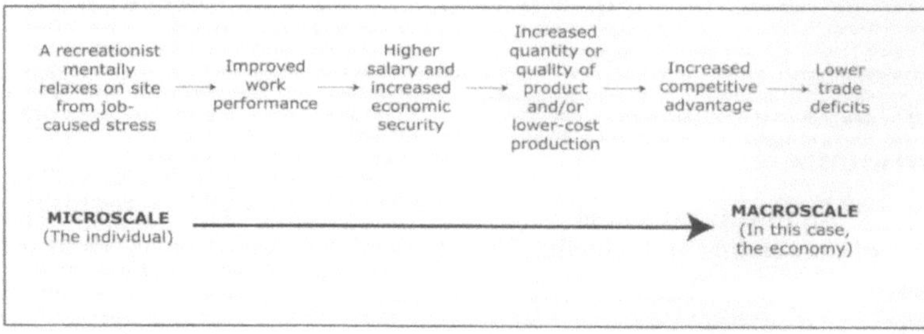

Figure 7.4: The Leisure Benefits "Chain of Causality" (Source: Crompton et al. (2005, p. 249).

7.5.5 Holistic Aspects of TEMM Therapy

The multimodal and experience-based nature of TEMM-LSM also has an element of holistic or integrative therapeutic effect; it would seem that the progress made by a patient during this kind of multimodal meditation would trickle into different facets of the patient's life, allowing him or her to carry the benefits of treatment over into issues that may be beyond the scope of initial symptoms or concerns. Various other analogous therapies (in the form of research projects) that look to enhance wellbeing are exploring the multimodal/multisensory approach to meditation/relaxation induction or training. Biofeedback used to regulate the TEMM experience based on user performance specifically looks at bringing not only the technology closer to the body, but also the experience. Measuring of respiration patterns to augment meditative experience is a trend observed in projects at both SFU's CPRM lab and Stanford's Calming Technology lab, as discussed in Section 2.1. The authors of this paper plan to launch a new TEMM research project that brings the body more intimately into the meditation/relaxation experience in the near future under a similar clinical study setup. The upcoming project involves teaching healthy breath-work while displaying visual imagery that depicts positive healing experienced by the user's body as he or she progresses with the experience. This approach ventures further into the realm of spiritual holistic health interaction while conditioning users in a way that refers to the concept of respiratory psychophysiology. It is also noteworthy that TEMM appears congruent with recent reports of utility of mindfulness exercises that include meditation, stretching, and acceptance of thoughts and emotions in veterans with combat-related post-traumatic stress disorder (King et al., 2013). In particular, the inclusion of haptic/somatosensory elements of TEMM may be congruent with the difficult-to-define mind-body benefit of stretching incorporated into meditation, which can also be seen in other forms of therapeutic exercises such as Tai Chi.

7.5.6 Personalized Medicine Aspects to TEMM and Immersive Wellbeing Environments

The ORGONA series, currently a collection of two TEMM-like experiences that engage users in healthy breath-work, serve as musings for innovative healthcare design that have also been tested and documented as well-received supportive therapy modalities (see *Figures 7.5* and *7.6*). ORGONA (the first iteration, http://harjotbal.com/?st_portfolio=orgona) interfaces primarily with the body in order to empower physicality; input is taken in the form of exhalation detected by a miniature microphone (shown in *Figure 7.5* The game allows users to stand in front of a screen onto which is projected a backdrop of a natural environment as well as a lively cloth with pseudo-realistic motion physics. The cloth responds to breath input and, upon interaction, shoots up into the air as if it were being swept up by a gust of wind.

The second iteration, ORGONA Prana (http://harjotbal.com/?st_portfolio=orgona-prana) is an engaging multimodal healing experience simulated by technology. The function of this experience is to reinforce healthy breathing technique, borrowed from yogic meditation, through physical and psychological conditioning. This is explored by using audiovisual cues that reference the holistic concept of chakras – a concept that brings the body into the healing experience through metaphor and analogy (shown in *Figure 7.6*). The visual symbolic acts of healing and transcendence through the subtle energy body are intended to positively impact the user – having effects that are both calming and empowering, ideally allowing for transformative shifts in attitude regarding personal health. Notions of embodiment, as related to autonomy and sense of agency over one's own wellbeing are emphasized by the design – superimposed healing led by the user's control.

Both iterations of the ORGONA series offer immediate interactive feedback that allows users to navigate the experiences with respect to individual performance, referred to as "responsive aesthetics". This feature allows the therapy modality to parallel and perhaps even refresh the concept of "personalized medicine" — the monitoring of performance and/or adjustment of treatment based on the individual patient more so than on a demographic or standard of treatment for a particular diagnosis. It is also likely that the ability to extract data via new technology devices, while patients/users are performing interactive wellbeing exercises, will be a leading innovative approach to tailoring therapy creating a performance history so that patients and practitioners can have a more detailed view of a user's trajectory.

Delving further into the concept and current trend of personalized medicine, while also working with the innovative affordances of new technology, TEMM-like experiences that foster a greater sense of autonomy and empowerment in the user (patient) seem to be an ideal design project for a truly innovative healthcare paradigm. In most of the mentioned related research projects (see Section 2), the use of physiological sensors attached to the user's body was a necessary means through which performance related data was collected. From a design perspective it is critical

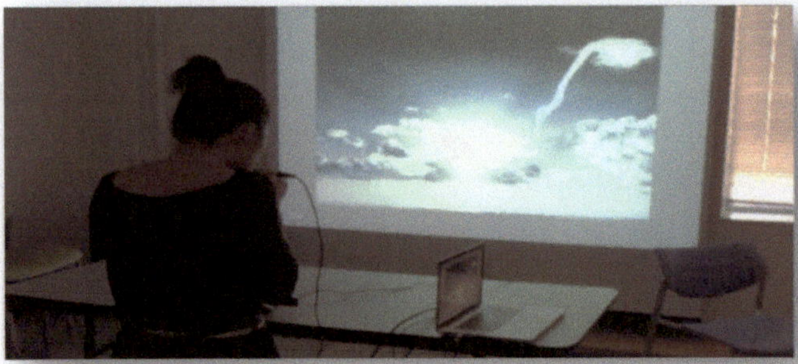

Figure 7.5: ORGONA

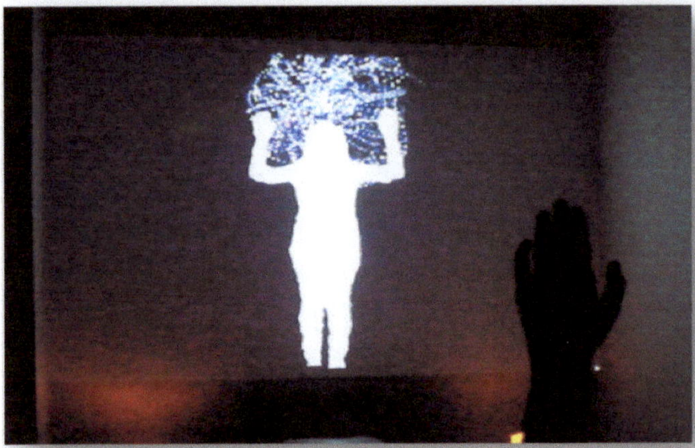

Figure 7.6: ORGONA Prana

to determine the dialogue that is imposed onto the user when he/she is ornamented in computing sensors that may act as physical and visual reminders of the user's connection to a machine that is used to make both the explicit and subtle workings of their body intelligible. Thus, an argument can be made against autonomy and agency over one's own healing experience in such projects, a paradigm similar to that associated with taking pharmaceuticals. In order for autonomy and empowerment to be realized in the context of an innovative wellbeing experience, the user should find that the system conforms to his/her reality and physicality, as opposed to the reverse – a concept that Patrizia Marti refers to as "enabling through design" in her research on responsive aesthetics for therapy and care (Marti 2012).

Certainly, there are rich opportunities for creating technologically-mediated inner presence states that may be a far more individualized and personalized approach to wellbeing, both mental and physical depending on the multimodal and sensory nature of the experience design process. A fundamental issue for the development of such technologies is to design inclusively for both accessibility by impaired people and effectiveness of the therapy. These technologies mostly refer to the concept of "cognitive orthoses" or "cognitive prosthetics", that is compensatory strategies that alter the patient's environment and are directed to an individual's functional skills (Marti, 2012). Through inclusive design conceptual frameworks, we are also actively exploring development of assessment tools with high usability for use in clinical and research endeavours involving individuals with a wide range of ages, abilities, cultural/linguisitic backgrounds.

An avenue to better understand how to personalize immersive environments with therapeutic intent will be to conduct focus groups with TEMM users who have interacted with and experienced presence in their healing and wellbeing journeys. Given the multifaceted, multimodal nature of TEMM, it is both a challenge and opportunity to have so many variables available to modify, ranging from light colour and frequency, to selected immersive visual naturescapes, to the audio content (both musical and textual content of any phrases contained within the meditation programs, and to the haptic elements of touch, warmth and vibration. Clarifying differences between individuals and linking qualitative "lived experience" reports to clinical data. This is part of the iterative process of designing for health and wellness that frames a creative scientific approach that allows for both methodical and serendipitous discovery. The possibilities of personalized experience design of immersive wellbeing environments appear wide open for future work, discovery and implementation.

7.6 Conclusion to Chapter 7

The initiative for this exploration of "recreating leisure" was primarily driven by clinical demand for safe, effective and tolerable mental health therapies. The demonstration of benefit in this broad-spectrum clinical population suggests that TEMM provides symptomatic relief from stress-related symptoms for a relatively wide range of symptoms. This is important to mental health clinicians as it may widen the range of therapeutic options, improve quality of life and reduce burden of suffering for a large number of patients in a standardized, replicable and easily administrable manner. The very positive qualitative and quantitative user feedback also suggests that as patients generally reported enjoying their TEMM sessions and programs, this form of therapy might have a low stigma that is possibly associated with other mental health therapies, and perhaps even contain some hedonic properties to contribute to a healing experience sought out by patients. This may set the stage not only in healthcare settings, but also in workplace wellness initiatives.

We have advocated for the creation and operationalization of simulated leisure-oriented states as an innovative and pragmatic wellbeing intervention on biomedical, public health and econo]mic development levels. We are intrigued by the consideration that it is the element of "flow" related to presence states also induced in leisure experiences may be a primary active ingredient. This notion of creating a state of wellbeing, rather than attacking a state of illness certainly is attractive both from a patient-centered perspective and from a clinician safety-tolerability standpoint, and highlights the potential of virtual environments as healthcare tools that may have a synthetic basis, but are still holistically oriented for therapeutic impact. If "feeling good" means freedom to be at your best, this is a compelling direction for therapeutic aspects of presence-enabling technologies to head towards vis-à-vis health and wellness.

References

Adrian, E.D. & Matthews, B.H. (1934). The Berger rhythm: Potential changes from the occipital lobes of man. *Brain*, 57, 355-385.

Adu Poku, D. (2013). *Flow in games: Aural conditioning*. Saarbrucken, Germany, Lambert Academic Publishing.

AHHA (2003) Wellness From Within: The First Step, S. Caton (Ed) *American Holistic Health Association*, Anaheim, CA.

Barlow, J.S. (1960). Rhythmic activity induced by photic stimulation in relation to intrinsical activity of the brain in man. *Electroencephalography and Clinical Neurophysiology*, 12, 317-326.

Budzynski, T., Jordy, J., Budzynski, H., Tang, H., & Claypoole, K. (1999). Academic performance enhancement with photic stimulation and EDR feedback. *Journal of Neurotherapy*, 3, 11-21.

Cantor, DS & Stevens S (2009). QEEG correlates of auditory-visual entrainment treatment efficacy of refractory depression. *Journal of Neurotherapy*, 13, 100-108.

Chen, J. (2012). Journey Breaks PSN Sales Records. Playstation.Blog. March 29, 2012. http://blog.eu.playstation.com/2012/03/29/journey-breaks-psn-sales-records/. Accessed December 13, 2013.

Crompton, J.L., Jackson, E.L., & Witt, P. (2005). Integrating benefits to leisure with constraints to leisure. In E.L. Jackson (Ed.) *Constraints to leisure* (244-257). State College, PA: Venture Publishing, Inc.

Csikszentmihalyi, M. (1975). *Beyond Boredom and anxiety*. San Francisco, CA: Jossey- Bass.

Csikszentmihalyi, M. (1990). *Flow: The psychology of optimal experience*. New York, NY: Harper Perennial.

Csikszentmihalyi, M., & Kleiber, D.A. (1991). Leisure and self-actualization. In B.L. Driver, P.J. Brown, & G.L. Peterson (Eds.) *Benefits of leisure* (91-102). State College, PA: Venture Publishing, Inc.

Difede J, Hoffman HG. (2002) Virtual reality exposure therapy for World Trade Center Post-traumatic Stress Disorder: a case report. *Cyberpsychology and Behaviour*, 5(6), 529-35.

Driver, B.L., & Bruns, D.H. (1999). Concepts and uses of the benefits approach to leisure. In E.L. Jackson & T.L. Burton (Eds.) *Leisure Studies: Prospects for the twenty-first century*. State College, PA: Venture Publishing Inc., 349-369.

Goetz, C.G.(2009) Jean-Martin Charcot and Movement Disorders: Neurological Legacies to the 21st Century International Parkinson and Movement Disorder Society. *Movement Disorders*. Aug/Sept 2009. http://www.movementdisorders.org/monthly_edition/2009/08/charcot.php). Accessed December 10, 2013.

Gromala, D., Song, M., Yim, J. D., Fox, T., Barnes, S. J., Nazemi, M. & Squire, P. (2011, May). Immersive VR: a non-pharmacological analgesic for chronic pain? In: *PART 1---Proceedings of the 2011 annual conference extended abstracts on Human factors in computing systems,* 1171-1176.

Heusser, M. (2013) M&M's, Stress and the Quest for a Sustainable Pace in the Tech Rat Race. Biztech Magazine. http://www.biztechmagazine.com/article/2013/08/mms-stress-and- quest-sustainable-pace-tech-rat-race. Accessed December 13, 2013.

Hobson, J.A. (2009). REM sleep and dreaming: towards a theory of protoconsciousness *Nature Reviews Neuroscience,* 10, 803-813.

Hwang, J.; Adamson, C.; Butler, D.; Janero, D. R.; Makriyannis, A.; Bahr, B. A. (2009). Enhancement of endocannabinoid signaling by fatty acid amide hydrolase inhibition: A neuroprotective therapeutic modality. *Life Sciences,* 86(15-16), 615-623.

Inouye, T., Sumitsuji, N., & Matsumoto, K. (1979). EEG changes induced by light stimuli modulated with the subject's alpha rhythm. *Electroencephalography and Clinical Neurophysiology,* 49, 135-142.

Janet, P. (1925). *Psychological healing: A historical and clinical study.* Paul E. & Paul C.,(Translation). London: Allen & Unwin.

King, A. P., Erickson, T. M., Giardino, N. D., Favorite, T., Rauch, S. A., Robinson, E., Kulkarni, M. Liberzon, I. (2013). A Pilot Study of Group Mindfulness-Based Cognitive Therapy (MBCT) for Combat Veterans with Posttraumatic Stress Disorder (PTSD). *Depression and Anxiety*, 30, 638-45.

Kleiber, D. A., Mannell, R. C., & Walker, G. J. (2011). *A social psychology of leisure.* State College, PA: Venture Pub. Incorporated.

Lipsman, N., Sankar, T., Downar, J., Kennedy, S.H., Lozano, A. Giacobbe, P. (2014) Neuromodulation for treatment-refractory major depressive disorder. *Canadian Medical Association Journal,* 186, 33-39.

Mannell, R.C., & Klieber, D.A. (1997). *A social psychology of leisure.* State College, PA: Venture Publishing, Inc.

Markland, O.N. (1990) Alpha Rythms. *Journal of Clinical Neurophysiology,* 1990. 7, 163-189.

Marti, P. (2012) *Enabling through design: exploration of aesthetic and embodied interaction in therapy and care.* Eindhoven Technical University Library, ISBN: 978-90-386-3089-2.

Marti, P. Giusti L. (2011) Bringing aesthetically minded design to devices for disabilities. *Proceedings of 5th International conference on Designing Pleasurable Products and Interfaces*, 22-25 June 2011, Milan, Italy.

Mechoulam, R., Fride E. (1995). The unpaved road to the endogenous brain cannabinoid ligands, the anandamides. In R.G. Pertwee (Ed.) *Cannabinoid receptors*. (233-258) Boston: Academic Press.

Meyer, J.S., and Quenzer, L.F. (2005). *Psychopharmacology: Drugs, the brain, and Behaviour.* Sunderland, MA. Sinauer Associates, Inc.

Moller H.J. (2006) The neurocognitive role of 'absence' in multimodal simulator protocols. *Proceedings, IEEE 2006 International Conference of the Engineering in Medicine and Biology Society, 5th International Workshop on Virtual Rehabilitation,* 116-120.

Moller H.J. (2008) Neural Correlates of "Absence" in Interactive Simulator Protocols. *Cyberpsychology and Behavior,* 11(2), 181-187.

Moller, H.J., Bal, H. (2013) Technology-enhanced multimodal meditation: Clinical results from an observational case series. *Proc 10th International Conference on Virtual Rehabilitation*, Philadelphia, PA, USA, 26-29 Aug. 2013, 1-9.

Moller H.J. & Barbera, J. (2006): Media Presence, Dreaming and Consciousness. Chapter 5, pp 97-123. In: *From Communication to Presence: the integration of cognition, emotions and culture towards the ultimate communicative experience.* Riva G, Anguera MT, Wiederhold BK, Mantovani F (Eds.), IOS Press, Amsterdam.

O'Connor, M., Brenninkmeyer, C., Morgan, A.,Bloomingdale K, Thall M, Vasile R, Pascual-Leone, A. (2003) Relative effects of repetitive transcranial magnetic stimulation and electroconvulsive therapy on mood and memory: a neurocognitive risk-benefit analysis. *Cognitive and Behavioral Neurology*, 16, 118-127.

Nieoullon, A. (2002). Dopamine and the regulation of cognition and attention. *Progress in Neurobiology,* 67(1), 53-87.

Pashler, H. & Wagenmakers, E.J (2012). Editors' Introduction to the Special Section on Replicability in Psychological Science: A Crisis of Confidence? *Perspectives on Psychological Science,* 7, 528-530.

Panzarino, M. (2013) The New Xbox One Kinect Tracks Your Heart Rate, Happiness, Hands and Hollers. Be Free News. http://bfreenews.com/bfn/showonenews?id=427809&s=2&f=3). Accessed December 6, 2013.

Patrick, G. J., (1996.) Improved neuronal regulation in ADHD: An application of fifteen sessions of photic-driven EEG neurotherapy. *Journal of Neurotherapy,* 1, 27-36.

Peters, T., Ghadiri, A., & Kohl, M. (2013, April). Betriebliches Gesundheitsmanagement: audio-visuelle Entspannung kann Krankenstand senken. *CO'MED* 19(4), 40-43.

Revonsuo, A. (2006). *Inner presence: Consciousness as a biological phenomenon. Cambridge,* MA, US: MIT Press.

Stickel, C., Ebner, M., Steinbach-Nordmann, S., Searle, G., & Holzinger, A. (2009). Emotion detection: application of the valence arousal space for rapid biological usability testing to enhance universal access. In *Universal Access in Human-Computer Interaction. Addressing Diversity* (615-624). Springer Berlin Heidelberg.

Smith, K.A., Fairburn, C.G., and Cowen, P.J. (1997). Relapse of depression after rapid depletion of tryptophan. *Lancet,* 349, 915-919.

Thrash, T. M., Elliot, A. J., Maruskin, L. A., & Cassidy, S. E. (2010). Inspiration and the promotion of well-being: Tests of causality and mediation. *Journal of Personality and Social Psychology,* 98(3), 488-506.

Thomas, N. & Siever, D. (1989). The effect of repetitive audio/visual stimulation on skeletomotor and vasomotor activity. *Hypnosis: 4th European Congress at Oxford.* London: Whurr Publishers., 238-245.

Toman, J. (1941). Flicker potentials and the alpha rhythm in man. *Journal of Neurophysiology,* 4, 51-61.

Vidyarthi, J., Riecke, B. E., & Gromala, D. (2012). Sonic Cradle: designing for an immersive experience of meditation by connecting respiration to music. In *Proceedings of the Designing Interactive Systems Conference,* June, 2012, 408-417.

Wallace RK, Benson H. (1972) The physiology of meditation. *Scientific American,* 226, 84-90.

Walter, V.J. & Walter, W.G. (1949). The central effects of rhythmic sensory stimulation. *Electroencephalography and Clinical Neurophysiology*, 1, 57-86.

Weiser, M., & Brown, J. S. (1996). Designing calm technology. *PowerGrid Journal*, 1(1), 75-85.

Wessinger, E., & Iso-Ahola, S.E. (1984). Intrinsic leisure motivation, personality and physical health. *Society and Leisure,* 7, 217-228.

Williams, P. & West, M. (1975). EEG responses to photic stimulation in persons experienced in meditation. *Electroencephalography and Clinical Neurophysiology*, 39, 519-522.

Woodcock, J. (2007). The prospects for "personalized medicine" in drug development and drug therapy. *Clinical Pharmacology & Therapeutics*, 81(2), 164-169.

Wongsuphasawat, K., Gamburg, A., Moraveji, N. (2012). You Can't Force Calm: Designing and Evaluating Respiratory Regulating Interfaces for Calming Technology. *Extended abstracts of ACM UIST*, Cambridge, MA, USA.

8 Therapeutic Presence in Mediated Psychotherapy: the Uncanny Stranger in the Room

Sheryl Brahnam

Abstract: Taking the perspective of the therapist, this chapter reflects on how both the lack of important physical cues and the addition of media artifacts, such as audio/video synchronization problems and technological glitches, in distance psychotherapy using the telephone and videoconferencing technologies can potentially affect the therapeutic relationship and therapeutic presence.

Keywords: Presence; Therapeutic Presence; Therapeutic Relationship; Distance Psychotherapy; Distance Psychoanalysis; Skype.

8.1 Introduction to Chapter 8

Mediated psychotherapy is as old as the profession of psychotherapy itself, which is said to have been invented as a medical profession in the 1890s when Sigmund Freud undertook a self-analysis thereby becoming the first analyst (Cushman, 1992). Freud's letters to his friend Wilhelm Fliess were an important instrument in his self-analysis, and it was Freud who first demonstrated the value of using correspondence therapeutically in his letters of advice to the father of "Little Hans," a five-year-old boy with a phobia of horses (Freud, 1959). By the end of the 1950s, many analysts were describing their ventures in analysis through letters (Grotijahn, 1955), but letter writing was not the sole form of mediation psychoanalysts were exploring that decade. In 1959 a closed-circuit link was set up between the University of Nebraska and Norfolk State Hospital to provide psychiatric and other health services (Rees & Haythornthwaite, 2004), and in 1953 the Samaritans started using the telephone as a crises intervention tool for suicide (Grumet, 1979), an intervention so successful that by the 1970s a plethora of community hotlines and crises call centers had been established (Hornblow & Sloane, 1980). The 1970s also witnessed a wave of experimentation with the telephone's potential for other therapeutic functions, ranging from distance psychotherapy (Grumet, 1979) to telephone hypnosis (Owens, 1970) to "videotelephone" consultations (Maxmen, 1976). In the 1990s the first forays into distance psychotherapy using the Internet were launched, beginning around 1995 with online advice services and rapidly developing by the end of the decade into offering a full range of psychological services via real-time chat, videoconferencing, and encrypted email (Ainsworth, 2002). Today videoconferencing technologies routinely link specialists at academic and regional mental health centers to remote centers around the world, and internet psychotherapy is slowly but increasingly being accepted, at least as an adjunctive modality, by psychotherapists and clients alike.

Despite the early adoption in psychiatry of videoconferencing technologies and the many studies indicating its reliability, effectiveness, and patient satisfaction (Hilty, Marks, Urness, Yellowlees, & Nesbitt, 2004) and despite the accessibility of similar technologies available on the Internet, such as Skype, and the many studies attesting to the Internet's therapeutic value (Barak, Hen, Boniel-Nissim, & Shapira, 2008), many psychotherapists continue to express skepticism and reservations about employing videoconferencing, the telephone, Skype, and other internet tools, such as chat and email, as the *primary* means of communicating and interacting with clients (Lester, 2006), citing concerns not only with opening a Pandora's box of legal and ethical issues (Koocher, 2007) but also, and more importantly, with having a negative impact on what is considered by many theoretic viewpoints to be the most vital instrument of change: the therapeutic relationship. Operationally defined as the feelings and attitudes the therapist and client have for one another and how these are expressed, the therapeutic relationship is held to account for the highest outcome variance (33% or more) across all theoretical orientations (Lambert, 1992).

The literature is mixed, however, regarding the impact mediation has on the therapeutic relationship, with some studies reporting positive or at least similar influences compared with face-to-face encounters (Reynolds, Stiles, & Grohol, 2006), while other studies report adverse mediation effects on the relationship (Rees & Stone, 2005). A limitation of many of these studies is that they have focused almost exclusively on one component of the therapeutic relationship: the alliance, defined as the affective bond between client and therapist and the extent to which they work together collaboratively and purposely (Bordin, 1979). There are at least two reasons for this focus. First, it is commonly asserted that alliance predicts outcome (Martin, Garske, & Davis, 2000); however, there is a small but growing body of literature that questions the validity of this assertion (Barber, Khalsa, & Sharpless, 2010). Second, there is a tendency to define the therapeutic relationship solely in terms of the alliance, which is a gross oversimplification (Stiles & Goldsmith, 2010). According to Gelso and Hayes (1998), for instance, all therapeutic relationships have at least three components: a working alliance, a transference/countertransference configuration (that is, the repetition and reliving of earlier relational patterns with significant others within the therapeutic relationship), and the real relationship. Norcoss (2010) presents an even more elaborate view of the therapeutic relationship, with the alliance being but one ingredient among many. Another limitation in these studies concerns the way in which the alliance is measured, which can be from the perspective of the client, the perspective of the therapist, or the perspective of the expert observer. Most studies measuring the impact mediation has on the alliance have taken the perspective of the client because research has shown the strongest correlation between the client's views of the working alliance and outcomes (Bachelor & Horavath, 1999), especially in the early stages of the relationship (Kokotovic & Tracey, 1990), while therapist reservations and expressions of concern using these technologies and their impact on the alliance, if addressed at all, are typically dismissed as normal resistances to change or as a lack of experience with the new technologies (Rees & Stone, 2005). Client-centric views of the alliance measured in the early stages, however, may present a premature picture of the alliance (Castonguay, Constantino, & Grosse, 2006). Many have argued that the alliance changes over time (Stiles & Goldsmith, 2010); it ruptures and is rebuilt (Eubanks-Carter, Muran, & Safran, 2010), providing corrective emotional experiences for the client and powerful opportunities for change (F. Alexander & French, 1946).

According to J.F. Alexander, Holtzworth-Munroe, and Jameson (1994), many psychotherapists find empirical research unappealing and remain largely uninfluenced by it because it fails to capture what they perceive to be essential aspects of the phenomenon. My intention in this chapter is to address the concerns of therapists, not by writing them off as mere discomfort working with unfamiliar technologies, but rather by acknowledging them for what they are reported to be: modalities affecting the clinician's ability to influence the relationship–to attend to the subtleties of client expressions and to the clinician's own reactions and experiences. Some of these concerns involve the sensorial imposition of what I have labeled elsewhere *media artifacts* (Brahnam, 2009, 2012), with the sense of the word *artifact* taken from *Webster's Third New International Dictionary* as "a product of artificial character due to extraneous agency" (Gove, 1986, p. 124). Media artifacts, such as synchronization problems between audio and video and technological glitches, can unconsciously alter and transform participants' impressions of each other, perturbing, for the clinician, the psychological and physical *presence* of the client–potentially introducing into the therapeutic frame the presence of something akin to an uncanny stranger in the room.

Although few in number and mostly in the field of telepsychiatry, there are papers and studies that have associated various media artifacts with a concept of presence. An early work is that of Cukor et al. (1998), who examined video artifacts in relation to *social presence* (see also Chapters 1, 5 and 6, this volume), a term first introduced by Short, Williams, and Christie (1976) and defined as "a quality of the communications medium" that expresses "the degree of the salience of the other person in the interaction and the consequent salience of the interpersonal relationships" (p. 65). Cukor et al. found video in telepsychiatry establishing a baseline sense of social presence; but video artifacts, some of which were acknowledged to be subtle, were speculated to reduce the effectiveness of the video channel for conveying information to psychiatrists about their patients. More recently, Turner (2006) related media artifacts to the idea of presence as it is conceptualized in the field of virtual reality, often as the "sensation of being there" in the virtual world (Barfeld, Zeltzer, Sheridan, & Slater, 1995) or as the "perceptual illusion of non-mediation" (Lombard & Ditton, 1997).[1] His goal was to show that the illusion of non-mediation creates the impression

1 It should also be noted that there are a number of papers that address presence in virtual reality psychotherapy, especially in relaxation therapy (Villani, Riva, & Riva, 2007) and in virtual exposure therapy (VET) (Lu, Harter, & Pierce, 2011; Meyerbröker & Emmelkamp, 2011; Riva, 2005), with the

that all the bodily cues relevant to a therapeutic interaction are available, when in fact they are not (for a broader discussion on the concept of presence see Chapters 1, 2 and 3, this volume).

My goal is to reflect both on what is missing in mediation (corporality) and what is being added (the presence of media artifacts/agencies) and to explore how the qualities of the media (specifically, the telephone and Skype) affect the therapeutic relationship by disturbing what is known as *therapeutic presence*, that is, the therapist's intricate and multifaceted awareness of the client. To accomplish this goal, I begin by briefly reviewing the concept of therapeutic presence, mostly as it is defined and described in humanistic and psychodynamic writings.[2] This overview of therapeutic presence is then followed by a discussion of media artifacts, or *mediation agencies* as they might best be described here, and how they perturb the ability of psychotherapists to "use their selves and their attuned bodily awareness as tools" for understanding their clients as well as for perceiving "how their responses are facilitating the client's therapeutic process and the therapeutic relationship" (Geller & Greenberg, 2012, p. 7).

8.2 Therapeutic Presence

As indicated above, researchers have not identified all client/therapist factors that contribute to the development of a beneficial therapeutic relationship, but according to Geller, Greenberg, and Watson (2010) therapeutic presence, which they define as being in the moment with the client on multiple levels (physical, emotional, cognitive, and spiritual), is a necessary condition for a positive therapeutic relationship; and they present empirical evidence to support this claim.[3] In an early exploratory paper on therapeutic presence, Geller and Greenberg (2002) found in their examination of solicited accounts from expert therapists practicing a range of theoretical

concern of the latter being primarily on providing patients with enough presence to feel anxiety when presented with a fear provoking stimulus. For more on presence in virtual reality stress management and in VET, see chapter 10.

2 My arguments in this chapter, however, equally apply to other therapeutic modalities, including cognitive behavioral therapy (CBT). Although not generally seen as highly central, the therapeutic relationship in all its complexity is still relevant in CBT (Gelso & Hayes, 1998). There are even CBT orientations that stress therapeutic presence (see, for example, Friedberg, Tabbaraha, & Poggesia, 2013).

3 As with many alliance studies, client perceptions of presence, and not therapist perceptions, are associated with positive outcome. Geller et al. (2010) note two possible reasons for this incongruity: 1) therapists may not always be able to communicate presence, even though they may be experiencing it, and 2) some clients may have difficulty experiencing presence as well as relational connectivity. The authors point out that studies are needed to isolate the qualities and attachment styles that allow a client to experience presence.

orientations–but all acknowledging the importance of presence–that presence prepares the ground for an attuned responsiveness to the client that is made possible by combining a kinesthetic and emotional sensing of the client's affect (receptivity) with an inward attendance to the way in which the experience of the client resonates in the therapist's own body (inward attendance). The receptivity that therapists report is a bodily receptivity achieved by listening "deeply to their clients with all of their senses and perceptions," perceiving what clients are saying beyond words and their expression. As one therapist put it, "it's just not listening to the words, listening to the tone, listening to what the person's bodily experience is...but somehow listening with my body to their bodily experience" (p. 78). Inward attendance is described as transforming the self of the therapist into a finely tuned instrument, where everything that is experienced inside (images, feelings, bodily sensations, and memories) is used to inform the therapeutic process. Through receptivity and inward attendance, the body of the therapist becomes a sensitive sensor attuned to the self, to the client, and to the relationship. The goal of therapeutic presence is to enable the client to feel fully perceived and understood. Thus, therapeutic presence (the inner resonance and feeling of connection to the client that the therapist experiences) needs to be communicated to the client. When clients feel understood, they elaborate and delve more deeply into what they are feeling in the moment and eventually learn to understand and validate their own experiences.[4]

The focus in therapeutic presence on the body is not surprising. From the start the development of interpersonal connections and the body are closely tied. Within the shared embodied space between infant and mother, the infant learns to locate its own body by exhibiting a "lived sense of corporeal equivalencies (your tongue, my tongue)" (Crossley, 1996, p. 51) and by actively assuming the gestures of those around it, eventually investing them with intentionality so that "here the others' intentions," as Merleau-Ponty (1964) observes of the infant, "somehow play across my body while my intentions play across his" (p. 119). According to Schore (2000), in the infant's first year, visual experiences play a predominant role in social and emotional development, with the mother's emotionally expressive face the site of the most potent visual stimulus. The choreographed oscillations and synchronizations of expressions and of glances in the mother-infant dyad create a mutual regulatory system of arousal that map, according to Tronick and Weinberg (1997), "elements of each interactant's state of consciousness into each of their brains" (p. 75). These researchers claim that the infant's limbic system, which is associated with the right hemisphere, is centrally involved in emotional communication (as well as in processing bodily experiences). Because this association persists into adulthood, the transfer of affect between infant

4 These three activities (receptivity, inward attendance, and communication/connection), define what the authors call the *process* of presence, as opposed to the therapist's *preparations* for presence and actual *experiences* when in presence (Geller & Greenberg, 2012).

and mother becomes a direct right brain linkage, forming the basis of what might best be described as *intersubjectivity*.

Intersubjectivity, or the shared relational space through which unconscious expressive material is communicated, has been described by many psychotherapists: Winnicott (1971), for example, speaks of *potential space*, Buber of the *I-thou* (1958), and Ogden (2004) of the *analytic third*. This is the space, according to Winnicott (1971), that both joins and separates the mother and child, the client and therapist, a space that is neither outside nor inside, neither objective nor subjective, a playful space where relationships are nourished and where culture begins. Ogden's description of the analytic third is particularly interesting in the way he describes the space between therapist and client as a separate agency, a third subjectivity that is "the product of a unique dialectic generated by/between the separate subjectivities of analyst and analysand within the analytic setting" and that "seems to take on a life of its own in the interpersonal field" (p. 169). The third position allows the analyst to attend to such relational psychodynamics as transference/countertransference and *projective identification*, a dynamic where subjectivities are subverted so that the recipient of the projection (the analyst) becomes for a moment the projector (the client). Through projective identification the therapist becomes a container for material the client is not yet ready to acknowledge or experience for himself.

How unconscious material is transferred directly from client to therapist is not fully understood. Schore (2000) suggests that "just as the left brain communicates its states to other left brains via conscious linguistic behaviors, so the right nonverbally communicates its unconscious states to other right brains *that are tuned to receive these communications*" (p. 76). This aligns with Trevarthen (1998), who states that intersubjectivity is manifested as an immediate sympathetic awareness of other's attentions, emotions, and intentions as these are transmitted through bodily movements and emotional expressions, especially those conveyed by the face, vocal tract, and hands. Nonverbal communication is pervasive in any human interaction and accompanies every utterance, with Beier and Young (1998) noting "even in written language authors convey 'nonverbal' structures, which tell us through channels such as continuity of words, unexpected phrasing, repetition, etc., more about the authors themselves than about their lexical message" (p. 243). For Beier and Young nonverbal behavior is the unconscious made visible, especially when there are discrepancies in messages between channels, such as facial expressions, verbal communication, tone of voice, gestures, and so on. They write, "because the cues and discrepancies among messages traveling in a variety of channels are subtle and appear ambiguous,...the meaning can stay hidden even from the sender and yet affect the emotions of the receiver" (p. 252).

To pick up these unconscious communications, Freud (1912) claimed the analyst "must adjust himself to the patient as a telephone receiver is adjusted to the transmitting microphone" (p. 115-116) and "turn his own unconscious like a receptive organ towards the transmitting unconscious of the patient" (p. 115). Freud called this state of attunement "evenly suspended attention" (p. 115). It was because the body inevitably gave away the unconscious that Freud was certain it could be known: "If his lips are silent, he chatters with his fingertips; betrayal oozes out of him at every pore. And thus the task of making conscious the most hidden recesses of the mind is one which is quite possible to accomplish" (Freud, 1997, p. 69).

8.3 Mediated Therapeutic Presence

So how do electronic representations of client and therapist affect therapeutic presence? What happens to the perceptions of client and therapist–and to the space in-between–when therapy is electronically mediated? How much do the media themselves intrude? For Stadter (2012) electronic media (smart phones, laptops, game controls, and tablets) insert themselves between two people, quite literally, as a clinging copresence he calls (echoing Ogden's analytic third) the *e-third*. The e-third "interferes with intimacy and reflection," Stadter claims, unlike "the intersubjective third which promotes reflective and intimate relating" (p. 11). Although appreciative of what the new communication technologies are offering his clients, Stadter (2013) describes many who are struggling hard in their lives to handle the social intrusiveness of this third thing that subsumes so many people's relational needs.[5] According to Turkle (2011), the social intrusion of communication devices is leaving a whole generation of young people–the so-called *digital natives*–feeling cheated because parents and friends are never really present. What these youths yearn for, Turkle says, is "the pleasure of full attention, coveted and rare" (p. 266). They desire "time and touch, attention and immediacy" (p. 272). Because therapeutic presence provides "the pleasure of full attention, coveted and rare", therapy today, according to Stadter, is more valuable than ever, but the question remains to what extent the relational depths obtainable in therapeutic presence can be mediated.[6]

Reflecting on her own experiences with telephone psychoanalysis using Skype, Dettbarn (2013) has come to regard technology in the therapeutic setting more as *the uncanny third*. In its magical power to connect and in its inexplicable malfunctions and disconnects, Dettbarn claims, "The machine, a third party who suddenly determines the rules, becomes a part of our work" (p. 18), an object like the therapist eliciting both positive and negative transferences. Dettbarn observes that the digital devices used

5 As Newitz (2007) describes so well in writing about his personal relationship with his laptop, "My laptop computer is irreplaceable...I love it. I would recognize the feel of its keyboard under my fingers in a darkened room...It doesn't just belong to me; I also belong to it" (p. 88).

6 Of course, therapists have as much difficulty as other people keeping their communications devices at bay–even during the therapeutic hour with a client. Wallwork, (2013), for instance, mentions psychotherapists confessing to reading emails, surfing the Internet, and checking text messages during telephone sessions.

to make connections with the therapist can metamorphose into "evocative objects" (Turkle, 2007) taken by the client to "symbolically make and potentially maintain the connection [to the therapist] eternally, as when a Skype participant looks to see if his analyst is online around the clock." She goes on to say that "The beloved object has, as it were, become a living object, having settled somewhere between living and dead matter" (p. 19). Moreover, if the therapist is experienced as a bad object, "malfunctions or disruptions in Skype are interpreted as confirmation of the analyst's aggression towards the analysand" (p. 20), with the uncanny third appearing to collude with the client against the therapist. If instead both client and therapist join forces against the uncanny third, forming a "double negative transference" (p. 22), working through can be prevented. In cases where the client has "attributed magical powers to the analyst" (p. 21), disruptions can result in premature disillusionment, upsetting the alliance. Because no one can control technological problems, Dettbarn claims, "the field of magic and the uncanny is activated" (p. 21).

Equally uncanny for Dettbarn (2013) is the disembodied voice. She asks, "Do our voices become disembodied on the computer? Are they ghostly voices? But who still believes in ghosts? Surely we have long since left this notion behind us. Or have we?... As the normally vibrant mark of our presence, does the voice lose its vitality in the absence of the body or does it lead us into an emotional area between the living and the dead?" (p. 20). Dettbarn is not alone here; other therapists and analysts have also spoken about the uncanniness of the disembodied voice in telephone sessions. For Brainsky (2003) the disembodied voice fosters "an unusually spectral relationship" (p. 23)–an "uncanny attachment" says Moses (2005, p. 28)–and hearing ghostly echoes in the room using a speakerphone left Leffert (2003) feeling "eerie." Freud (1915/1955), in his famous essay on the uncanny, connects uncanny feelings to a resurrection of outmoded animistic beliefs: "Nowadays we no longer believe in them, we have surmounted these modes of thought; but we do not feel quite sure of our new beliefs, and the old ones still exist within us ready to seize upon any confirmation" (p. 246). The telephone, as Connor (2000) in his history of ventriloquism writes, "still retains a tincture of the old supernatural explanations, and indeed begins to bring about a kind of re-enchantment of the world" (p. 42).

For other therapists, the telephone magnifies the presence of the absent body through the voice. Connor (2000) describes what is magnified by the telephone as a confluence of "pants, gasps, and hisses, pops, and percussions, of the breath sounding amid its originating body and amid the sensitive body of the telephone apparatus," making the sensorial experience of talking on the phone "like being coiled alongside your speaking twin, their lips pressed to your ear, and your lips murmuring into theirs" (p. 381). This coiled communication becomes for some therapists a connection that supports containment (Scharff, 2014), as reflected in Leffert's (2003) observation that the telephone "results in a purer, more intensely, even hyper-analytic process" (p. 124) that is especially effective because it echoes the holding presence of the mother. Metaphorical references to the womb and the bonds between mother and child abound in descriptions of therapy by telephone.[7] However, as Connor (2000) is quick to note, the voice over the telephone is "both *more mechanical* and *more human* than ordinary voices" (p. 381, emphasis added). Whereas Leffert emphasizes some of the more human, hyper-analytic aspects of therapy by telephone, Argentieri and Mehler (2003) are convinced that the mechanical inflections of the voice–the telephone's distortions of tones and inflections–interfere with communication between client and therapist. Indeed, one might ask how it is possible for the "hisses, pops, and percussions, of the breath"–the nonverbal expressions through which, as noted in the last section, the unconscious is revealed–are to be distinguished from the "hisses, pops, and percussions" of the interference on the line? As I have observed elsewhere, these interferences, or artifacts, are problematic precisely "because of their tendency to perturb (write over, jostle, and shove aside) the unconscious...expressions of human subjects," producing "impressions that do not originate with the subject but yet are often unconsciously confused with him" (Brahnam, 2012, p. 81).

Conventional wisdom would assume that adding a visual channel to distance psychotherapy would reunite voice and body, thereby enriching therapeutic presence. But that does not appear to be the case. Evidence suggests that, unlike face-to-face interactions, when a visual channel is available, it is used mostly to situate the interaction, with the audio channel becoming the focus of attention like it is with the telephone (Cukor et al., 1998). O'Donnell (1997), after presenting some evidence that bandwidth and screen size have little effect on people's preference for the audio channel in videoconferencing, speculates that video conferencing is missing some subtle yet unidentifiable elements that are essential for the proper utilization of the visual channel, rendering it "a sterile medium of limited value compared with a face-to-face meeting" (p. 315). Neuroscience provides clues to what might be missing. Schore (2000), for instance, presents powerful scientific evidence that subtle and implicit bodily interactions involving elaborate exchanges with others of corporeal expression matching, synchronizations, and rhythmical patterning, form the core of intersubjectivity. Beebe (2004) notes that "Interactions in the nonverbal and implicit modes are rapid, subtle, co-constructed, and generally out of awareness. And yet they profoundly affect moment-to-moment communication and the affective climate" (p. 49). In most teleconferencing systems available today, synchronization of audio and visual channels is imperfect, images are often distorted, and there are noticeable delays. Although Bayles (2012) realizes most therapists and clients accommodate the time lags that occur on Skype, she is concerned about the costs, "about the impact of the mismatching that can happen on Skype–both the minute, singular mismatches as well as ongoing failure to consistently meet and match" (p. 578).

7 As reflected, for instance, in these two quotes: "Does the offer of phone treatment break the boundary...stretching the umbilical cord?" (Moses, 2005, p. 29) and "The ringing of the phone symbolically represented 'the cry of the infant'...." (Rosenbaum, 1974, p. 490-491).

Bayles's concerns are supported by evidence suggesting that audio/video mismatches, speed/pitch changes, timing misalignments, and delays have the potential of interrupting and attenuating the subtle nonverbal exchanges between people–sometimes producing unexpected effects. Massaro and Egan (1996), for example, found mismatches between visual and auditory displays registering as a third emotion (for instance, when *happy* audio content was played simultaneously with a video of a *fearful* facial expression, the resulting perception was *surprise*), and Tinwell and Grimshaw (2009) found that lack of synchronization between sound and lip movements in virtual characters produced perceived *eeriness*. In general, misalignment of audio and visual cues has been found to be confusing to viewers and to elicit negative emotions (Bruce, 1996). Recall in the last section how the unconscious is revealed through "discrepancies among messages traveling in a variety of channels...[where]...the meaning can stay hidden even from the sender and yet affect the emotions of the receiver" (Beier & Young, 1998, p. 252). For therapists these audio/video mismatches and discrepancies can be unconsciously deceptive and disruptive, perturbing the feeling tones produced by the client's subtle and unconscious communications.

Tightly bound with the experience of the uncanny (*unheimlich*), as Freud (1915/1955) observed, is the experience of the familiar (*heimlich*). Mediated psychotherapy provokes the uncanny in part because it commingles the *Heimlich* with the *Unheimlich*. In our society people ordinarily communicate with each other using electronic devices, thus it seems perfectly natural to conduct therapy online or via telephone.[8] Yet just as unresolved relational dynamics are magnified and intensified within the therapeutic setting, so too are media artifacts magnified and intensified. Echoes are heard, and a sort of ghost, a stranger in the room appears, in whose face and in whose voice is reflected, not so much a mirroring of the self as some shadow self. Cultures around the world tell stories of a mischievous shadow twin: one's doppelgänger and harbinger of death (Rank, 1925/1971).

In reading the accounts of psychotherapists conducting therapy by telephone or Skype, there is a notable undercurrent of anxiety, often expressed as a rush to explain away an impending threat that makes being together in silence nearly intolerable:

> Sometimes I have a feeling or experience, usually accompanied by mild anxiety, that the mechanical/psychological connection itself has been lost or broken. Patients may experience the same thing, asking, "Are you still there?" or saying, "I'm not hearing you."...If I feel troubled by a silence or experience a sense of having "lost" the patient somewhere in it, I am more likely to interrupt it with a neutral question such as, "What's going on?" or "What's your thought?" or, more specifically, "I feel I've lost you."...For some patients the activity provides necessary evidence of both the analyst's presence and empathic contact, while for others it can remove

8 In fact, this is a major argument for doing psychotherapy via the telephone or the Internet (see, for example, Scharff, 2014).

> a silence that could verge on a traumatic pressure to say too much too soon (Leffert, 2003, p. 121-122).

Accounts of sessions using Skype or the telephone are often punctuated, as in the example above, by expressions that eerily echo a medium's conjuring of spirits: "Are you there?...Are you still there?" Silence, rather than being a moment of communion, or of resistance, or of reflection, or of an emotional loss for words, becomes, instead, a reminder of loss, and for some, an occasion to panic.

At the moment of malfunction–when Dettbarn's uncanny third asserts itself with its power to connect and to disconnect–the absence of therapeutic presence can become painfully present. For Scharff (2014) such moments offer opportunities. For instance, she describes a situation early in therapy with a client when her headset failed: the client could hear her, but she could not hear him. The incident ended up revealing important dynamics between the client and his mother, which, through the process of working through, eventually fostered the therapeutic alliance. For Argentieri and Mehler (2003), however, mediated therapy is essentially traumatizing for both therapist and client precisely because it denies separation and loss and deprives the client of the bodily presence of the therapist, a traumatization poignantly described by this psychoanalytic candidate's account of her experiences with her training analyst:

> On several occasions my analyst's phone was actually not working and he was not aware of the problem, which meant that I could not reach him. At other times there were problems with static in the line, poor reception, and dropped calls which required hanging up and redialing. These technical interferences in the line interrupted time, thought, and a sense of connection. It felt unsafe to have my analyst so far away and so silent, hidden from my emotions....It was not possible to jump on a plane and travel in the middle of a painful period where I needed the physical holding of my analyst's presence and the visual constancy of his office" (de Benaim, de Varela, de Setton, & Anonymous, 2013, p. 200).

8.4 Conclusion to Chapter 8

In this chapter I have addressed how mediated psychotherapy (mostly via telephone and Skype) affects therapeutic presence and the shared relational space through which unconscious expressive material is communicated between therapist and client. Ogden (2004) calls this shared relational space the *analytic third*, which he describes in terms of a third subjectivity that "seems to take on a life of its own in the interpersonal field" (p. 169). For some therapists and psychoanalysts, technology becomes yet another presence that seems to take on a life of its own, an uncanny third (Dettbarn, 2013) or e-third (Stadter, 2012) that disrupts and intrudes upon the relational space between therapist and client. After discussing the uncanny third and e-third, I go on to show how therapeutic presence is potentially affected not only by the missing bodies of therapist and client (an important expressive modality of the unconscious and source of intersubjective resonance) but also by the addition of media artifacts that may unconsciously become confused with and alter the therapist's impressions and emotional reactions to the client's nonverbal expressions.[9]

A major goal of this chapter has been to bring to attention the effects media artifacts can potentially have on therapeutic presence and on the therapists who use their minds and bodies as sensitive instruments for receiving the unconscious communications of their clients.[10] While some therapists are adapting to the new technologies, acknowledging the many conveniences offered by distance psychotherapy and its necessity in some cases, other therapists are expressing reservations about adopting these technologies, especially as the primary means of conducting therapy. Too often, however, their concerns are dismissed out of hand as resistances to change or as a lack of familiarity with the new technologies. However, as Short, Williams, and Christie (1976) early observed, people are aware of the degree of social presence offered by communications media and tend to avoid using a medium if they feel the degree of social interaction requires more social presence than the medium offers. It is reasonable to assume that therapists are equally aware of the degree of therapeutic presence offered by communications media and tend to avoid using a medium if they feel their interactions with clients require more therapeutic presence than the medium offers. Another goal of this chapter has been to show that therapist reservations are tenable and should be listened to carefully and taken more seriously.

Because the reader may be involved in the enterprise of designing technologies, my intention in this chapter is also to challenge researchers to do more to investigate the effects of media artifacts on person perception and on social presence and to encourage interface designers to consider the more subtle effects technologies can have on deeper forms of interpersonal communication and to think of ways of ameliorating some of their more obvious deleterious effects, especially when designing applications for distance psychotherapy. For example, can walls be stitched together virtually so that clients undertaking distance psychotherapy can have the feeling of containment that is offered by the visual constancy of a therapist's brick and mortar office? Or is it possible for a shared aural space or an unobtrusive sonic background to be designed such that it produces a feeling of containment and constancy? Or can methods be devised for gently alerting communication partners of a disconnection or of a device failure, such as a faulty headset? It is my hope that understanding more about therapeutic presence and how it is affected when mediated will put designers

9 Media artifacts potentially alter clients' impressions of therapists as well, but my focus in this chapter is on therapists since they use these feelings and impressions therapeutically in their work with clients.

10 I wish to stress that only a few media artifacts have been considered in this chapter; there are many more (see, for instance, Cukor et al., 1998).

and developers in a better position to appreciate the necessity of supporting and of protecting it when designing future systems for distance psychotherapy.[11]

References

Ainsworth, M. (2002). ABC's of "internet therapy": E-therapy history and survey. http://www.metanoia.org/imhs/history.htm. Accessed December, 2013.

Alexander, F., & French, T. M. (1946). *Psychoanalytic therapy*. New York: Ronald Press.

Alexander, J. F., Holtzworth-Munroe, A., & Jameson, P. B. (1994). The process and outcome of marital and family therapy: Research review and evaluation. In A. E. Bergin & S. L. Garfield (Eds.), *Handbook of psychotherapy and behavior change* (4th ed., pp. 595-630). New York: John Wiley & Sons, Inc.

Argentieri, S., & Mehler, J. A. (2003). Telephone 'anaysis': 'Hello, who's speaking?' *Insight, 12*, 17-19.

Bachelor, A., & Horavath, A. (1999). The therapeutic relationship. In M. A. Hubble, B. L. Duncan & S. D. Miller (Eds.), *The heart and soul of change: What works in therapy* (pp. 133-178). Washington, DC: American Psychological Association.

Barak, A., Hen, L., Boniel-Nissim, M., & Shapira, N. (2008). A comprehensive review and a meta analysis of the effectiveness of internet-based psychotherapeutic intervention. *Journal of Technology in Human Services, 26*(2/4), 109-160.

Barber, J. P., Khalsa, S.-R., & Sharpless, B. A. (2010). The validity of the alliance as a predictor of psychotherapy outcome. In J. C. Muran & J. P. Barber (Eds.), *The therapeutic alliance: An evidence-based guide to practice* (pp. 29-43). New York: John Wiley and Sons.

Barfeld, W., Zeltzer, D., Sheridan, T. B., & Slater, M. (1995). Presence and performance within virtual environments. In W. Barfield & T. A. Furness (Eds.), *Virtual environments and advanced interface design* (pp. 473-541). Oxford: Oxford University Press.

Bayles, M. (2012). Is physical proximity essential to the psychoanalytic process? An exploration through the lens of skype? *Psychoanalytic Dialogues, 22*, 569-585.

Beebe, B. (2004). Faces in relation. *Psychoanalytic Dialogues, 14*(1), 1-51.

Beier, E. G., & Young, D. M. (1998). *The silent language of psychotherapy: Social reinforcement of unconscious process* (3rd ed.). New York: Aldine De Gruyter.

Bordin, E. S. (1979). The generalizability of the psychoanalytic concept of working alliance. *Psychotherapy: Theory, Research, Practice, Training, 16*, 252–260.

Brahnam, S. (2009). Building character for artificial conversational agents: Ethos, ethics, believability, and credibility. *PsychNology Journal, 7*(1), p. 9-47.

Brahnam, S. (2012). To hear—to say: The mediating presence of the healing witness. *AI & Society, 27*(1), 53-90.

Brainsky, S. (2003). Adapting to, or idealizing, technology? *Insight, 12*, 22–24.

Bruce, V. (1996). The role of the face in communication: Implication for video design. *Interacting with Computers, 8*, 166-176.

Buber, M. (1958). *I-Thou* (R. G. Smith, Trans.). New York: Charles Scribner's Sons.

Castonguay, L. G., Constantino, M. J., & Grosse, H. M. (2006). The working alliance: Where are we and where should we go? *Psychotherapy: Theory, Research & Practice, 43*, 271-279.

11 Interface and systems designers might at least consider the effect their systems have on therapeutic presence by measuring it when designing products for distance psychotherapy (see, for instance, the instrument for measuring therapeutic presence devised by Geller, Greenberg, & Watson, 2010).

Connor, S. (2000). *Dumbstruck: A cultural history of ventriloquism*. Oxford: Oxford University Press.
Crossley, N. (1996). *Intersubjectivity: The fabric of social becoming*. London: Sage.
Cukor, P., Baer, L., Willis, B. S., Leahy, L., O'Laughlen, J., Murphy, M., M., Withers, M., & Martin, E. (1998). Use of videophones and low-cost standard telephone lines to provide a social presence in telepsychiatry. *Telemedicine Journal, 4*(4), 313-321.
Cushman, P. (1992). Psychotherapy to 1992: A historically situated interpretation. In D. K. Freedheim & H. J. Freudenberger (Eds.), *History of psychotherapy: A century of change* (pp. 21-64). Washington, DC: American Psychological Association.
de Benaim, B. S., de Varela, Y. G., de Setton, L. S., & Anonymous. (2013). Four women analysts reflect on their teleanalyses when candidates. In J. S. Scharff (Ed.), *Psychoanalysis online: Mental health, teletherapy and training* (pp. 195-207). London: Karnac.
Dettbarn, I. (2013). Skype as the uncanny third. In J. S. Scharff (Ed.), *Psychoanalysis online: Mental health, teletherapy, and training* (pp. 15-25). London: Karnac Books Ltd.
Eubanks-Carter, C., Muran, J. C., & Safran, J. D. (2010). Alliance ruptures and resolution. In J. C. Muran & J. P. Barber (Eds.), *The therapeutic alliance: An evidence-based guide to practice* (pp. 74-94). New York: John Wiley and Sons.
Freud, S. (1912). Recommendations to physicians practicing psycho-analysis. In J. Strachey (Ed.), *The standard edition of the complete psychological works of Sigmund Freud* (Vol. 12, pp. 111-120). New York: W. W. Norton & Company.
Freud, S. (1915/1955). *The Uncanny. The standard edition of the complete psychological works of Sigmund Freud* (Vol. 17). London: Hogarth.
Freud, S. (1959). *Analysis of a phobia in a five-year-old boy. Collected Papers* (Vol. 3). New York: Basic Books.
Freud, S. (1997). *Dora: An analysis of a case of hysteria*. New York: Touchstone.
Friedberg, R. D., Tabbaraha, S., & Poggesia, R. M. (2013). Therapeutic presence, immediacy, and transparency in CBT with youth: Carpe the moment! *The Cognitive Behaviour Therapist, 6*(Jan): e12.
Geller, S. M., & Greenberg, L. S. (2002). Therapeutic presence: Therapists' experience of presence in the psychotherapeutic encounter. *Person-Centered and Experiential Psychotherapies, 1*, 71-86.
Geller, S. M., & Greenberg, L. S. (2012). *Therapeutic Presence: A mindful approach to effective therapy*. Washington, DC: American Psychological Association.
Geller, S. M., Greenberg, L. S., & Watson, J. C. (2010). Therapist and client perceptions of therapeutic presence: The development of a measure. *Psychotherapy Research, 20*, 599-610.
Gelso, C. J., & Hayes, J. A. (1998) *The psychotherapy relationship: Theory, research, and practice*. New York: John Wiley & Sons, Inc.
Gove, P. B. (Ed.). (1986). *Webster's third new international dictionary of the english language unabridged*. Springfield, MA: Merriam-Webster Inc., Publishers.
Grotijahn, M. (1955). *Six letters to an analyst by an adolescent Girl*. Jake Gimbel Lectures. Stanford University.
Grumet, G. W. (1979). Telephone therapy: A review and case report. *American Journal of Orthopsychiatry, 49*, 574-584.
Hilty, D. M., Marks, S. L., Urness, D., Yellowlees, P. M., & Nesbitt, T. S. (2004). Clinical and educational telepsychiatry applications: A review. *Canadian Journal of Psychiatry, 49*(1), 12-23.
Hornblow, A. R., & Sloane, H. R. (1980). Evaluating the effectiveness of a telephone counseling service. *British Journal of Psychiatry, 137*, 337-338.
Kokotovic, A. M., & Tracey, T. J. (1990). Working alliance in the early phase of counseling. *Journal of Counseling Psychology, 37*, 16–21.
Koocher, G. P. (2007). Twenty-first century ethical challenges for psychology. *American Psychologist, 62*(5), 375-384.

Lambert, M. J. (1992). Psychotherapy outcome research: Implications for integrative and eclectical therapists. In M. R. Goldfried (Ed.), *Handbook of psychotherapy integration* (pp. 94–129). New York: Basic Books.
Leffert, M. (2003). Analysis and psychotherapy by telephone: Twenty years of clinical experience. *Journal of the American Psychoanalytic Association, 51*, 101-130.
Lester, D. (2006). Etherapy: Caveats from experiences with telephone therapy. *Psychological Reports, 99*, 894–896.
Lombard, M., & Ditton, T. (1997). At the heart of it all: The concept of presence. *Journal of Computer-Mediated Communication, 3*(2). DOI: 10.1111/j.1083-6101.1997.tb00072.x.
Lu, S., Harter, D., & Pierce, D. (2011). Potentials and challenges of using virtual environments in psychotherapy. *Annals of Psychotherapy & Integrative Health, 14*(1), 56-66.
Martin, D. J., Garske, J. P., & Davis, M. K. (2000). Relation of the therapeutic alliance with outcome and other variables: A meta-analytic review. *Journal of Consulting and Clinical Psychology, 68*(3), 438-450.
Massaro, D. W., & Egan, P. B. (1996). Perceiving affect from the voice and the face. *Psychonomic Bulletin and Review, 3*(2), 215-221.
Maxmen, J. (1976). *The post-physician era: Medicine in the 21st century*. New York: John Wiley & Sons.
Merleau-Ponty, M. (1964). *The primacy of perception*. Evanston, IL: Northwestern University Press.
Meyerbröker, K., & Emmelkamp, P. M. G. (2011). Virtual reality exposure therapy for anxiety disorders: The state of the art. In S. Brahnam & L. C. Jain (Eds.), *Virtual reality in psychotherapy, rehabilitation, and assessment* (pp. 47-62). Berlin Heidelberg: Springer-Verlag.
Moses, I. (2005). Controversial discussions: Telephone analysis, treatment by telephone: An uncanny attachment. *Psychologist-Psychoanalyst Official Publication of Division 39 of APA, 15*(4), 28-29.
Newitz, A. (2007). My laptop. In S. Turkle (Ed.), *Evocative objects* (pp. 88-91). Cambridge: MIT Press.
Norcoss, J. C. (2010). The therapeutic relationship. In B. L. Duncan, S. D. Miller, B. E. Wampold & M. A. Hubble (Eds.), *The heart and soul of change: Delivery what works* (2nd ed., pp. 113-141). Washington, DC: American Psychological Association.
O'Donnell, C. P. (1997). A nod is as good as a wink...or is it? A critical review of social psychology involved in video conferencing. http://www.psy.gla.ac.uk/~steve/crvid.html. Accessed December, 2013.
Ogden, T. H. (2004). The analytic third: Implications for psychoanalytic theory and technique. *Psychoanalytic Quarterly, LXXIII*, 167-195.
Owens, H. (1970). Hypnosis by phone. *American Journal of Clinical Hypnosis, 13*, 57-60.
Rank, O. (1925/1971). *Double: A psychoanalytic study* (H. Tucker, Trans.). Chapel Hill: The University of North Carolina Press.
Rees, C. S., & Haythornthwaite, S. (2004). Telepsychology and videoconferencing: Issues, opportunities and guidelines for psychologists. *Australian Psychologist, 39*(3), 212-219.
Rees, C. S., & Stone, S. (2005). Therapeutic alliance in face-to-face versus videoconferenced psychotherapy. *Professional Psychology: Research and Practice, 36*, 649–653.
Reynolds, D. J., Jr., Stiles, W. B., & Grohol, J. M. (2006). An investigation of session impact and alliance in Internet based psychotherapy: Preliminary results. *Counseling and Psychotherapy Research, 6*, 164–168.
Riva, G. (2005). Virtual reality in psychotherapy: Review. *CyberPsychology & Behavior, 8*(3), 220-230.
Rosenbaum, M. (1974). Continuation of psychotherapy by "long distance" telephone. *International Journal of Psychoanalytic Psychotherapy, 3*, 483-495.
Scharff, J. S. (2014). Clinical issues in analyses over the telephone and the internet. In A. Lemma & L. Caparrotta (Eds.), *Psychoanalysis in the technoculture era* (pp. 47-61). London and New York: Routledge.

Schore, A. (2000). *Affect regulation and the repair of the self.* Hillsdale, NJ: Erlbaum.
Short, J., Williams, E., & Christie, B. (1976). *The social psychology of telecommunications.* London, New York, Sydney, Toronto: John Wiley & Sons.
Stadter, M. (2012). *Presence and the present: Relationship and time in contemporary psychodynamic therapy.* New York: Jason Aronson.
Stadter, M. (2013). The influence of social media and communications technology on self and relationships. In J. S. Scharff (Ed.), *Psychoanalysis online: Mental health, teletherapy and training* (pp. 3-14). London: Karnac Books Ltd.
Stiles, W. B., & Goldsmith, J. Z. (2010). The alliance over time. In J. C. Muran & J. P. Barber (Eds.), *The therapeutic alliance: An evidence-based guide to practice* (pp. 44-62). New York: John Wiley and Sons.
Tinwell, A., & Grimshaw, M. (2009). *Survival horror games: An uncanny modality.* Paper presented at the Thinking After Dark Conference, Montreal, Canada. http://data.bolton.ac.uk/cet/JGVW_Tinwell_et_al.pdf. Accessed December, 2013.
Trevarthen, C. (1998). Intersubjectivity. In R. Wilson & F. Keil (Eds.), *The MIT Encyclopedia of Cognitive Science* (pp. 415-419). Cambridge: MIT Press.
Tronick, E. Z., & Weinberg, M. K. (1997). Depressed mothers and infants: Failure to form dyadic states of consciousness. In L. Murray & P. J. Cooper (Eds.), *Postpartum depression and child development* (pp. 54-81). New York: Guilford Press.
Turkle, S. (2007). *Evocative Objects.* Cambridge: MIT Press.
Turkle, S. (2011). *Alone together: Why we expect more from technology and less from each other.* New York: Basic Books.
Turner, J. W. (2006). Telepsychiatry as a case study of presence: Do you know what you are missing? *Journal of Computer-Mediated Communication, 6*(4). DOI: 10.1111/j.1083-6101.2001.tb00132.x.
Villani, D., Riva, F., & Riva, G. (2007). New technologies for relaxation: The role of presence. *International Journal of Stress Management, 14*(3), 260-274.
Wallwork, E. (2013). Skype as the uncanny third. In J. S. Scharff (Ed.), *Psychoanalysis online: Mental health, teletherapy, and training* (pp. 85-94). London: Karnac Books Ltd.
Winnicott, D. W. (1971). *Playing and reality.* London: Routledge.

9 Coping with Stress and Anxiety: the Role of Presence in Technology Mediated Environments

Daniela Villani, Pietro Cipresso, and Claudia Repetto

Abstract: Several studies in the last decades have demonstrated that exposure therapy is an effective way to treat anxiety and stress and Virtual Reality Exposure Therapy (VRET) acts as a completely controlled experience. A new perspective is represented by the use of Virtual Reality (VR) for triggering a broad empowerment process to learn coping skills and emotional regulation to cope with stress and anxiety. The link between these approaches is constituted by the sense of presence. In this view, the experience of "being there" is influenced by the ability of "making sense there" and by the possibility to learn by living real experiences in technology-mediated environments. Thanks to the integration of several advanced technologies (virtual reality, advanced sensors and smartphones), as supported by the Interreality approach, it is possible to take advantage of the sense of presence to overcome the limitations of existing protocols for psychological stress and anxiety. Furthermore, a larger availability of unobtrusive biosensors makes possible the effective measurement of presence (and the related affective states) during the interaction instead of using post-experience self-assessments.

Future mediated platforms will provide the following advantages: 1) increased accuracy in assessment of ongoing intervention processes; 2) the ability to correlate specific mental states with specific activities executed in the environments; 3) the ability to study the variables related to stress and anxiety in the framework of simulations representing realistic situations and daily contexts, thus increasing the ecological validity of gathered data.

Keywords: Stress; Anxiety; Presence; New Technologies; Mobile Devices; Interreality.

9.1 Introduction to Chapter 9

To answer to the growing need to find innovative and effective interventions in healthcare services to cope with stress and anxiety, an increasing number of studies show how interactive media may improve traditional stress management interventions (Gorini & Riva, 2008a, 2008b; Powers & Emmelkamp, 2008; Preziosa A., 2009; Repetto et al., 2013; Villani & Riva, 2012; Gaggioli & Riva, 2014).

Three different approaches of interactive media used to cope with stress and anxiety emerge from literature.

The Virtual Reality Exposure Therapy (VRET) represents the traditional one. Following this approach, the users, immersed within a computer-generated simulation or virtual environment (VE), can be systematically exposed to specific feared stimuli within a contextually relevant setting. The rationale for this view typically derives from early evidence that VRET produces better outcomes than imaginal exposure, provides equivalent outcomes and is a pragmatically attractive alternative to in vivo exposure, such as the real-world confrontation of feared stimuli (Emmelkamp et al., 2002). According to Parsons and colleagues (Parsons & Rizzo, 2008) empirical data from research positively assessed the efficacy of VRET on affective outcomes and consensus exists about the good potential of VRET as a treatment approach for several anxiety disorders (Botella et al., 2004; Goncalves, Pedrozo, Coutinho, Figueira, & Ventura, 2012; Krijn, Emmelkamp, Olafsson, & Biemond, 2004; Meyerbroker & Emmelkamp, 2010; Pull, 2005).

The second new and applied approach, the Positive Technology (PT), aims to improve the quality of the personal experience with the goal of increasing wellness and generating strengths and resilience. (Botella et al., 2012; Riva, Banos, Botella, Wiederhold, & Gaggioli, 2012). Within this perspective, in the last 10 years several studies have shown the possibility of interactive media to support empowerment processes in terms of relaxation training and improvement in self-efficacy and emotional management (Plante et al., 2003; Plante, Cage, Clements, & Stover, 2006; Valtchanov, 2010; Villani et al., 2013; Villani, Riva, & Riva, 2007; Villani & Riva, 2012). Findings indicate that a sense of flourishing and resilience can be promoted by interventions leading to a positive evaluation of one's self and to the capacity to manage one's life effectively. Furthermore, according to Fredrickson (2001; 2009), positive emotions can play a critical role for mental and physical health because, even though a positive emotional state is only momentary, benefits can last in the form of traits, social bonds, and abilities that endure well into the future and that can help people to cope with several stressors.

A third approach is represented by the use of Cyber-interventions based on the Stress Inoculation Training protocol (Cyber-SIT). The general objectives of SIT (Meichenbaum, 1977; 1996) are threefold: to acquire active coping strategies; to develop an activity of self-regulation; to explore and modify dysfunctional cognitive appraisal related to stressful events. According to the systematic review recently presented by Serino and colleagues (Serino et al., 2013), Cyber-SIT appears a promising clinical approach, and there are interesting researches that effectively combined traditional SIT clinical protocol within advanced technologies. (Grassi, Gaggioli, & Riva, 2011; Villani et al., 2013). Specifically, Cyber-SIT combines aspects deriving both from the traditional perspective of VRET and from the innovative perspective of Positive Technology. These aspects are evident in two phases of SIT. As far as the skill acquisition and rehearsal phase is concerned, advanced technologies can help individuals in acquiring effective coping skills, such as relaxation strategies (Manzoni et al., 2009; Stetz et al., 2011; Villani, Grassi, et al., 2012) by doing exercises, with technology administering positive reinforcement of healthy conduct (Fox & Bailenson, 2009). As far as the application and follow-through phase is concerned, it is possible to create controlled, graded and safe simulations of stressful scenarios to allow participant to use the acquired coping skills based on the exposure approach. Nevertheless, there are still few studies in the literature meeting the requirement of using cyber-SIT in all its clinical elements and phases. Work has to be done to achieve rigor and generalizability from a methodological point of view.

What is the key factor that links together these approaches apparently so different from each other? We consider that a key role in supporting the change process allowed by all these approaches is played by the sense of presence.

9.2 Presence as a Link Among Different Approaches

Although the concept of presence has been investigated from various perspectives that have accordingly proposed different definitions, we would like to overcome these conflicting standpoints by emphasizing that the experience of "being there" is influenced by the ability of "making sense there" and by the possibility of learning by living real experiences in virtual environments (see also Chapters 1 and 2, this volume).

To achieve the ability of "making sense there" is important to take in consideration several aspects of action. First, it is important to work not only on the environmental features but also on the proposed content inside the mediated experience (Grassi, Gaggioli, & Riva, 2009; Riva et al., 2007; Villani, & Riva, 2009). In accordance with Scherer et al.'s (Scherer, Schorr, & Johnstone, 2001) theory we consider the coherence between the content and the goal of the multimedia experience to be critical. We suggest that it is important to critically choose the sampling strategies according to the specific aim of the protocol. Participants may feel more engaged if they consider the experience to be crucial for their needs and goals, and this is also true for mediated experiences (Riva & Mantovani, 2012).

A second perspective suggests that it is possible to work on the content a priori, but the assignment of meaning is a subjective process emerging during the experience. This issue has been showed in experimental research carried out by Villani and colleagues (Villani, Repetto, Cipresso, & Riva, 2012). Authors compared the experienced feeling of presence in two different settings: an immersive virtual reality job interview simulation and a real world simulation that was identical to its VR counterpart (same interviewer, same questions) but without technological mediation and without any social and cultural cues in the environment that could give a better meaning to both the task and its social context. Results suggested that a virtual experience could elicit a higher sense of presence if the meaning and the emotional engagement are higher than in real experience. This result supports a conception of presence as a social construction (Mantovani, 1996; Riva, 1999) that is different from the "perceptual illusion of non-mediation" suggested by Lombard and Ditton (Lombard & Ditton, 1997).. In this sense, "reality" is not out there in the world, somewhere "outside" people's minds, escaping social negotiation and cultural mediation; reality is co-constructed in the relationship between actors and their environments through the mediation of the artifacts (Riva & Galimberti, 1997).

The third level we have to consider is that related to the emotional experience. The relationship between presence and emotions in mediated environments has been explored by Riva and colleagues (Riva et al., 2007). Their data showed a circular interaction between presence and emotions: on the one hand, the feeling of presence was greater in the "emotional" environments; on the other hand, the level of presence influenced the emotional state. Taken together these results underline the existence of a bi-directional relationship between presence and emotions. Furthermore, as recently investigated by Wirth and colleagues (Wirth, Hofer, & Schramm, 2012) emotional involvement influences presence in terms of assigning relevance to the mediated environment and to embedded objects. Both processes of assigning relevance and generating meaning are related and can be seen as inextricably interwoven.

As stated above, the sense of presence is influenced also by the possibility of learning by living real experiences in technology-mediated environments. The potential to include protocols to cope with stress and anxiety in the patient's real-life context is emphasized by the Ubiquitous and Interreality approaches, presented below.

9.3 From the Ubiquitous to the Interreality Approach

The ubiquitous approach to healthcare refers to the provision of healthcare and health-related information through mobile applications and devices (e.g., tablets and smartphones). The interest demonstrated toward these devices is shown by their wide diffusion: if the use of tablets is still rising and rapidly increasing, the penetration of mobile phones across the worldwide population is enormous, and makes it the ideal candidate to support the Ubiquitous approach. In fact, the advanced technology now available makes mobile phones something more than a calling device: new generation smartphones are able to achieve broader communication capabilities, supporting 3D graphics, pictures, musical sounds and software programs. Thanks to these features, VR applications can be uploaded on the smartphones and launched in everyday life.

The opportunity to access the virtual experiences during real life situations, at times convenient to the individual, is especially important in the treatment of symptoms strictly related to concrete events (e.g., phobias), symptoms occurring repeatedly during the day (e.g., anxiety-related symptoms), and in the empowerment of people experiencing negative emotions (e.g., stress).

Recently, the capabilities of mobile phones as a tool for responding to a variety of clinical needs have been investigated. (Preziosa, Grassi, Gaggioli, & Riva, 2009). Authors reported two experiments aimed at investigating the efficacy of the use of mobile phones to cope with different stress situations. In the first experiment, a Stress

Inoculation Training was used to reduce examination stress: the data supported the hypothesis that the combination of video and audio narratives administered via Universal Mobile Telecommunications Systems - UMTS - induced more relaxation when compared with the other experimental conditions (either video or narratives administered with alternative means, such as CD and MP3 players). In the second study, mobile phones were used to train the ability to relax in a group of stressed patients by administering mobile narratives. The outcome of this research, together with other experimental studies on mobile phones, suggests that this technology is promising in the treatment of anxiety disorders, since it offers the opportunities to bridge the gap between inpatient and outpatient sessions.

The first attempt to transfer an integrated VR system to train relaxing abilities during patient's real life was performed in the INTREPID project (Repetto et al., 2009; Repetto & Riva, 2011). In this study the ubiquitous approach was employed to reduce anxiety symptoms in patients suffering from Generalized Anxiety Disorder, a clinical condition that has pervasive effects on patients' personal, professional and affective life. Researchers compared the use of a virtual environment uploaded on mobile phone and designed to treat anxiety symptoms by means of relaxation, with a condition of absence of treatment. Results indicated that the VR portable system was effective in reducing anxiety, either with or without biofeedback; furthermore, when interviewed about the usefulness of the mobile system, the majority of patients (91%) answered that they were very satisfied with it because it helped them to consolidate the relaxation training in the absence of the therapist (Pallavicini, Algeri, Repetto, Gorini, & Riva, 2008a).

Even if VR-based treatments for anxiety symptoms and stress management proved to be effective, the ubiquitous approach provides new opportunities and overcomes VR limitations by reducing the gap between clinical settings and real life context. In fact, often the virtual experience is a distinct realm, separate from the emotions and behaviours experienced by the patient in the real world: the behaviour of the patient in mediated contexts has no direct effects on the real life experience and the emotions and problems experienced by the patient in the real world are not directly addressed in laboratory.

The availability of living virtual experiences during real life situations is the first step to promote the sense of presence. Thanks to the integration of several devices, the content is available anywhere and anytime. The weakest link in the ubiquitous approach is that behavior in the physical world still does not influence the virtual world experience.

A further advance aiming at the integration of assessment and treatment within a hybrid, closed-loop empowering experience, bridging physical and virtual worlds into one seamless reality is represented by a new e-Health paradigm, named Interreality (IR) (Riva, 2009). The clinical experience becomes more comprehensive thanks to the combination of virtual experiences – which are fully controlled by the therapist, and used to learn coping skills and emotional regulation – with real experincces – which allow both the identification of any critical stressors and the assessment of what has been learned.

Within this paradigm, the interconnections between the virtual and real world become bidirectional. Behaviour in the virtual world influences real life: for example, if I participate in a virtual support group to cope with generalized anxiety I can interact with other participants during the day via instant messaging service for smartphones, such as Whatsapp. Behaviour in the real world influences the virtual environment. For example, if emotional regulation is poor during a stressful day, then some exercises in the virtual environment can help participants to train this ability with cognitive or relaxation exercises.

A recent project which used the Interreality approach in the Management and Treatment of Stress-Related Disorders was the EU-funded INTERSTRESS research program (FP7- 247685). The project was aimed at helping teachers and nurses, who represent two typical high-stress professions, to manage their psychological state by using Interreality based protocols (Pallavicini et al., 2013). It is easy to comprehend that the sense of presence benefits from the link between real behaviour, virtual experience and therapist's monitoring. From a clinical standpoint, IR offers some innovations to current VR protocols: objective and quantitative assessment of symptoms using biosensors, provision of warnings, and motivating feedback to improve compliance and long-term outcome.

9.4 Advances in Presence Measurement

Traditionally, the sense of presence has been evaluated through the use of self-reports, developed according to the different concepts of presence, administered to the user after the virtual experience (Lessiter, Freeman, Keogh, & Davidoff, 2001; Lombard et al., 2000; Schubert, Friedman, & Regenbrecht, 2001; Witmer & Singer, 1998). Regardless of the ease of administration it is possible to identify two major biases in the reliability of this approach. On one side, many items of the questionnaires are difficult to understand or ambiguous to interpret. On the other side, introspection requests the participants to be able to analyze their experience in different ways, producing answers that are not easy to classify.

To overcome users' difficulties in accessing and evaluating their own experience, the measurement of sense of presence encompassed quantitative indexes - such as galvanic skin response, respiration rate and others (Villani et al., 2007; Villani & Riva, 2012). The rationale is easy to understand: the higher the sense of presence experienced in virtual environments, the higher will be the possibility of observing a modification of physiological indexes related to the stressful event. The measurement of this modification does not require a retrospective judgement but can be done simultaneously with the mediated experience, and without interpretative bias. This approach is useful to assess sense of presence in terms of engagement within the mediated experience but it does not allow participants to be aware of their psycho-physiological state and to learn how to control and manage their reactions to stressful events.

Recent progress in the sophistication and feasibility of biosensor technology and the remarkable spread of mobile electronic devices have led to ubiquitous and unobtrusive recorder systems that allow naturalistic and multimodal assessment of psycho-physiological parameters (Barrett & Barrett, 2001; Houtveen & de Geus, 2009; Intille, 2004). Since psychological stress could be defined as a continuous person-environment transaction, such as a series of interactions and adjustments between the person and the environment (Cohen, Janicki-Deverts, & Miller, 2007; Gaggioli et al., 2011, 2014; Riva et al., 2010), this integrated and mobile assessment offers the opportunity to analyze the real-time interaction between challenges and skills occurring in daily life situations.

Thanks to the integration of sensors in contemporary VR systems (for example, biosensors, cranial movements tracking sensors, sensors for superior limbs, datagloves, etc.) it is possible to record a high quantity of data with regard to actions executed by the patient inside the virtual scenario, and to use these data to create some indexes of performance in order to measure in a quantitative and objective way the performance improvement observable in the course of intervention process (Pallavicini et al., 2013).

Sense of presence measurement and clinical outcomes can be extended beyond the traditional research and clinical setting by using emerging mobile technology to deliver real-time interventions and assessment during daily activities. In particular, an interesting focus is Heart Rate Variability (HRV) Biofeedback as a promising approach aimed at treating psychological diseases. HRV Biofeedback involves training participants to adjust their breathing rate to a resonant frequency (RF), a breathing rate (usually slower than normal breathing) at which respiratory sinus arrhythmia (RSA) is maximized. In fact, by acting on their breath, the participants are able to change HRV levels and reduce stress and anxiety (Lagos et al., 2008).

Low HRV is associated with a wide variety of medical and psychological health problems, such as cardiovascular diseases, metabolic syndrome, depression, anxiety and psychological stress (Lehrer, 2013). An HRV biofeedback at helping subjects manage and cope with psychological stress has been developed within the INTERSTRESS project (http://www.interstress.eu). The first step was to collect data from the wireless wearable electrocardiogram (ECG). Then, the mobile application, running on a smartphone with Android SO, provided a real-time and graphical visualization of user's physiological parameters. For example, by controlling the respiration rate, variations in the HRV indexes modified a virtual environment by controlling the increase or the decrease of the size of a campfire in a valley or the movement of the waves in a beach. In this way patients can become aware of their psychophysiological changes and learn to modify their activation state. Thanks to the use of mobile biofeedback in support of traditional clinical methods for stress management both participants and clinicians can be supported. Participants can have the opportunity to immediately apply newly-acquired skills to their actual experiences and clinicians can be helped to assign to subjects relaxing exercises or "homework" and to schedule the timing and the modality of these exercises beyond a research or clinical setting (Serino et al., 2012).

Recently, the importance of understanding and assessing activity-related behavioural features has been emphasized. One of the first attempts towards a system for activity-related automatic stress detection has been carried out by Giakoumis and colleagues (Giakoumis et al., 2012) by using low cost interactive devices from the home gaming market. This attempt represents a new challenge towards presence measurement based on the integration of psycho-physiological and behavioral indexes.

9.5 Conclusion to Chapter 9

The present chapter illustrated the role of presence in protocols aiming at helping people to cope with anxiety and stress.

In the literature, different approaches of interactive media have been demonstrated to be effective in the reduction of anxiety symptoms and in stress managing, such as the traditional virtual reality exposure (VRET) and, more recently, the paradigm of positive technology (PT) and Cyber-interventions based on the Stress Inoculation Training protocol (Cyber-SIT).

The sense of presence represents the key factor that links together these approaches. The definition proposed here overcomes the conflicting perspectives often reported in literature, by claiming that presence is influenced primarily by the "ability of making sense" in a given environment. Technologies aiming at supporting an emotional and behavioral change in people suffering from anxiety or stress should take into account three key elements that promote presence:

1. the content of the proposed experience, which should be congruent with the goal of the multimedia experience;
2. the meaning and the emotional engagement elicited by the experience, which should be kept higher than in the real experience;
3. the emotional experience, as a goal to achieve inside the virtual experiment, inextricably interwoven with the potential to assign meaning to the experience.

As far as technologies enhancing presence are concerned, it appears that the Interreality (IR) approach opens new opportunities of treatment and empowerment.

What is the core of the improvement? Beyond the advances in computer graphics, speed of execution, interactive capabilities, which surely account for greater appeal, willingness to use, and richness of the offered experience, the main element of the IR approach is the bidirectional interconnection between the virtual and real world.

IR allows the integration of assessment and treatment bridging physical and virtual worlds into one seamless reality.

Furthermore, IR offers some clinical innovations to current VR protocols: objective and quantitative assessment of symptoms using biosensors, provision of warnings, and motivating feedback to improve compliance and long-term outcomes. Nowadays, indeed, quantitative and objective measures related to presence can be obtained by means of recording psycho-physiological parameters. This approach has multiple applications and gives several advantages to both therapist and patient: on the one hand it bypasses the biases inherently presented by self-reporting instruments, but more importantly it provides the opportunity to directly access the individual's emotional states, and to use this knowledge to tailor the training, provide real time feedback and quantify the performance and the outcomes of the exercises.

Take the example of considering an experience strongly characterized by emotional involvement: the job interview. Typically, applicants feel anxious and stressed both because talking to strangers could provoke anxiety and because they could perceive a lack of control of the situation. Thanks to the sense of presence, mediated interventions could enhance skills to cope with a job interview. Cyber-interventions based on the SIT protocol can give applicants useful information, help them in acquiring effective coping skills, such as relaxation strategies, and let them experience, with controlled, graded and safe simulations, their competences to cope with a job interview. Applicants can do this training anytime and anywhere thanks to mobile technologies. Thanks to psycho-physiological assessment enabled by biosensors, the applicant's emotional states can be monitored during training to tailor the proposed experiences, to provide real time feedback and administer positive reinforcement of good conduct. Furthermore, this assessment is possible until just a few minutes before undertaking a job interview: if biosensors reveal a high level of anxiety, the system could increase the comfort level by proposing ad hoc relaxation exercises and, by lessening anxiety, the system can support the applicant's performance. *Figure 9.1* shows the virtual job interview available by using different technologies and draws attention to the bidirectional interconnection between the virtual and real world allowed by biosensors. In particular, the technologies shown in *Figure 9.1* can be seen as more than devices. The interconnection among them through Internet or other devices (like PCs or smartphones) allows a continuous information transmission to a central repository that collects and processes all the information received through data fusion and classification. This computational approach is changing the way to use devices allowing an effective and continuous exchange between real and virtual world.

In summary, the concept of presence seems a critical feature to consider when designing technology-mediated protocols, and future investigations will give researchers and clinicians important indications on how to create increasingly effective virtual experiences.

Figure 9.1: A representation of cyber-intervention to help candidate to cope with stress related to job interview

References

Barrett, L. F., & Barrett, D. J. (2001). An introduction to computerized experience sampling in psychology. *Social Science Computer Review, 19*(2), 175-185.

Botella, C., Quero, S., Banos, R. M., Perpina, C., Garcia Palacios, A., & Riva, G. (2004). Virtual reality and psychotherapy. *Studies in Health Technology and Informatics, 99*, 37-54

Botella, C., Riva, G., Gaggioli, A., Wiederhold, B. K., Alcaniz, M., & Banos, R. M. (2012). The present and future of positive technologies. *Cyberpsychology, Behavior and Social Networking, 15*(2), 78-84.

Cohen, S., Janicki-Deverts, D., & Miller, G. E. (2007). Psychological stress and disease. *JAMA, 298*(14), 1685-1687.

Emmelkamp, P. M., Krijn, M., Hulsbosch, A. M., de Vries, S., Schuemie, M. J., & van der Mast, C. A. (2002). Virtual reality treatment versus exposure in vivo: a comparative evaluation in acrophobia. *Behaviour Research & Therapy, 40*(5), 509-516.

Fox, J., & Bailenson, J. (2009). Virtual self modeling: the effects of vicarious reinforcement and identification on exercise behavior. *Media Psychology, 12*, 1-25.

Fredrickson, B. L. (2001). The role of positive emotions in positive psychology. The broaden-and-build theory of positive emotions. *American Psychologist, 56*(3), 218-226.

Fredrickson, B. L. (2009). *Positivity: Groundbreaking research reveals how to embrace the hidden strength of positive emotions, overcome negativity, and thrive.* New York: New York: Crown.

Gaggioli, A., Pallavicini, F., Morganti, L., Serino, S., Scaratti, C., Briguglio, M., . . . Riva, G. (2014). Experiential virtual scenarios with real-time monitoring (interreality) for the management of psychological stress: a block randomized controlled trial. *J Med Internet Res, 16*(7), e167. doi: 10.2196/jmir.3235

Gaggioli, A., Raspelli, S., Grassi, A., Pallavicini, F., Cipresso, P., Wiederhold, B. K., & Riva, G. (2011). Ubiquitous health in practice: the interreality paradigm. *Studies in Health Technology and Informatics, 163*, 185-191.

Gaggioli, A., & Riva, G. (2014). Psychological treatments: Smart tools boost mental-health care. *Nature, 512*(7512), 28. doi: 10.1038/512028b

Giakoumis, D., Drosou, A., Cipresso, P., Tzovaras, D., Hassapis, G., Gaggioli, A., & Riva, G. (2012). Using activity-related behavioural features towards more effective automatic stress detection. *PLoS One, 7*(9), e43571.

Goncalves, R., Pedrozo, A. L., Coutinho, E. S. F., Figueira, I., & Ventura, P. (2012). Efficacy of Virtual Reality Exposure Therapy in the Treatment of PTSD: A Systematic Review. *Plos One 7*(12).

Gorini, A., & Riva, G. (2008a). The potential of Virtual Reality as anxiety management tool: a randomized controlled study in a sample of patients affected by Generalized Anxiety Disorder. *Trials, 9*, 25.

Gorini, A., & Riva, G. (2008b). Virtual reality in anxiety disorders: the past and the future. *Expert Review of Neurotherapeutics, 8*(2), 215-233.

Grassi, A., Gaggioli, A., & Riva, G. (2009). The Green Valley: The Use of Mobile Narratives for Reducing Stress in Commuters. *CyberPsychology & Behavior, 12*(2), 1-7.

Grassi, A., Gaggioli, A., & Riva, G. (2011). New technologies to manage exam anxiety. *Studies in Health Technology and Informatics, 167*, 57-62.

Houtveen, J. H., & de Geus, E. J. C. (2009). Noninvasive Psychophysiological Ambulatory Recordings Study Design and Data Analysis Strategies. *European Psychologist, 14*(2), 132-141.

Intille, S. S. (2004). A new research challenge: Persuasive technology to motivate healthy aging. *IEEE Transactions on Information Technology in Biomedicine, 8*(3), 235-237.

Krijn, M., Emmelkamp, P. M., Olafsson, R. P., & Biemond, R. (2004). Virtual reality exposure therapy of anxiety disorders: a review. *Clinical Psychology Review, 24*(3), 259-281.

Lagos, L., Vaschillo, E., Vaschillo, B., Lehrer, P., Bates, M., & Pandina, R. (2008). Heart rate variability biofeedback for dealing with competitive anxiety: A case study. *Applied Psychophysiology and Biofeedback, 36*(3), 109–115.

Lehrer, P. (2013). How Does Heart Rate Variability Biofeedback Work? Resonance, the Baroreflex, and Other Mechanisms. *Biofeedback: Spring 41*(1), 26-31.

Lessiter, J., Freeman, J., Keogh, E., & Davidoff, J. (2001). A Cross-Media Presence Questionnaire: The ITC-Sense of Presence Inventory. *Presence: Teleoperators, and Virtual Environments, 10*(3), 282-297.

Lombard, M., & Ditton, T. (1997). At the heart of it all: The concept of presence. *Journal of Computer Mediated-Communication* [On-line], 3(2). http://www.ascusc.org/jcmc/vol3/issue2/lombard.html. Accessed on October 30, 2013

Lombard, M., Ditton, T. B., Crane, D., Davis B., Gil-Egui, G., Horvath K., Rossman, J., Park S., (2000). *Measuring presence: A literature-based approach to the development of a standardized paper-and-pencil instrument.* Paper presented at the Third International Workshop on Presence, Delft, The Netherlands.

Mantovani, G. (1996). *New communication environments: from everyday to virtual.* London: Taylor & Francis.

Manzoni, G. M., Pagnini, F., Gorini, A., Preziosa, A., Castelnuovo, G., Molinari, E., & Riva, G. (2009). Can relaxation training reduce emotional eating in women with obesity? An exploratory study with 3 months of follow-up. *Journal of the American Dietetic Association, 109*(8), 1427-1432.

Meichenbaum, D. (1977). *Cognitive behavior modification*. New York: Plenum Press.

Meichenbaum, D. (1996). Stress inoculation training for coping with stressors. *The Clinical Psychologist, 49*, 4-7.

Meyerbroker, K., & Emmelkamp, P. M. G. (2010). Virtual Reality Exposure Therapy in Anxiety Disorders: A Systematic Review of Process-and-Outcome Studies. *Depression and Anxiety, 27*(10), 933-944.

Pallavicini, F., Algeri, D., Repetto, C., Gorini, A., & Riva, G. (2009). Biofeedback, virtual reality and mobile phones in the treatment of generalized anxiety disorder (GAD): A phase-2 controlled clinical trial. *Journal of CyberTherapy and Rehabilitation, 2(4)*, 315-327.

Pallavicini, F., Gaggioli, A., Raspelli, S., Cipresso, P., Serino, S., Vigna, C., Grassi, A., Morganti, L., Baruffi, M., Wiederhold, B., Riva, G. (2013). Interreality for the management and training of psychological stress: study protocol for a randomized controlled trial. *Trials, 14*:191.

Parsons, T. D., & Rizzo, A. A. (2008). Affective outcomes of virtual reality exposure therapy for anxiety and specific phobias: a meta-analysis. *Journal of Behaiorv Therapy and Experimental Psychiatry, 39*(3), 250-261.

Plante, T. G., Aldridge, A., Su, D., Bogdan, R., Belo, M., & Kahn, K. (2003). Does Virtual Reality enhance the management of stress when paired with exercise? An exploratory study. *International Journal of Stress Management, 10*, 203–216.

Plante, T. G., Cage, S., Clements, S., & Stover, A. (2006). Psychological benefits of exercise paired with virtual reality: Outdoor Exercise energizes whereas indoor virtual exercise relaxes. *International Journal of Stress Management, 13*, 108–117.

Powers, M. B., & Emmelkamp, P. M. (2008). Virtual reality exposure therapy for anxiety disorders: A meta-analysis. *Journal of Anxiety Disorders, 3(22)*, 561-569.

Preziosa, A., Grassi, A., Gaggioli, A., & Riva, G. (2009). Therapeutic applications of the mobile phone. *British Journal of Guidance & Counselling, 37*(3), 313-325.

Pull, C. B. (2005). Current status of virtual reality exposure therapy in anxiety disorders: Editorial review. Current Opinion in Psychiatry, 18, 7–14. *Current Opinion in Psychiatry, 18*, 7-14.

Repetto, C., Gaggioli, A., Pallavicini, F., Cipresso, P., Raspelli, S., & Riva, G. (2013). Virtual reality and mobile phones in the treatment of generalized anxiety disorders: a phase-2 clinical trial. *Personal and Ubiquitous Computing 17*(2), 253-260.

Repetto, C., Gorini, A., Vigna, C., Algeri, D., Pallavicini, F., & Riva, G. (2009). The use of biofeedback in clinical virtual reality: the INTREPID project. *Journal of Visualized Experiments: JoVE*, (33): e1554.

Repetto, C., & Riva, G. (2011). From virtual reality to interreality in the treatment of anxiety disorders. *Neuropsychiatry, 1*(1), 31-43.

Riva, G. (1999). Virtual Reality as a communication tool: a socio-cognitive analysis. *Presence, Teleoperators, and Virtual Environments, 8*(4), 460-466.

Riva, G. (2009). Interreality: A New Paradigm for E-health. *Studies in Health Technology and Informatics, 144*, 3-7.

Riva, G., Banos, R. M., Botella, C., Wiederhold, B. K., & Gaggioli, A. (2012). Positive technology: using interactive technologies to promote positive functioning. *Cyberpsychology, Behavior, and Social Networking, 15*(2), 69-77.

Riva, G., & Galimberti, C. (1997). The psychology of cyberspace: a socio-cognitive framework to computer mediated communication. *New Ideas in Psychology, 15*(2), 141-158.

Riva, G., & Mantovani, F. (2012). From the body to the tools and back: a general framework for presence in mediated interactions. *Interacting with Computers, 24*(4), 203-210.

Riva, G., Mantovani, F., Capideville, C. S., Preziosa, A., Morganti, F., Villani, D Gaggioli, A., Botella, C., Alcaniz, M. (2007). Affective interactions using virtual reality: the link between presence and emotions. *Cyberpsychology and Behavior, 10*(1), 45-56.

Riva, G., Raspelli, S., Pallavicini, F., Grassi, A., Algeri, D., Wiederhold, B. K., & Gaggioli, A. (2010). Interreality in the management of psychological stress: a clinical scenario. *Studies in Health Technology and Informatics, 154*, 20-25.

Scherer, K. R., Schorr, A., & Johnstone, T. (Eds.). (2001). *Appraisal Processes in Emotion: Theory, Methods, Research.* New York: Oxford University Press.

Schubert, T., Friedman, F., & Regenbrecht, H. (2001). The experience of presence: Factor analytic insights. *Presence: Teleoperators, and Virtual Environments, 10*(3), 266-281.

Serino, S., Cipresso, P., Gaggioli, A., Pioggia, G., Tartarisco, G., Baldus, G., Corda, D., Riva, G. (2012). *Beyond the Lab: Towards the Mobile Assessment.* Paper presented at the Applied Psychophysiology and Biofeedback Meeting.

Serino, S., Triberti, S., Villani, D., Cipresso, P., Gaggioli, A., & Riva, G. (2013). Toward a validation of cyber-interventions for stress disorders based on stress inoculation training: a systematic review. *Virtual Reality, 18*(1), 73-87. doi: Doi 10.1007/S10055-013-0237-6.

Stetz, M. C., Kaloi-Chen, J. Y., Turner, D. D., Bouchard, S., Riva, G., & Wiederhold, B. K. (2011). The effectiveness of technology-enhanced relaxation techniques for military medical warriors. *Military Medicine, 176*(9), 1065-1070.

Valtchanov, D., Barton, K. R., Ellard, C. (2010). Restorative effects of virtual nature settings. *Cyberpsychology, Behavior, and Social Networking, 13(5),* 503-512.

Villani, D., & Riva, G. (2009). The role of interactive media features on the affective response: a virtual reality study. *E-minds. International Journal on Human- Computer Interaction, 1*(5), 35-55.

Villani, D., Grassi, A., Cognetta, C., Cipresso, P., Toniolo, D., & Riva, G. (2012). The effects of a mobile stress management protocol on nurses working with cancer patients: a preliminary controlled study. *Studies in Health Technology and Informatics, 173*, 524-528.

Villani, D., Grassi, A., Cognetta, C., Toniolo, D., Cipresso, P., & Riva, G. (2013). Self-help stress management training through mobile phones: An experience with oncology nurses. *Psychological Services, 10*(3), 315-322.

Villani, D., Repetto, C., Cipresso, P., & Riva, G. (2012). May I experience more presence in doing the same thing in virtual reality than in reality? An answer from a simulated job interview. *Interacting with Computer, 24*, 265-272.

Villani, D., Riva, F., & Riva, G. (2007). New technologies for relaxation: The role of presence. *International Journal of Stress Management, 14*(3), 260-274.

Villani, D., & Riva, G. (2012). Does Interactive Media Enhance the Management of Stress? Suggestions from a Controlled Study. *Cyberpsychology, Behavior, and Social Networking, 15*(1), 24-30.

Wirth, W., Hofer, M., & Schramm, H. (2012). The Role of Emotional Involvement and Trait Absorption in the Formation of Spatial Presence. *Media Psychology, 15*, 19-43.

Witmer, B. G., & Singer, M. J. (1998). Measuring Presence in Virtual Environments: A Presence Questionnaire. *Presence: Teleoperators and Virtual Environments, 7*(3), 225-240.

10 Does Gender Matter? Exploring Experiences of Physical and Social Presence in Men and Women

Anna Felnhofer and Oswald D. Kothgassner

Abstract: It has repeatedly been suggested that gender may play a constituting role in the formation and experience of presence when interacting with a mediated environment or with a virtual character. However, studies looking into possible gender differences in presence are still rather scarce. Existing studies use environments with a differing degree of interactivity (e.g., television, simulators) thus producing conflicting results. This diversity of methods and ambiguity of findings both call for a more thorough literature review to be able to draw valid conclusions and to add to a more robust theoretical basis. Therefore, this chapter will first outline past research on gender differences in both social and physical presence. The focus will especially be on virtual reality applications commonly used for social interaction or therapy purposes. Accordingly, three studies focusing on gender differences will then be described in more detail; the first two studies look at students' presence experiences in both a stressful and a non-stressful virtual environment. The third study expands its scope and focuses on gender differences in younger and older adults when interacting with virtual characters in a collaborative virtual environment. Overall, the results are conflicting but point toward an advantage of men over women, regardless of their age, in physical but not in social presence. It becomes clear, however, that there might be a range of factors mediating the relationship between gender and presence. The conclusion discusses these factors and elaborates recommendations for future research.

Keywords: Physical Presence; Social Presence; Gender Differences; Collaborative Virtual Environments.

10.1 Introduction to Chapter 10

Examining user characteristics seems to be a particularly promising approach on the road to a better understanding of the presence concept which to date still has no commonly acknowledged solid theoretical basis (c.f. Schubert, 2009). This approach is based on the frequent observation that participants using the same Virtual Environment (VE) may still fundamentally differ in the amount of presence they report. Considering this, it is apparent that alongside characteristics of the technology such as media form and content, user characteristics and related differences between users may also critically shape VE experiences. It has been repeatedly suggested that the differences between men and women be examined more closely (IJsselsteijn, 2004;

ISPR, 2000; Lombard & Ditton, 1997). Even though there is no theoretical assumption linked to examining gender differences, including them as an independent variable in data analyses may still allow promising inferences as to the factual nature of presence. However, caution is warranted as the variable 'gender' may act as a disguise for other, more differentiated latent individual differences.

10.1.1 Sex or Gender?

A book chapter dealing with gender differences is naturally challenged to first clarify the term 'gender' in order to enable readers to understand the underlying preconceptions. In the related literature, the terms sex and gender are usually both used (e.g., Kryspin-Exner, Lamplmayr, & Felnhofer, 2011). Both concepts have to be considered separately. On the one hand "sex" is commonly defined on the basis of genetic, physiological and endocrinological factors, while on the other hand "gender" refers to socially and culturally learned aspects of being male or female, defined by the role as perceived social position and its associated typical behaviors. The latter also rather reflects psychological and social constructs related to the terms masculinity and femininity (Delphy, 1993; Unger, 1979; West & Zimmerman, 1987). Below, we will predominantly refer to the term gender. However, the meaning of both sex and gender as described above shall be incorporated in this term.

10.1.2 Presence Equals Presence?

From a theoretical and a practical perspective it is useful and reasonable to distinguish between physical and social presence even though most VEs – especially so called collaborative VEs – usually evoke both. However, physical and social presence underlie separate theoretical assumptions: while physical presence is thought to rely mostly on the interaction with the given environment, social presence requires another social entity with which reciprocal communication is possible (IJsselsteijn et al., 2000). In other words, physical presence is the engagement or interaction with a virtual environment, while social presence is the engagement or interaction with another virtual being (see also Chapter 1, this volume). In this sense, physical presence may be regarded a "perceptual illusion of non-mediation" (Lombard & Ditton, 1997) within which the person perceives a given mediated environment as if it was a 'real' physical environment (Slater, Lotto, Arnold, & Sanchez-Vives, 2009). In contrast, social presence may be understood as the sense of being together and perceiving a virtual other as if he or she was a physically present person (IJsselsteijn et al., 2000). For both, congruence in reactions to virtual stimuli and comparable physical stimuli seems to be a crucial hallmark: only if one reacts to a virtual snake or a virtual imposter the same way one would in comparable 'real-life' circumstances, satisfactory presence levels may be assumed (Slater, 2003).

10.2 Physical Presence

10.2.1 Background

To date, only few studies have exclusively set their research focus to examining differences between men and women in presence experiences. Those which actually do so demonstrate a large variance in methods and design. Some, for instance, concentrate mainly on non-interactive environments such as television (Bracken, 2005; Lombard, Reich, Grabe, Bracken, & Ditton, 2000) or non-collaborative VEs (Almog, Wallach, & Safir, 2009). These studies predominantly find women to show a stronger emotional reaction and a stronger response to changes in screen size (Lombard, 1995; Lombard et al., 2000) as well as higher levels of perceived realism than men when watching TV (Bracken, 2005), all of which are regarded as physical presence correlates. Despite these encouraging results in non-interactive environments, generalizations to highly interactive and collaborative VEs have to be undertaken with great care. A VE involving direct interaction with virtual objects and communication with other virtual characters is naturally expected to tap into different perceptional, cognitive and behavioral processes than merely watching a TV-scene. The remaining chapter shall therefore exclusively concentrate on collaborative VEs.

Studies exploring male and female presence experiences in interactive VEs mostly contradict the results reported for non-interactive settings. For instance, Nicovich, Boller and Cornwell (2005), who exposed their participants to a flight simulator, found men to report higher levels of physical presence when interacting and controlling the simulator while women showed more physical presence when merely watching the simulation. Similarly, Lachlan and Krcmar (2011) described an overall advantage of men in their physical presence experiences while playing a video game. Altogether, their male participants showed more control over the environment and more related sensory presence than female participants. Apart from the interactivity of the environment, task complexity seems to be another influencing factor affecting gender differences in presence: Slater and colleagues (1998) examined the impact of body movements on physical presence when counting virtual trees with diseased leaves and found men to report higher presence levels than women when the task was more complex.

A pressing question often encountered in gender research is why a gender difference is detected at all and what may be the underlying cause of it? In light of the above described results a possible explanation is the commonly assumed greater familiarity of males with diverse interactive VEs such as video games (Hartmann & Klimmt, 2006). The idea behind this assumption and its link to physical presence is quite evident: The more familiar a person is with VEs in general, the easier it will be to interact with a specific VE because fewer factors will prove detrimental to presence (e.g., cumbersome handling of the equipment, problems with navigation and orientation etc.). Hence, a person familiar with VEs is expected to report more presence. Past research has indeed detected a positive effect of previous experiences with video games on presence levels (Lachlan & Krcmar, 2011). This notion is supported by one of the few theoretical presence models: the *Process Model of the Formation of Spatial Presence Experiences* (Wirth et al., 2007). It assumes that cognitive processes (i.e., attention, spatial orientation etc.) are involved in the formation of physical presence. These processes are thought to rely on pre-existing spatial knowledge and previous spatial experiences. Considering this, it is apparent how frequent computer or video game players might experience more presence than non-gamers.

Furthermore, one might consider spatial or navigational abilities. There is a long tradition of reporting a male advantage across the lifespan in spatial abilities, i.e., rotating three-dimensional objects mentally, reading maps or navigating through a maze (Kryspin-Exner, Lamplmayr, & Felnhofer, 2011; Lautenbacher, Güntürkün, & Hausmann, 2009; Maylor, Reimers, Choi, Collaer, Peters, & Silverman, 2007). Extending the study of navigation and spatial orientation to VEs, studies were able to replicate the male advantage in a virtual Morris water maze task - the person is required to find an underwater platform while swimming in a circular pool of water (Astur, Ortiz & Sutherland, 1998) - as well as in a number of VEs with differing orientation and navigation tasks (Cutmore, Hine, Maberly, Langford, & Hawgood, 2000). These findings may prove particularly insightful for the explanation of a male advantage especially for spatial presence. The nature of physical presence is one that is thought to be (at least partially) reliant on the spatial abilities of a person. The perception of one's body being physically located in a mediated environment as well as the construction of a coherent mental model of space and the subsequent exploration and interaction with this space all seem to depend on proper spatial orientation as well as navigational abilities (Nash, Edwards, Thompson, & Barfield, 2000; Wirth et al., 2007).

Last, it is possible that the emotional content of the environment may trigger gender specific reactions to it, which in turn might influence reported presence levels. Next to form factors (i.e., head tracking, stereoscopic view, rendering etc.) media content such as the ability to interact with the environments, the story line and the meaningfulness of the environment has frequently been regarded a factor crucially shaping VE-experiences (c.f. IJsselsteijn et al., 2000). Previous results support this notion by showing a positive relationship between the meaningfulness of a VE and presence (Hoffman, Prothero, Wells, & Groen, 1998). Thus, it is safe to assume that two VEs triggering opposite emotional states (e.g., stressful vs. non-stressful) will elicit different individual reactions to them. These reactions in turn might account in large parts for gender differences in presence.

10.2.2 Physical Presence in a Stressful vs. a Non-stressful VE

Two studies were conducted to analyze differences in physical presence between men and women when exposed to a stressful VE including social cues (Felnhofer et al., 2012) and to compare them to gender specific presence experiences in a non-stressful, rather relaxing VE (Felnhofer et al., 2014). The above mentioned possible confounders (i.e., previous experience with VEs, spatial abilities, emotional content of the VE) were all assessed in order to control for their influences on gender differences. In the first study, 20 student participants (10 males, 10 females) were assigned to hold a speech in front of a virtual audience, whereas the other group (10 males, 10 females) formed the control group which was asked to merely imagine a lecture hall. The virtual scenario used in this experiment was presented via a head mounted display, HMD (*eMagin Z800 3D*) and consisted of a virtual lecture hall with an audience of 20 males and females which showed both contented and discontented facial expressions (see *Figure 10.1*). After exposure, all participants were asked to fill out a German version of the igroup Presence Questionnaire, IPQ (Schubert, Friedmann, & Regenbrecht, 2001) consisting of the three sub-scales Spatial Presence, Realism and Involvement. Additionally, the single item Sense of Being There was evaluated.

In sum, male participants were found to score higher on all IPQ (Spatial Presence, Realness, Sense of Being There). Only the scale Involvement did not reveal any significant gender differences. Interestingly, this clear male advantage was only found in the virtual condition. The control group, however, showed comparable levels of physical presence for men and women. Moreover, women reported stronger experiences of physically being there in the imagined environment as compared to the virtual one. Both male and female students showed comparable levels of prior computer experience.

In a second study we opted to assess male and female presence experiences in a non-stressful, sunny virtual park (see *Figure 10.2*). Again, the VE was presented via a HMD (Sony, HMZ-T1) and all 28 student participants (14 males, 14 females) were asked to freely explore the park. In contrast to the above described stressful VE (Felnhofer et al., 2012) no gender differences were detected on the IPQ scales for the non-stressful VE. Also, an additional measure of spatial abilities (i.e., rotating three dimensional cubes mentally) did not reveal a male advantage. Furthermore, men and women both found the park equally relaxing.

10.2.3 Discussion

Study 1 (Felnhofer et al., 2012) supports past literature reporting higher presence levels in males (e.g., Lachlan & Krcmar, 2011), whereas study 2 (Felnhofer et al., 2014) did not replicate these results. Interestingly, two of the three potential influencing factors (i.e., previous experience and spatial ability) showed no effect and no differences

Figure 10.1: Virtual lecture hall as seen by the participants

between males and females. In both samples, female participants were found to have the same amount of computer experience as their male counterparts (Felnhofer et al., 2012; Felnhofer et al., 2014). It is therefore safe to assume that previous experiences with VEs might not have accounted for the observed gender differences (Felnhofer et al., 2012) and may altogether prove to be a rather poor explanation of different VE experiences in males and females.

Taking a closer look at current gaming developments, one encounters recent statistics which contradict the above mentioned assumption that males play more computer and video games (Hartmann & Klimmt, 2006). Instead, literature now reports up to 50% of female game players in gaming communities (ESA, 2012). Furthermore, we found the same levels of spatial abilities for males and females in our second sample (Felnhofer et al., 2014). This is in line with recent studies which start calling the male advantage in spatial abilities into question. Findings show that women demonstrate better spatial and orientation abilities in certain phases of their menstrual cycle when estradiol levels are low and testosterone levels high (Hausmann, Slabbekoorn, Van Goozen, Cohen-Kettenis, & Güntürkün, 2000). Also, the so called 'stereotype threat' (Steele 1997) has to be taken into account when looking at gender gaps in spatial abilities. It pertains to the often replicated phenomenon that women tend to show a worse spatial performance in a subsequent task when previously being primed with negative stereotypes about female spatial abilities (Lautenbacher, Güntürkün, & Hausmann, 2009).

The importance of the VE's content and emotional appeal has to be stressed in this context since conflicting results were found in two opposed VEs – a stressful vs. a non-stressful one. Congruence between the emotional state of a person and the affective quality of an environment may be thought of as an additional factor possibly influencing presence (Robillard, Bouchard, Fournier, & Renaud, 2003). Therefore, assessing a person's affective appraisal and emotional reaction to a VE in future studies might shed more light on presence experiences. However, gender specific

Figure 10.2: A view on the virtual park

preferences for emotional contents as well as differing reactions to stressful vs. non-stressful situations may also be held accountable for confounding the relationship between gender and presence in emotionally charged VEs.

10.3 Social Presence

10.3.1 Background

Compared to physical presence, research targeting gender differences in social presence experiences is even scarcer. This is in fact quite surprising since past results point towards gender differences in online social interaction with avatars and agents (Szell & Thurner, 2013). In this context, one study particularly seems worth mentioning: Bailenson, Blascovich, Beall and Loomis (2003) evaluated the interaction between gender and agency by asking participants to approach either an avatar (human controlled virtual character) or an agent (computer controlled virtual character). Both subjective (self-report questionnaires) and objective measures (interpersonal distance and mutual gaze) were used to assess social presence levels. This study found only limited evidence for gender differences, but male participants were found to be more sensitive to mutual gaze, whereas females responded with the highest social presence with male avatar. Another study (Bracken, 2005) found no gender differences in social presence at all, but in a non-interactive television scenario.

However, in general, females tend to be more focused on social interaction and intimacy than males. Some authors state that women are socialized to form more intimate and close relationships than men (Cyranowski et al., 2000). According to this, women tend to react differently to threat than men would do. Thus, while men rather show a fight or flight reaction, women tend to engage in befriending, which can be seen as the creation of a social network that provides protection and (social) resources for females and their offspring (Taylor et al., 2002). Additionally, females show higher levels of empathy than men (e.g., Derntl et al., 2010; Toussaint & Webb, 2005). Given the association of empathy to social presence (e.g., Bouchard et al., 2013; Nowak & Biocca, 2003) it may be assumed that women will experience more social presence of another social entity, because of their greater empathic abilities. Yet, to date only little research has been conducted in this area.

10.3.2 Social Presence in a Collaborative VE

A study was recently conducted to debunk differences in social presence and the intention to use a collaborative virtual environment between older men and women (Kothgassner, Felnhofer, Beutl, Heinzle, Gomm, Kastenhofer, Hauk, Hlavacs, & Kryspin-Exner, 2013). Participants (25 females, 25 males) between 55 and 90 years of age were tested using a collaborative virtual environment using an HMD (*Sony HMZ-T1 3D Visor, Tokyo*) with an adapted head-tracking system (*TrackIR 5.0, NaturalPoint*). All participants were immersed in the VE in which they were invited to a virtual café (see *Figure 10.3*). There, a 5 minute experimental phase started, within which the participants had to interact with a waiter and another guest in the café. After that, participants had to rate their experience of social presence and to evaluate the system. Results indicate no differences between men and women regarding social presence experiences, but reveal that social presence highly influences the intention to use of such a system.

10.3.3 Discussion

Surprisingly, no gender differences in social presence could be found in the reported study. The tested population of elderly people might in part be responsible for these results. Another study using a similar VE (Kothgassner, Felnhofer, Hlavacs, Beutl, Gomm, Hauk, Kastenhofer, & Kryspin-Exner, 2013) revealed an influence of age on the ratings of social presence. Also, research suggests that interactions in virtual environments are valued differently among males and females (e.g., Szell & Thurner, 2013). In sum, this finding is particularly surprising in the light of research by Bouchard and colleagues (2013) as well as previous research done by Nowak and Biocca (2003). Nevertheless, it has to be considered that in this context gender differences might be a vehicle for other factors which influence technology usage per se, for example technology anxiety, technology acceptance and usability perceptions or personality structure of the user (e.g. Kothgassner, Felnhofer, Beutl, Hlacavcs, Lehenbauer, & Stetina, 2012; Venkatesh & Morris, 2000).

10.4 Conclusion to Chapter 10

In sum, previous research indicates an advantage of men over women regardless of their age in physical but not in social presence. Yet, considering null findings such as the one reported for the relaxing park environment (Felnhofer et al., 2014) it becomes clear, that there might be a range of factors mediating the relationship between gender and presence. In other words, gender effects may simply be an artifact of the effect of other individual characteristics or even of different responses to certain characteristics of the VE (i.e., interactivity, emotional content, meaningfulness and affective quality). Non-interactive environments (i.e., TV) seem to produce exactly the opposite effect to highly interactive collaborative VEs. This can be regarded an indication for the importance of an environment's interactivity in shaping male and female presence experiences. Indeed, some work reports women to be more visually oriented than males (Holbrook, 1986). Thus, it might be hypothesized that women may engage in presence via merely watching the environment and therefore report higher levels when watching TV, whereas men may rely more on the interaction provided by the environment and may therefore profit more from interactive VEs (Nicovich et al., 2005).

Furthermore, taking into account the emotional content of the VE (Robillard et al., 2003) may prove helpful in delineating the relationship between gender and physical presence in future studies. The line of reasoning for this approach would be that gender differences are to be considered an artifact of the environment's emotional impact and appeal. Here, gender specific expectations, experiences and evaluations of the content are thought to mediate the observed differences in presence.

Interestingly, in social presence there is a lack of knowledge about gender differences. It is frequently stated that empathy is closely related to social presence, hence differences in men and women concerning empathy might indicate gender differences in social presence (Bouchard et al., 2013; Nowak & Biocca, 2003). Yet, other factors should also be taken into consideration when investigating gender differences

Figure 10.3: Virtual characters starting an interaction with the participant

for collaborative virtual environments (e.g., Kothgassner et al., 2012). Future studies should focus on technological aspects as well as on personality structure when investigating gender differences in social presence.

At this point it still not clear whether examining gender differences in VE experiences may actually shed more light on the nature of the presence concept. While the body of literature focusing predominantly on this research question is still rather slim, the impression arises that there might be a bias in publishing only studies revealing significant gender differences. Reporting gender differences on a more regular basis for every study (if the composition of the sample allows it) would certainly help estimate whether studying gender related aspects is a subject worth pursuing or a dead end for presence research.

References

Almog, I., Wallach, H.S., & Safir, M.P. (2009). Ethnicity and sense of presence in a virtual environment: Arab women - A case in point. In Virtual Rehabilitation International Conference, 2009 (pp. 78-82). IEEE.

Astur, R. S., Ortiz, M. L., & Sutherland, R. J. (1998). A characterization of performance by men and women in a virtual Morris water task: A large and reliable sex difference. *Behavioural Brain Research, 93(1)*, 185-190.

Bailenson, J.N., Blascovich, J., Beall, A.C., & Loomis, J.M. (2003). Interpersonal distance in immersive virtual environments. *Personality and Social Psychology Bulletin, 29*, 819-833.

Bracken, C.C. (2005). Presence and image quality: The case of high-definition television. *Media Psychology, 7(2)*, 191-205.

Cutmore, T. R., Hine, T. J., Maberly, K. J., Langford, N. M., & Hawgood, G. (2000). Cognitive and gender factors influencing navigation in a virtual environment. *International Journal of Human-Computer Studies, 53(2)*, 223-249.

Cyranowski, J. M., Frank, E., Young, E., & Shear, M. K. (2000). Adolescent onset of the gender difference in lifetime rates of major depression: a theoretical model. *Archives of General Psychiatry, 57(1)*, 21-27.

Delphy, C. (1993). Rethinking sex and gender. *Women's Studies International Forum, 16(1)*,1-9.

Derntl, B., Finkelmeyer, A., Eickhoff, S., Kellermann, T., Falkenberg, D. I., Schneider, F., & Habel, U. (2010). Multidimensional assessment of empathic abilities: neural correlates and gender differences. *Psychoneuroendocrinology, 35(1)*, 67-82.

ESA (2012). Essential Facts about the Computer and Video Game Industry 2012: Sales, Demographic and Usage Data. Retrieved 20.01.2014 from http://www.theesa.com/facts/pdfs/esa_ef_2012.pdf

Felnhofer, A., Kothgassner, O.D., Beutl, L., Hlavacs, H., & Kryspin-Exner, I. (2012). Is virtual reality made for men only? Exploring gender differences in the sense of presence. *Proceedings of the International Society on Presence Research,* Philadelphia, USA.

Felnhofer, A., Hetterle, T., Schmidt, M., Kryspin-Exner, I. & Kothgassner, O.D. (2014). Challenging gender differences in physical presence: Affective states, spatial abilities and presence in a relaxing virtual park. *Challenging Presence. Proceedings of the International Society for Presence Research*, 161-166.

Hartmann, T., & Klimmt, C. (2006). Gender and computer games: Exploring females' dislikes. *Journal of Computer-Mediated Communication, 11(4)*, 910-931.

Hausmann, M., Slabbekoorn, D., Van Goozen, S. H., Cohen-Kettenis, P. T., & Güntürkün, O. (2000). Sex hormones affect spatial abilities during the menstrual cycle. *Behavioral neuroscience, 114(6)*, 1245-1250.

Hoffman, H. G., Prothero, J., Wells, M. J., & Groen, J. (1998). Virtual chess: Meaning enhances users' sense of presence in virtual environments. *International Journal of Human-Computer Interaction, 10(3)*, 251-263.

Holbrook, M. B. (1986). Aims, concepts, and methods for the representation of individual differences in esthetic responses to design features. *Journal of Consumer Research, 13(3)*, 337-347.

IJsselsteijn, W.A. (2004). *Presence in depth*. Eindhoven: University of Technology.

IJsselsteijn, W.A., de Ridder, H., Freeman, J. and Avons, S.E. (2000). Presence: Concept, determinants and measurement. In *Proceedings of the SPIE, Human Vision and Electronic Imaging V*, 3959-76.

ISPR. International Society for Presence Research. (2000). *The Concept of Presence: Explication Statement*. Retrieved 20.01.2014 from http://ispr.info/

Kothgassner, O. D., Felnhofer, A., Beutl, L., Hlavacs, H., Lehenbauer, L. & Stetina, B. U. (2012). A virtual training tool for giving talks. *Lecture Notes in Computer Science, 7522*, 53-66.

Kothgassner, O.D., Felnhofer, A., Hlavacs, H., Beutl, L., Gomm, J., Hauk, N., Kastenhofer, E., & Kryspin-Exner, I. (2013). Debunking differences between younger and older adults using a collaborative virtual environment. *Lecture Notes in Computer Science, 8215*, 36-47.

Kothgassner, O.D., Felnhofer, A., Beutl, L., Heinzle, A.-K., Gomm, J., Kastenhofer, E., Hauk, N., Hlavacs, H., & Kryspin-Exner, I. (2013). Geschlechtsunterschiede in der Nutzung von kollaborativen virtuellen Umwelten bei gesunden Älteren: Der Einfluss von Sozialer Präsenz, Benutzerfreundlichkeit und Technikängstlichkeit. *Proceedings of the 11th Usability Day on Natural User Interfaces*. Austria, Dornbirn.

Kryspin-Exner, I., Lamplmayr, E., & Felnhofer, A. (2011). Geropsychology: The Gender Gap in Human Aging – A Mini-Review. *Gerontology, 57(6)*, 539-548.

Lachlan, K. & Krcmar, M. (2011). Experiencing Presence in Video Games: The Role of Presence Tendencies, Game Experience, Gender, and Time Spent in Play. *Communication Research Reports, 28(1)*, 27-31.

Lautenbacher, S., Güntürkün, O., & Hausmann, M. (Hrsg.) (2009). *Gehirn und Geschlecht: Neurowissenschaft des kleinen Unterschieds zwischen Mann und Frau. Auflage: 1.* Berlin: Springer.

Lombard, M. & Ditton, T. (1997). At the heart of it all: The concept of presence. *Journal of Computer Mediated Communication, 3(2)*.

Lombard, M., Reich, R.D., Grabe, M.E., Bracken, C.C., & Ditton, T.B. (2000). Presence and television. *Human Communication Research, 26(1)*, 75-98.

Maylor, E.A., Reimers, S., Choi, J., Collaer, M.L., Peters, M., & Silverman, I. (2007). Gender and sexual orientation differences in cognition across adulthood: age is kinder to women than to men regardless of sexual orientation. *Archives of Sexual Behavior, 36*, 235-249.

Nicovich, S.G., Boller, G.W., & Cornwell, T.B. (2005). Experienced Presence within Computer-Mediated Communications: Initial Explorations on the Effects of Gender with Respect to Empathy and Immersion. *Journal of Computer-Mediated Communication, 10(2)*.

Nowak, K. L., & Biocca, F. (2003). The effect of the agency and anthropomorphism on users' sense of telepresence, copresence, and social presence in virtual environments. *Presence: Teleoperators and Virtual Environments, 12(5)*, 481-494.

Robillard, G., Bouchard, S., Fournier, T., & Renaud, P. (2003). Anxiety and presence during VR immersion: A comparative study of the reactions of phobic and non-phobic participants in therapeutic virtual environments derived from computer games. *CyberPsychology & Behavior, 6(5)*, 467-476.

Schubert, T.W. (2009). A New Conception of Spatial Presence: Once Again, with Feeling. *Communication Theory, 19*, 161-187.
Schubert, T., Friedmann, F., & Regenbrecht, H. (2001). The experience of presence: Factor analytic insights. *Presence: Teleoperators and Virtual Environments, 10(3)*, 266-281.
Slater, M., McCarthy, J., & Maringelli, F. (1998). The influence of body movement on subjective presence in virtual environments. *Human Factors: The Journal of the Human Factors and Ergonomics Society, 40(3)*, 469-477.
Slater, M., Lotto, B., Arnold, M.M., & Sanchez-Vives, M.V. (2009). How we experience immersive virtual environments: the concept of presence and its measurement. *Anuario de psicología, 40(2)*, 193-210.
Steele, C.M. (1997). A threat in the air. How stereotypes shape intellectual identity and performance. *American Psychologist, 52*, 613-629.
Szell, M., & Thurner, S. (2013). How women organize social networks different from men. *Scientific Reports, 3*, 1214.
Taylor, S. E., Klein, L. C., Lewis, B. P., Gruenewald, T. L., Gurung, R. A., & Updegraff, J. A. (2000). Biobehavioral responses to stress in females: tend-and-befriend, not fight-or-flight. *Psychological Review, 107(3)*, 411.
Toussaint, L., & Webb, J. R. (2005). Gender differences in the relationship between empathy and forgiveness. *The Journal of Social Psychology, 145(6)*, 673-685.
Unger, R. K. (1979). Toward a redefinition of sex and gender. *American Psychologist, 34(11)*, 1085.
Venkatesh, V., & Morris, M. G. (2000). Why don't men ever stop to ask for directions? Gender, social influence, and their role in technology acceptance and usage behavior. *MIS Quarterly, 24(1)*, 115-139.
West, C., & Zimmerman, D. H. (1987). Doing gender. *Gender & Society, 1(2)*, 125-151.
Wirth, W., Hartmann, T., Böcking, S., Vorderer, P., Klimmt, C., Schramm, H., Saaris, T., Laarni, J., Ravaja, N., Gouveia, F.R., Biocca, F., Sacau, A., Jäncke, L., Baumgartner, T., & Jäncke, P. (2007). A Process Model of the Formation of Spatial Presence Experiences. *Media Psychology, 9*, 493-525.

11 The Experience of Presence in Persuasive Virtual Environments

Jesse Fox, Katheryn R. Christy, and Mao H. Vang

Abstract: The examination of presence is important, as previous studies have shown that the subjective experience of presence can impact the effectiveness of virtual treatments (Villani, Riva, & Riva, 2007) and the degree to which these stimuli translate into real world behavior (e.g., Fox, Bailenson, & Binney, 2009; Persky & Blascovich, 2008; Price & Anderson, 2007). In this chapter, we will explore three components of presence (self, social, and spatial; Lee, 2004) and how they relate to persuasion in virtual environments. Relevant theoretical approaches including media richness and Blascovich's (2002) model of social influence in virtual environments will be discussed. We will also elaborate on studies examining the experience of presence in virtual environments designed with various persuasive goals, including health (e.g., Girard, Turcotte, Bouchard, & Girard, 2009; Skalski & Tamborini, 2007), advertising (e.g., Li, Daugherty, & Biocca, 2002; Shin & Shin, 2011; Yim, Cicchirillo, & Drumwright, 2012), education (e.g., Allmendinger, 2010; Caudle, 2013; Mikropoulos & Strouboulis, 2004), and work collaboration (e.g., Bente, Rüggenberg, Krämer, & Eschenburg, 2008; Ratan & Hasler, 2010). We will draw upon this literature to develop practical suggestions for designing virtual environments to cultivate presence while also achieving persuasive goals.

Keywords: Presence; Persuasion; Virtual Environments; Social Influence; Avatars.

11.1 Introduction to Chapter 11

Homebound, Joe visits with his doctor in an avatar-based virtual world. Given the avatar's brief, generic answers, Joe has his doubts about whether the person he is communicating with is really his doctor or if it is a pre-programmed bot. Skeptical, Joe opts to ignore the advice offered by the doctor's avatar.

Amanda joins a virtual conference hoping to convince a client to hire her to design a new office building. The potential client, however, keeps complaining that the lag and quality of the video feed makes Amanda's presentation difficult to follow; the client says it feels like she's transmitting from another planet. Amanda is unable to persuade the client to hire her.

Max visits an online retailer to buy a new pair of glasses. The website encourages him to link up with his webcam so that he can see what the glasses will look like on his own face. Max is disturbed by his disembodied presence on the screen and the odd, floating glasses on his virtual face. He leaves the website, convinced he would rather visit a shop in person.

As virtual environments become more commonplace for communication across persuasive contexts such as health, work collaboration, and advertising, it is important to assess how the experience of presence in these environments may influence persuasive outcomes. Self, social, and spatial presence can be important determinants in whether a source succeeds or fails in persuading a targeted user. In this chapter we will discuss how various conceptualizations of presence are tied to persuasive outcomes. We will then outline theoretical frameworks that may be implemented in the study of presence in persuasive environments. Finally, we will address several contexts in which presence has been demonstrated to influence persuasive outcomes and discuss what these findings indicate for the design of successful persuasive virtual environments.

11.2 Defining Presence in the Context of Persuasion

Presence has been defined in a variety of ways across the literature (Lombard & Ditton, 1997; Witmer & Singer, 1998), sometimes being referred to as *telepresence* (e.g., Minsky, 1980; Schloerb, 1995), *virtual presence* (Sheridan, 1992), or *mediated presence* (Biocca, Kim, & Choi, 2001). For the purposes of evaluating the utility of virtual environments for persuasive means, Lee's (2004) clarification is useful. Lee (2004) defines presence as "a psychological state in which virtual...objects are experienced as actual objects in either sensory or non-sensory ways" (p. 37). This overall construct can be further divided into three types of presence: *self, social,* and *spatial.*

Self-presence occurs when users experience their avatar (or other virtual self-representation) as if it were their actual self, physically or cognitively (Lee, 2004 ; see also Chapters 1 and 4, this volume). Self-presence may entail a feeling of embodying an avatar and feeling its body as one's own physical form (Ratan & Hasler, 2010). Self-presence may also be experienced cognitively as identification with a character. In this case, individuals feel as though they share the character's self (Klimmt, Hefner, & Vorderer, 2009). Self-presence may be important to persuasion because users need to feel connected to their virtual presence. Otherwise, they may not care what outcomes their virtual presence experiences. Alternatively, if users do not feel linked with their avatar or virtual self-presence, they may be resistant to persuasion because they are merely observing, rather than participating in, the experience.

The second category of presence, social presence, was first elaborated by Short, Williams, and Christie (1976). Lee (2004) defines social presence as a psychological and physical awareness of other social actors in the virtual environment. The representations of these social actors may be vary in their level of anthropomorphism (e.g., a virtual human as opposed to a virtual dog; Nowak, 2004), physical realism (e.g., a virtual human could look realistic or cartoon-like), and behavioral realism (e.g., a virtual human could emote naturally or unrealistically; Blascovich et al., 2002). These representations can be controlled by a human (an avatar), a computer (an agent), or a hybrid of the two (e.g., a human controls speech while the computer controls the representation's animations). It is also important to note that social presence does not require the user and the social actor to be virtually co-located, or even communicating simultaneously. Lee uses the example of reading a letter from a dear friend to suggest a situation in which social presence is felt, but the communication is asynchronous. In regard to persuasion, Allport (1985) suggests that human actions and psychological experiences are shaped by the actual, imagined, and implied presence of others; that is, people behave in accordance with some degree of social influence. Thus, the degree to which others perceive social presence in a virtual environment will likely shape persuasive outcomes. Low social presence may therefore motivate users to question the credibility of the source, which would be detrimental to persuasive efforts.

Finally, spatial or environmental presence is a psychological state in which people feel like they are physically located within a virtual environment and interacting with virtual objects (Schubert, 2009; Wirth et al., 2007). Lee (2004) originally conceptualized this interaction of the body with virtual objects as physical presence, but his conceptualization was too limiting for many scholars. Subsequently, the concept has been expanded to include the virtual environment more holistically. Spatial presence may be key to persuasion because it may promote more natural interaction with the user's surroundings. If users do not experience spatial presence, they may not be immersed enough in the virtual environment to attend to the persuasive message. Alternatively, low spatial presence may degrade the user experience, which may negativity skew the user's response to the persuasive message.

There are a wide range of factors that have been suggested to impact an individual's overall experience of presence (see also Chapters 1, 2 and 3, this volume). Witmer, Jerome, and Singer (2005) have theorized that the experience of presence is predicated upon two fundamental psychological states, involvement and immersion, and suggest that there are four factors that significantly affect the experience of presence. *Control* refers to the user's control over the virtual environment, whereas the *sensory* dimension encompasses features such as modality (e.g., visual, audio) and environmental richness. *Distraction* refers to the degree to which distractions (both internal and external) exist. Finally, *realism* consists of not only the degree to which the virtual environment adheres to real-world features (e.g., shadows reacting correctly to light sources), but also the meaningfulness of the experience. Lombard and Ditton (1997) also provide a highly-elaborated list of formal (e.g., image fidelity, aural features, interactivity), content (e.g., social realism, nature of the task), and individual (e.g., prior experience, willingness to suspend disbelief) factors that may play a role in the experience of presence.

In terms of empirical research, several factors have been found to influence the experience of the various dimensions of presence. Perceptions of self-presence, for example, tend to increase when there is a high degree of visual similarity between the real self and the virtual self (Bailenson, Blascovich, & Guadagno, 2008; Ratan, Santa Cruz, & Vorderer, 2007), and when avatars speak with a user's voice (Aymerich-Franch, Karutz, & Bailenson, 2012).

Perceptions of social presence, on the other hand, are increased when participants can interact with a virtual actor (Skalski & Tamborini, 2007), when participants have a previous relationship with a virtual actor (Bailenson et al., 2004), and when participants perceive a virtual actor as similar to themselves (Lee & Nass, 2003). A virtual actor's tone of voice can also influence perceptions of presence. Sources whose tone of voice matches the content of their words are perceived to be more socially present than those with tone/content inconsistencies, and sources whose voices are extroverted in tone are perceived to be more socially present than those whose voices are introverted (Lee & Nass, 2003).

Finally, recent research on spatial presence has suggested that there are two steps involved in a user experiencing spatial presence: the construction of a mental model of the virtual environment and the suppression of external cues that signal the artificiality of the virtual environment (Hofer, Wirth, Kuehne, Schramm, & Sacau, 2012). The first stage is influenced by the user's attention to the virtual environment and, to a lesser degree, their innate ability to create visual representations of the virtual environment in their mind. The second stage relies primarily on the degree to which a user is involved with the virtual environment, which was found to be strongly linked to the amount of interest the user had in the content found in the virtual world (Hofer et al., 2012).

11.3 Theoretical Frameworks for Examining Presence in Persuasive Environments

11.3.1 Media Richness

The concept of media richness was derived from Short et al.'s (1976) exploration of the experience of social presence in various forms of telecommunication and incorporates both a medium-based and user-based conceptualization. *Media richness* refers to the sensory quality of a medium and how it is experienced by the user (Trevino, Lengel, & Daft, 1987). Daft, Lengel, and Trevino (1987) assessed media richness by comparing mediated and face-to-face communication on four criteria: 1) immediate feedback; 2) transmission of multiple cues, such as nonverbal communication or graphics; 3) language variety; and 4) personal focus. In general, richer media are predicted to be more effective in managing equivocal or complex tasks, and greater richness has been associated with better outcomes (e.g., Scheck, Allmendinger, & Hamann, 2008; Timmerman & Kruepke, 2006).

In terms of persuasion, the original postulation of media richness suggests that richer media create more social presence, which can lead to more persuasion. For example, Rockmann and Northcraft (2008) found that media richness influences trust, which in turn affects levels of cooperation. Other studies have found that existing relationships, goals, and strategies predict the use of more or less rich media in persuasive interactions, suggesting that higher levels of media richness are not always desired or necessary to achieve persuasive outcomes (Schmitz & Fulk, 1991; Wilson, 2003). At this stage, further research is necessary to ascertain whether relationships exist between the medium-based conceptualizations of media richness and user-based conceptualizations of media richness (i.e., social presence), and whether these are able to predict the effectiveness of persuasive messages.

11.3.2 Computers as Social Actors

According to Nass and colleagues' computers as social actors (CASA) framework (Nass, Fogg, & Moon, 1996; Nass & Steuer, 1993), including Reeves and Nass's (1996) media equation, humans have limited abilities to distinguish between real and mediated representations, as the brain has not evolved in response to the latter. Therefore, interactions with media are "fundamentally social and natural" (Reeves & Nass, 1996, p. 5).

The primary force behind CASA is the concept of "mindlessness" (Nass & Moon, 2000). People often process stimuli automatically, conserving cognitive effort and maximizing response efficiency (Langer, 1989). According to CASA, rather than scrutinize a message or evaluate the symbolic representations therein, humans respond in an automatic way to mediated stimuli. If a computer demonstrates social behavior, people do not exert the cognitive effort to determine how to behave with a social machine; rather, they respond and react to computers in a manner similar to how they respond to other people (Nass & Moon, 2000). Thus, CASA would predict high levels of social presence during social interactions in VEs.

11.3.3 Model of Social Influence in Virtual Environments

The model of *Social Influence in Virtual Environments* (SIVE) elaborates several variables believed to affect how persuasive virtual social beings can be (Blascovich, 2002; Blascovich et al., 2002). Perceived agency is important because it affects the degree of social presence an individual feels and thus the likelihood of influence occurring. Blascovich et al. (2002) posit that computers (agents) elicit less social presence than humans (avatars) in virtual interactions, but that this difference diminishes the more behavioral realism agents portray. We tend to automatically experience more social presence—and thus are more persuaded by—human-controlled avatars. Thus, computer-controlled agents must act in a realistic manner to bolster social presence. In essence, when greater social presence is experienced with a virtual representation, more social influence will occur because users will perceive and interact with the representation as they would with a real person.

Several studies have indicated support for this model of social influence in virtual environments. In a gaming study, players who believed they were playing a video game with other people were more cooperative than people who believed they were playing the game with a computer (Merritt, McGee, Chuah, & Ong, 2011). Guadagno and colleagues (2007) found that avatars were more effective at changing a user's attitudes than agents, and that higher levels of behavioral realism made agents more persuasive. A recent meta-analysis further supported SIVE by demonstrating that avatars are more influential than agents (Fox et al., 2010).

It is important to understand theories related to the experience of presence, as they help us predict what outcomes may be affected by both designers' manipulations and users' experiences of presence. These theories can lend further insight into findings about presence in persuasive virtual environments across several contexts.

11.4 Contexts for Virtual Persuasion

11.4.1 Health

Research has shown that perceptions of presence in persuasive health contexts can significantly increase the effectiveness of health messages communicated via virtual environments and communicators. For example, Skalski and Tamborini (2007) found that when participants experienced social presence during an interaction with a health information agent, they were more likely to feel that the health topic under discussion was important and more likely to report increased behavioral intentions related to that health topic. Greater spatial presence has also been shown to lead to greater enjoyment in an exercise-promoting VE (IJsselsteijn, Kort, Westerink, Jager, & Bonants, 2006).

More subtle behavioral interventions can also benefit from perceptions of presence. In one study, participants in a smoking-cessation program were asked to play a game where they found and crushed cigarettes with their virtual hand as part of their therapy (Girard, Turcotte, Bouchard, & Girard, 2009). The researchers found that increases in participants' perceptions of presence in the virtual environment significantly contributed to reductions in their addictive behaviors (e.g., frequency of smoking). A similar pattern was found in a study by Fox, Bailenson, and Binney (2009). In this study, women experienced a virtual world where their avatar gained or lost weight based on their in-world food choices (chocolate or carrots). Participants were then told they could help themselves to a bowl of candy while they completed a survey. Women who experienced high levels of presence subsequently inhibited their appetites and ate fewer candies in real life as compared to those who experienced lower levels of presence. In both of these studies, presence in the VE influenced participants' subsequent health behaviors and choices.

There has also been an increasing amount of research done on the ways that presence can enhance the efficacy of virtual experiences during cognitive behavioral therapy (see also Chapter 9, this volume), known as *Virtual Reality Exposure Therapy* (VRET). Krijn and colleagues (2004) found that participants that experienced high levels of presence during VR acrophobia exposure therapy were more likely to complete the course of therapy. Bouchard, Robillard, and Dumoulin (2006) found a similar pattern of results in their investigation of the use of VR in the treatment of individuals with flight phobias; the experience of presence during therapy sessions was predictive of reduction in fear of flying and improved attitude towards flying.

11.4.2 Advertising and E-commerce

Brand attitudes may be affected by presence experienced in response to various electronic advertising formats. When interactivity increases in advertising contexts, those high in need for cognition also experience greater social presence (Fortin & Dholakia, 2005). Positive brand attitudes increased when presence increased in 3D environments (Li, Daugherty, & Biocca, 2002; Yim, Cicchirillo, & Drumwright, 2012) and video games with product placements (Nelson, Yaros, & Keum, 2006). Increases in presence are also associated with a greater ability to recall and recognize brands (Keng & Lin, 2006).

Presence and interactivity with items on e-commerce websites and in virtual environments also affect consumer attitudes and behaviors. The mere presence of others, whether interactive or non-interactive, can influence users' positive and negative emotions (Argo, Dahl, & Manchanda, 2005), trust in a website (Keeling, McGoldrick, & Beatty, 2010; Shin & Shin, 2011), perceived security and risk (Shin & Shin, 2011), and purchase intentions (Luo, 2005). Interestingly, perceived social presence may increase loyalty for a website among women (Cyr, Hassanein, Head, & Ivanov, 2007), whereas men may be more affected by the social presence of a word-of-mouth system (Awad & Ragowsky, 2008). Purchase intention and feelings of presence within the environment may also be affected by perceived usefulness and perceived risk (Dash & Saji, 2007), perceived integrity of the online environment (Gefen & Straub, 2004), and trust and past purchasing behaviors (Weisberg, Te'eni, & Arman, 2011). In an e-commerce environment, presence may also be positively influenced by increased levels of interactivity (Animesh, Pinsonneault, Yang, & Oh, 2011). For instance, text-to-speech technologies increase the social presence of speakers and predict more favorable attitudes toward products (Lee & Nass, 2004; Lee & Nass, 2005).

11.4.3 Education

In online educational settings, social presence plays a crucial role in the learning experience. Social presence influences course satisfaction (Cobb, 2011; Johnson, Hornik, & Salas, 2008), motivation (Allmendinger, 2010), and perceived learning (Cobb, 2011). Student age (e.g., children, adults) may differentially affect the influence of presence (Caudle, 2013). One important factor may be how the instructor's virtual presence in the environment influences students' perceptions of presence (Garrison, Cleveland-Innes, & Fung, 2010) and initiation of the course development process (Ke, 2010).

The structure of online learning may also influence feelings of presence. Persky and colleagues (2009) found that interactive learning promotes greater social presence than more passive learning (e.g., lectures) in virtual environments. When the course develops into a highly collaborative learning environment, social presence may also increase as well. So and Brush (2008) found that offering a variety of communication channels heightens collaborative interaction and social presence (e.g., enabling students to communicate through private chat and email in addition to group chat). By interacting directly with individual students, instructors can promote social presence in virtual settings (Garrison et al., 2010).

11.4.4 Organizations and Work Collaboration

Among organizations and small groups, the use of telecommunications and virtual environments can serve to enhance the group dynamic. For example, social presence may influence trust among groups of varying sizes (Lowry, Roberts, Romano, Cheney, & Hightower, 2006) and cultures (Lowry, Zhang, Zhou, & Fu, 2010). In addition, social presence may enhance trust across different media such as video and audio (Bente, Rüggenberg, Krämer, & Eschenburg, 2008), videoconferencing (Moody & Wieland, 2010), and face-to-face versus computer-mediated communication (Lowry et al., 2010). Among organizations, the effect of social presence may influence decisions made by recruiters (Allen, Van Scotter, & Otondo, 2004), managers and directors (Atkinson, 2008), and trainers (Warkentin & Beranek, 1999). Within groups, social presence affects a variety of variables that can enhance the group dynamic as well as the leaders within the group.

11.5 Implications for Design

Although designers cannot control the amount of presence a user experiences in an environment, they can design VEs to maximize the potential for presence. The goal should be to create immersive environments with behaviorally realistic representations, naturally mapped movement, and appropriately interactive objects.

Maximizing the experience of social presence is perhaps the most crucial aspect of designing persuasive virtual environments. As noted by the SIVE model and supported by numerous studies (see Fox et al., 2010), if an avatar or agent is incorporated as a persuasive source, it is important to convince the user that they are interacting with a human, not a computer. Thus, it is key for the designer to focus on making the agent behave in a realistic manner (e.g., body movement, natural speech, context appropriateness) to enhance the likelihood of influence. Although physical realism may be persuasive in some contexts, it is not required for many interactions if behavioral realism is well-designed. Indeed, designers should note that there are downsides to focusing too much on physical realism with virtual humans as these representations may begin to approach the *uncanny valley*, a point at which people are unsettled by the not-quite-human nature of anthropomorphic representations (Mori, 1970).

Even when avatars are being used, human controllers may need to emphasize their humanness. In many contexts, users have learned to become skeptical about who is controlling a representation. Thus, the persuader may need to reinforce human agency by incorporating appropriate nonverbal behaviors (Bente et al., 2008), emotions (Gratch et al., 2002), and even disfluencies (McFarlane & Latorella, 2002) to promote greater social presence. Regardless of whether agents or avatars are employed, perceived agency should be measured as it can affect social presence and persuasive outcomes (Fox et al., 2010; Vang & Fox, in press).

Spatial or environmental presence may also augment or detract from persuasion. Much as Blascovich et al. (2002) argue for the role of realism in social presence, realism within the VE (e.g., appropriateness of the environment, realistic feedback, or natural mapping) may influence feelings of spatial presence (Skalski, Tamborini, Shelton, Buncher, & Lindmark, 2011). From a hardware perspective, when possible, designers should consider the size, quality, and depth (i.e., stereoscopy) of the depicted virtual environment as this may influence the experience of spatial presence (Bracken & Skalski, 2009; IJsselsteijn, de Ridder, Freeman, Avons, & Bouwhuis, 2001). A fully immersive virtual environment is different than a large desktop computer monitor or a mobile phone (Fox, Arena, & Bailenson, 2009); some features which may work in larger or more immersive environments may be ineffective or even counter-effective via different media as they vary in image and rendering quality, modality, and methods of interactivity. For example, proximity to a target can influence persuasive outcomes, but proximity will be experienced differently in a fully immersive environment as opposed to a mobile interface.

Similarly, virtual environments vary in their ability to promote the feeling of self-presence, although less is known about self-presence in persuasion and further research is needed. One possibility is that identity cues may promote feelings of self-presence, which may lead to persuasive outcomes. For example, photorealistic versions of the self in virtual environments (i.e., doppelgängers; Fox & Bailenson, 2010) have been shown to be powerful persuasive tools, convincing people to exercise (Fox & Bailenson, 2009), eat or restrain eating (Fox, Bailenson, et al., 2009), or save money (Ersner-Hershfield et al., 2011). Further investigation is necessary to determine if self-presence is driving this influence.

Revisiting the cases of Joe, Amanda, and Max from the introduction, the literature presented here has provided some insight on how to alleviate these issues. To get Joe to adhere to the virtual doctor's advice, Joe's experience of social presence should be bolstered by making sure the doctor is responsive and behaves in a natural, realistic manner (Blascovich et al., 2002). If Amanda's client feels distant and separated, Amanda could give up on a traditional video conference and instead create a virtual model of the building that the client could walk through, thus bolstering the client's feelings of spatial presence and perhaps earning Amanda the contract (Skalski et al., 2011). The online retailer should make sure Max's representation looks like him and is comfortably realistic so that he experiences self-presence when interacting with products and is more persuaded to buy them (Ratan et al., 2009).

11.6 Conclusion to Chapter 11

Presence is an important consideration for both the designers of persuasive environments and the researchers who study them. In the studies presented here, presence is often studied as the mechanism explaining why a virtual environment is successful in persuasion, but future research should also investigate the mechanisms that explain presence as an outcome in persuasive VEs. Further, the role of presence should be tested as a potential mechanism in existing theories of persuasion. For example, the elaboration likelihood model suggests message involvement and level of cognitive processing predict persuasion (Petty & Cacioppo, 1986). In a persuasive VE, how do self-presence, spatial presence, and social presence in a virtual environment influence message involvement and cognitive processing? Future study must probe the role of these forms of presence in the process of persuasion. This way, virtual environments can be created to maximize influence and more readily facilitate persuasive goals.

References

Allen, D. G., Van Scotter, J. R., & Otondo, R. F. (2004). Recruitment communication media: Impact on prehire outcomes. *Personnel Psychology, 57*, 143-171.

Allmendinger, K. (2010). Social presence in synchronous virtual learning situations: The role of nonverbal signals displayed by avatars. *Educational Psychology Review, 22*, 41-56.

Allport, G. (1985). The historical background of social psychology. In G. Lindzey & E. Aronson (Eds.), *Handbook of social psychology*, (3rd ed., Vol. 1, pp. 1-46). New York: Random House.

Animesh, A., Pinsonneault, A., Yang, S.-B., & Oh, W. (2011). An odyssey into virtual worlds: Exploring the impacts of technological and spatial environments on intention to purchase virtual products. *MIS Quarterly, 35*, 789-810.

Argo, J. T., Dahl, D. W., & Manchanda, R. V. (2005). The influence of a mere social presence in a retail context. *Journal of Consumer Research, 32*, 207-212.

Atkinson, D. (2008). Dancing "the management": On social presence, rhythm and finding common purpose. *Management Decision, 46*, 1081-1096.

Awad, N. F., & Ragowsky, A. (2008). Establishing trust in electronic commerce through online word of mouth: An examination across genders. *Journal of Management Information Systems, 24*, 101-121.

Aymerich-Franch, L., Karutz, C., & Bailenson, J. N. (2012, October). *Effects of facial and voice similarity on presence in a public speaking virtual environment.* Paper presented at the International Society for Presence Research Annual Conference, Philadelphia, PA.

Bailenson, J. N., Aharoni, E., Beall, A. C., Guadagno, R. E., Dimov, A., & Blascovich, J. (2004, October). Comparing behavioral and self-report measures of embodied agents' social presence in immersive virtual environments. *Proceedings of the 7th Annual International Workshop on Presence*, 216-223.

Bailenson, J. N., Blascovich, J., & Guadagno, R. E. (2008). Self-representations in immersive virtual environments. *Journal of Applied Social Psychology, 38*, 2673-2690.

Bente, G., Rüggenberg, S., Krämer, N. C., & Eschenburg, F. (2008). Avatar-mediated networking: Increasing social presence and interpersonal trust in net-based collaborations. *Human Communication Research, 34*, 287-318.

Biocca, F., Kim, J., & Choi, Y. (2001). Visual touch in virtual environments: An exploratory study of presence, multimodal interfaces, and cross-modal sensory illusions. *Presence: Teleoperators & Virtual Environments, 10*, 247-265.

Blascovich, J. (2002). Social influence within immersive virtual environments. In R. Schroeder (Ed.), *The social life of avatars: Presence and interaction in shared virtual environments* (pp. 127-145). London: Springer-Verlag.

Blascovich, J., Loomis, J., Beall, A. C., Swinth, K. R., Hoyt, C. L., & Bailenson, J. N. (2002). Immersive virtual environment technology as methodological tool for social psychology. *Psychological Inquiry, 13*, 103-124.

Bouchard, S., Robillard, G., & Dumoulin, S. (2006). *Why would VR work in the treatment of anxiety disorders?* Paper presented at the 36th Annual Congress of the European Association for Behavioral and Cognitive Therapy (EABCT), Paris, France.

Bracken, C. C., & Skalski, P. (Eds.). (2009). *Immersed in media: Telepresence in everyday life.* New York: Routledge.

Caudle, L. A. (2013). Using a sociocultural perspective to establish teaching and social presences within a hybrid community of mentor teachers. *Adult Learning, 24*, 112-120.

Cobb, S. C. (2011). Social presence, satisfaction, and perceived learning of RN-to-BSN students in web-based nursing courses. *Nursing Education Perspectives, 32*, 115-119.

Cyr, D., Hassanein, K., Head, M., & Ivanov, A. (2007). The role of social presence in establishing loyalty in e-service environments. *Interacting with Computers, 19*, 43-56.

Daft, R. L., Lengel, R. H. & Trevino, L. K. (1987). Message equivocality, media selection, and manager performance: Implications for information systems. *MIS Quarterly, 11*, 355-366.

Dash, S., & Saji, K. B. (2007). The role of consumer self-efficacy and website social-presence in customers' adoption of B2C online shopping: An empirical study in the Indian context. *Journal of International Consumer Marketing, 20*, 33-48.

Ersner-Hershfield, H., Goldstein, D. G., Sharpe, W. F., Fox, J., Yeykelis, L., Carstensen, L. L., & Bailenson, J. N. (2011). Increasing saving behavior through age-progressed renderings of the future self. *Journal of Marketing Research, 48*, S23-S37.

Fortin, D. R., & Dholakia, R. R. (2005). Interactivity and vividness effects on social presence and involvement with a web-based advertisement. *Journal of Business Research, 58*, 387-396.

Fox, J., Ahn, S. J., Janssen, J., Yeykelis, L., Segovia, K. Y., & Bailenson, J. N. (2010, November). *A meta-analysis quantifying the effects of avatars and agents on social influence*. Paper presented at the 96th Annual Conference of the National Communication Association, San Francisco, CA.

Fox, J., Arena, D., & Bailenson, J. N. (2009). Virtual reality: A survival guide for the social scientist. *Journal of Media Psychology, 21*, 95-113.

Fox, J., & Bailenson, J. (2009). Virtual self-modeling: The effects of vicarious reinforcement and identification on exercise behaviors. *Media Psychology, 12*, 1-25.

Fox, J., & Bailenson, J. N. (2010). The use of doppelgängers to promote health behavior change. *Cybertherapy & Rehabilitation, 3*, 16-17.

Fox, J., Bailenson, J., & Binney, J. (2009). Virtual experiences, physical behaviors: The effect of presence on imitation of an eating avatar. *Presence: Teleoperators & Virtual Environments, 18*, 294-303.

Garrison, D. R., Cleveland-Innes, M., & Fung, T. S. (2010). Exploring causal relationships among teaching, cognitive and social presence: Student perceptions of the community of inquiry framework. *Internet & Higher Education, 13*, 31-36.

Gefen, G., & Straub, D. W. (2004). Consumer trust in B2C e-commerce and the importance of social presence: Experiments in e-products and e-services. *OMEGA-International Journal of Management Science, 32*, 407-424.

Girard, B., Turcotte, V., Bouchard, S., & Girard, B. (2009). Crushing virtual cigarettes reduces tobacco addiction and treatment discontinuation. *CyberPsychology & Behavior, 12*, 477-483.

Gratch, J., Rickel, J., André, E., Cassell, J., Petajan, E., & Badler, N. (2002). Creating interactive virtual humans: Some assembly required. IEEE Intelligent Systems, 17, 54-63.

Guadagno, R. E., Blascovich, J., Bailenson, J. N., & McCall, C. (2007). Virtual humans and persuasion: The effects of agency and behavioral realism. *Media Psychology, 10*, 1-22.

Hofer, M., Wirth, W., Kuehne, R., Schramm, H., & Sacau, A. (2012). Structural equation modeling of spatial presence: The influence of cognitive processes and traits. *Media Psychology, 15*, 373-395.

IJsselsteijn, W. A., Kort, Y. D., Westerink, J. H. D. M., Jager, M. D., & Bonants, R. (2006). Virtual fitness: stimulating exercise behavior through media technology. *Presence: Teleoperators & Virtual Environments, 15*, 688-698.

IJsselsteijn, W., de Ridder, H., Freeman, J., Avons, S. E., & Bouwhuis, D. (2001). Effects of stereoscopic presentation, image motion, and screen size on subjective and objective corroborative measures of presence. *Presence: Teleoperators & Virtual Environments, 10*, 298-311.

Johnson, R. D., Hornik, S., & Salas, E. (2008). An empirical examination of factors contributing to the creation of successful e-learning environments. *International Journal of Human-Computer Studies, 66*, 356-369.

Ke, F. (2010). Examining online teaching, cognitive, and social presence for adult students. *Computers & Education, 55*, 808-820.

Keeling, K., McGoldrick, P., & Beatty, S. (2010). Avatars as salespeople: Communication style, trust, and intentions. *Journal of Business Research, 63*, 793-800.

Keng, C. J., & Lin, H. Y. (2006). Impact of telepresence levels on Internet advertising effects. *CyberPsychology & Behavior, 9*, 82-94.

Klimmt, C., Hefner, D., & Vorderer, P. (2009). The video game experience as "true" identification: A theory of enjoyable alterations of players' self-perception. *Communication Theory, 19*, 351-373.

Krijn, M., Emmelkamp, P. M. G., Biemond, R., de Wilde de Ligny, C., Schuemie, M. J., & van der Mast, C. A. P. G. (2004). Treatment of acrophobia in virtual reality: The role of immersion and presence. *Behaviour Research & Therapy, 42*, 229-239.

Lee, K. M. (2004). Presence, explicated. *Communication Theory, 14*, 27-50.

Lee, K. M., & Nass, C. (2003). Designing social presence of social actors in human computer interaction. *Proceedings of the SIGCHI Conference on Human Factors in Computing Systems, 5*, 289-296.

Lee, K. M., & Nass, C. (2004). The multiple source effect and synthesized speech: Doubly-disembodied language as a conceptual framework. *Human Communication Research, 30*, 182-207.

Lee, K. M., & Nass, C. (2005). Social-psychological origins of feelings of presence: Creating social presence with machine-generated voices. *Media Psychology, 7*, 31-45.

Li, H., Daugherty, T., & Biocca, F. (2002). Impact of 3-D advertising on product knowledge, brand attitude, and purchase intention: The mediating role of presence. *Journal of Advertising, 31*(3), 43-57.

Lombard, M., & Ditton, T. (1997). At the heart of it all: The concept of presence. *Journal of Computer-Mediated Communication, 3*, n.p.

Lowry, P. B., Roberts, T. L., Romano, N. C., Cheney, P. D., & Hightower, R. T. (2006). The impact of group size and social presence on small-group communication: Does computer-mediated communication make a difference? *Small Group Research, 37*, 631-661.

Lowry, P. B., Zhang, D., Zhou, L., & Fu, X. (2010). Effects of culture, social presence, and group composition on trust in technology-supported decision-making groups. *Information Systems Journal, 20*, 297-315.

Luo, X. M. (2005). How does shopping with others influence impulsive purchasing? *Journal of Consumer Psychology, 15*, 288-294.

McFarlane, D. C., & Latorella, K. A. (2002). The scope and importance of human interruption in human-computer interaction design. *Human-Computer Interaction, 17*, 1-61.

Merritt, T., McGee, K., Chuah, T. L., & Ong, C. (2011, June). Choosing human team-mates: Perceived identity as a moderator of player preference and enjoyment. *Proceedings of the 6th International Conference on Foundations of Digital Games*, 196-203.

Mikropoulos, T. A., & Strouboulis, V. (2004). Factors that influence presence in educational virtual environments. *CyberPsychology & Behavior, 7*, 582-591.

Minsky, M. (1980). Telepresence. *Omni, 2*(9), 45-51.

Moody, R. A., & Wieland, R. L. (2010). Using videoconferencing to establish and maintain a social presence in online learning environments. *Educational Considerations, 37*(2), 18-21.

Mori, M. (1970). The uncanny valley. *Energy, 7*, 33-35.

Nass, C., Fogg, B. J., & Moon, Y. (1996). Can computers be teammates? *International Journal of Human-Computer Studies, 45*, 669-678.

Nass, C., & Moon, Y. (2000). Machines and mindlessness: Social responses to computers. *Journal of Social Issues, 56*, 81-103.

Nass, C., & Steuer, J. (1993). Voices, boxes, and sources of messages: Computers and social actors. *Human Communication Research, 19*, 504-527.

Nelson, M. R., Yaros, R. A., & Keum, H. (2006). Examining the influence of telepresence on spectator and player processing of real and fictitious brands in a computer game. *Journal of Advertising, 35*, 87-99.

Nowak, K. (2004). The influence of anthropomorphism and agency on social judgment in virtual environments. *Journal of Computer-Mediated Communication, 9*(2).

Persky, S., & Blascovich, J. (2008). Immersive virtual video game play and presence: Influences on aggressive feelings and behavior. *Presence: Teleoperators & Virtual Environments, 17*, 57-72.

Persky, S., Kaphingst, K. A., McCall, C., Lachance, C., Beall, A. C., & Blascovich, J. (2009). Presence relates to distinct outcomes in two virtual environments employing different learning modalities. *CyberPsychology & Behavior, 12*, 263-268.

Petty, R. E., & Cacioppo, J. T. (1986). *Communication and persuasion: Central and peripheral routes to attitude change*. New York: Springer-Verlag.

Price, M., & Anderson, P. (2007). The role of presence in virtual reality exposure therapy. *Journal of Anxiety Disorders, 21*, 742-751.

Ratan, R., & Hasler, B. S. (2010). Exploring self-presence in collaborative virtual environments. *PsychNology Journal, 8,* 11-31.

Ratan, R., Santa Cruz, M., & Vorderer, P. (2008). Multitasking, presence, and self-presence on the Wii. In L. Moreno (Ed.), *Proceedings of the 10th Annual International Workshop on Presence* (pp. 167-190). Barcelona, Spain: Starlab Barcelona.

Reeves, B., & Nass, C. (1996). *The media equation: How people treat computers, television, and new media like real people and places.* New York: Cambridge.

Rockmann, K. W., & Northcraft, G. B. (2008). To be or not to be trusted: The influence of media richness on defection and deception. *Organizational Behavior & Human Decision Processes, 107,* 106-122.

Scheck, S., Allmendinger, K., & Hamann, K. (2008). The effects of media richness on multilateral negotiations in a collaborative virtual environment. *Journal of Media Psychology: Theories, Methods, & Applications, 20,* 57-66.

Schloerb, D. W. (1995). A quantitative measure of telepresence. *Presence: Teleoperators & Virtual Environments, 4,* 64-80.

Schmitz, J., & Fulk, J. (1991). Organizational colleagues, media richness, and electronic mail: A test of the social influence model of technology use. *Communication Research, 18,* 487-523.

Schubert, T. W. (2009). A new conception of spatial presence: Once again, with feeling. *Communication Theory, 19,* 161-187.

Sheridan, T. B. (1992). Musings on telepresence and virtual presence. *Presence: Teleoperators & Virtual Environments, 1,* 120-126.

Shin, D.-H., & Shin, Y.-J. (2011). Consumers' trust in virtual mall shopping: The role of social presence and perceived security. *International Journal of Human-Computer Interaction, 27,* 450-475.

Short, J., Williams, E., & Christie, B. (1976). *The social psychology of telecommunications.* New York: Wiley.

Skalski, P., & Tamborini, R. (2007). The role of social presence in interactive agent-based persuasion. *Media Psychology, 10,* 385-413.

Skalski, P., Tamborini, R., Shelton, A., Buncher, M., & Lindmark, P. (2011). Mapping the road to fun: Natural video game controllers, presence, and game enjoyment. *New Media & Society, 13,* 224-242.

So, H.-J., & Brush, T. A. (2008). Student perceptions of collaborative learning, social presence and satisfaction in a blended learning environment: Relationships and critical factors. *Computers & Education, 51,* 318-336.

Timmerman, C. E., & Kruepke, K. A. (2006). Computer-assisted instruction, media richness, and college student performance. *Communication Education, 55,* 73-104.

Trevino, L. K., Lengel, R. H., & Daft, R. L. (1987). Media symbolism, media richness, and media choice in organizations: A symbolic interactionist perspective. *Communication Research, 14,* 553-574.

Vang, M. H., & Fox, J. (accepted). Race in virtual environments: Competitive versus cooperative games with black or white avatars. To appear in *CyberPsychology, Behavior, & Social Networking.*

Villani, D., Riva, F., & Riva, G. (2007). New technologies for relaxation: The role of presence. *International Journal of Stress Management, 14,* 260-274.

Warkentin, M., & Beranek, P. M. (1999). Training to improve virtual team communication. *Information Systems Journal, 9,* 271-289.

Weisberg, J., Te'eni, D., & Arman, L. (2011). Past purchase and intention to purchase in e-commerce: The mediation of social presence and trust. *Internet Research, 21,* 82-96.

Wilson, E. V. (2003). Perceived effectiveness of interpersonal persuasion strategies in computer-mediated communication. *Computers in Human Behavior, 19,* 537-552.

Wirth, W., Hartmann, T., Böcking, S., Vorderer, P., Klimmt, C., Schramm, H., Jäncke, P. (2007). A process model of the formation of spatial presence experiences. *Media Psychology, 9,* 493-525.

Witmer, B. G., & Singer, M. J. (1998). Measuring presence in virtual environments: A presence questionnaire. *Presence: Teleoperators & Virtual Environments, 7,* 225-240.

Witmer, B. G., Jerome, C. J., & Singer, M. J. (2005). The factor structure of the presence questionnaire. *Presence: Teleoperators & Virtual Environments, 14*, 298-312.

Yim, M., Cicchirillo, V. J., & Drumwright, M. E. (2012). The impact of stereoscopic three-dimensional (3-D) advertising: The role of presence in enhancing advertising effectiveness. *Journal of Advertising, 41*, 113-128.

Bios

Chapter 1

Giuseppe Riva, Ph.D., is Director of the Interactive Communication and Ergonomics of NEw Technologies Laboratory (ICE-NET Lab.) at the Catholic University of Milan, Italy, and Head Researcher of the Applied Technology for Neuro-Psychology Laboratory (ATN- P Lab.) at the Istituto Auxologico Italiano, Milan, Italy. He also Professor (tenure position) of General Psychology and Communication Psychology, and member of the steering committee of the Ph.D. programme in Psychology at the Catholic University of Milan, Italy. According to the scientific databases ISI Web of Science, PubMed/Medline and PsycInfo, Riva is the scholar who authored the highest number of peer-reviewed scientific publications in the fields of "Virtual Reality" in the world (as of July 2014). These papers range from specialistic journals such as "Presence: Teleoperators and Virtual Reality" (MIT Press) to general scientific journals such as "Science" (AAAS). In its first decade, Riva pioneered much of the applications that enabled the diffusion of Virtual Reality and Internet in the field of health care. Specifically, his research work led to the development of a new scientific discipline - Cyberpsychology - integrating innovative research ranging from usability and ergonomics, clinical psychology and cognitive science, to mobile devices and simulation apparatus. Through the analysis of the cognitive processes involved in simulated realities he expanded the concept of "Presence" the feeling of being there - originally developed by communication and technology scholars.

Fabrizia Mantovani, Ph.D., is Research Professor of Communication Psychology at the Università degli Studi di Milano-Bicocca. She is also Senior Researcher of the Centre for Studies in Communication Sciences (CESCOM) and member of the international research network on "Methodology for the Analysis of Social Interaction" (MASI). Her research work focuses on the concepts of "presence" and "human adaptability" embedding the bits of the digital realm with the atoms of our physical world. Specifically, the main contribution of her research work is related to the impact of serious games - computer or video games, considering also the involvement of emotions in this learning process.

Chapter 2

Eva Lindh Waterworth is manager of the Q-Life research group and a full professor of informatics (since 2010) at Umeå University in Sweden. Her own research focuses on the relationship between quality of life and IT, with a particular interest in creating technology that meets the needs of special groups such as the elderly, the young and the physically and mentally disadvantaged. She has a PhD in Informatics (2001), and a first degree in informatics and business administration.

John Waterworth is a full professor of Informatics (since 2001) and a member of the Q-life research group at Umeå University in Sweden. His funded research focuses on actual and potential effects of using ICT on quality of life and health, especially among the elderly. He has a PhD in Experimental Psychology (1984) and is a Chartered Psychologist of the British Psychological Society. With almost 200 publications to his name, he is best known for his work on topics such as information exploration, the experience of presence and creativity in mediated environments.

Chapter 3

Daniel Sjölie has a Ph.D. in Computing Science with a focus on human-computer interaction and cognitive neuroscience in a context of virtual realities and interactive 3d-graphics. Building on several years of practical experience of virtual reality as a research engineer, his research has focused on the foundations of presence in cognitive neuroscience, including brain imaging studies, and on how this may guide the design of VR applications and complex visualizations.

Chapter 4

Andrea Stevenson Won is a Ph.D. candidate in the Department of Communication at Stanford University, currently working in the Virtual Human Interaction Lab on the capture and expression of nonverbal behavior and the physical and psychological effects of mediated embodiment. Her interests include homuncular flexibility and health applications for virtual reality. Her M.S. in Biomedical Visualization from the University of Illinois at Chicago focused on modeling anatomy for virtual reality applications.

Antal Haans is assistant professor of Environmental Psychology in Human-Technology Interaction at Eindhoven University of Technology (TU/e) in The Netherlands. He received his Ph.D. from TU/e in 2010 on the topic of embodiment and corporeal awareness in media technologies. His research interest is in understanding the interplay between humans and their everyday socio-physical surroundings, including those offered by media technologies. Part of his work involves the scientific investigation of telepresence, and the potential of media technologies in the aid of psychological research; investigating the use and validity of immersive virtual environments for urban lighting research, or the potential of mediated social touch technologies for touch research.

Wijnand A. IJsselsteijn has a background in cognitive neuropsychology and artificial intelligence. In 2004, he received his PhD from Eindhoven University of Technology (TU/e) on the topic of telepresence. Since 2012, he is full professor of Cognition and Affect in Human-Technology Interaction at Eindhoven University of Technology in The Netherlands. Wijnand's focus is on conceptualizing and measuring human experiences in relation to advanced media environments (immersive 3D media, serious games, affective computing) in the service of human learning, communication, health, and wellbeing. Wijnand has a keen interest in technological innovations (e.g., sensor-enabled mobile technologies, virtual environments) that make possible novel forms of human behaviour tracking, combining methodological rigor with ecological validity.

Jeremy Bailenson is founding director of Stanford University's Virtual Human Interaction Lab, an Associate Professor in the Department of Communication at Stanford, and a Senior Fellow at the Woods Institute for the Environment. He explores the manner in which people are able to represent themselves when the physical constraints of body and veridically-rendered behaviors are removed. Furthermore, he designs and studies virtual reality systems that allow physically remote individuals to meet in virtual space, and explores the manner in which these systems change the nature of verbal and nonverbal interaction. In particular, he explores how virtual reality can change the way people think about education, environmental behavior, and health.

Chapter 5

John M. Carroll is Distinguished Professor of Information Sciences and Technology at Pennsylvania State University. Recent books include *Learning in Communities* (Springer, 2009), *The Neighborhood in the Internet: Design Research Projects in Community Informatics* (Routledge, 2012), and *Creativity and Rationale: Enhancing Human Experience by Design* (Springer, 2012). Carroll is editor of the Synthesis Lectures on Human-Centered Informatics. Carroll received the Rigo Award and CHI Lifetime Achievement Award from ACM, the Goldsmith Award from IEEE. He is a fellow of AAAS, ACM, APS, HFES, and IEEE. In 2012, he received an honorary doctorate in engineering from Universidad Carlos III de Madrid.

Patrick C. Shih received the B.S. degree in Computer Science and Engineering from the University of California, Los Angeles, in 2003, the M.S. degree in Information Networking from Carnegie Mellon University in 2005, and the Ph.D. degree in Information and Computer Science from the University of California, Irvine in 2011. In 2012, he joined the College of Information Sciences and Technology at The Pennsylvania State University as a Research Associate. His current research interests include community informatics, healthcare informatics, virtual communities, and educational technologies. Dr. Shih is a member of IEEE and ACM.

Blaine Hoffman is a user experience researcher. He earned a Bachelor of Science degree from Denison University, majoring in Computer Science and in Communication. Blaine went on as a graduate student within the College of Information Sciences and Technology at the Pennsylvania State University, exploring the roles of technology in social interaction. As a researcher, his interests and work included communication structures in open-source software communities, virtual communities, mobile computing, civic engagement and awareness, and user experience. Since completing his Ph.D. research and graduating in the summer of 2013, Blaine has been exploring career opportunities in industry to evaluate and inform design of more useful and engaging software.

Jing Wang received her Ph.D. degree in Information Sciences and Technology at Pennsylvania State University in 2013. Her research interests include human-computer interaction, computer-supported cooperative work, social computing, online communities, persuasive technologies, and creativity. She has published studies in a variety of domains, such as software development, education, and healthcare.

Kyungsik Han is a Ph.D. candidate in Information Sciences and Technology at Pennsylvania State University. He is interested in HCI and CSCW, especially the application of mobile technology in a geographical community context. Han received his B.S. in Computer Science from Kyungpook National University (2009) and M.S. in Computer Science from UCLA (2011).

Chapter 6

Dr. **Paul Cairns** is a Reader in Human-Computer Interaction at the University of York. He has a long-standing interest in immersion in digital games as well as broader gaming experiences. He was formerly at UCL where, with Anna Cox, he produced the first book on Research Methods for Human-Computer Interaction. His favourite cheese is Norwegian Jarlsberg.

Matthew Hudson is an Engineering Doctorate student at the University of York. His studies focus on Social Presence in virtual environments, specifically team-based games and mixed reality training simulations. He is supervised by Paul Cairns and sponsored by BAE Systems. He enjoys miniature compressors and avoiding virtual artillery.

Chapter 7

Dr. **Henry Moller**, B.Sc. (Hons.), MD, MSc, MPP, FRCPC, is a physician, researcher and theorist, board-certified in psychiatry, somnology and holistic/integrative medicine. His career began with a keen interest in the neuroscience of consciousness, and the impact of technology on wellbeing. Researching human-environment design vis-a-vis personal and public health promotion, he has successfully pioneered integration of immersive wellbeing programs in health and wellness settings. Current academic affiliations include University of Toronto's Faculty of Medicine, Music and Health Research Collaboratory and Knowledge Media Design Institute, as well as University of Waterloo Faculty of Applied Health Sciences.

Harjot Bal, M.Des., is an interdisciplinary designer in the emergent field of wellbeing technology, with an affiliation to OCAD University (Toronto, Ontario, Canada), Digital Futures Initiative Program. Interaction design works that aid in fostering empathy, sense of self, and wellbeing make up the range of his most recent work. Current focus is holistic health practices brought to technology in the form of audiovisual interaction pieces.

Kunal Sudan, B.Sc., studied psychology, neuroscience and behavior at McMaster University (Hamilton, Ontario, Canada), where he furthered his knowledge with studies in addictions and mental health at Ryerson University (Toronto, Ontario, Canada). He has a particular interest in neurochemistry, and integration of music into health care. He also has an interest in the neuroscience of sleep consciousness and interrelationships between immersive virtual realities and mental health therapies.

Luke R. Potwarka, Ph.D., is an Assistant Professor in the Department of Recreation and Leisure Studies at the University of Waterloo, in Ontario Canada. Luke earned his B.A. from the University of Waterloo (2002), his MA from Brock University (2004), and his Ph.D. from the University of Waterloo (2011). All of his degrees were completed in Recreation and Leisure Studies. His research is focused on understanding the behaviors and experiences of sport spectators and leisure participants. He is particularly interested in exploring relationships between cognitive function and sport and leisure participation.

Chapter 8

Sheryl Brahnam (M.F.A. Intermedia, Ph.D. Computer Science, and psychoanalytic candidate) is a full professor in the department of Computer Information Systems at Missouri State University and is the Director/Founder of the Infant COPE (Classification Of Pain Expressions) project. Her interests focus on medical decision support systems, machine learning, embodied conversational agents, computer abuse, and, recently, virtual reality psychotherapy. She has served as guest editor of several books and special issues on virtual reality and rehabilitation, technologies for inclusive well-being, agent abuse, and computational systems for medicine. She has published extensively in such journals as *Pattern Recognition*, *Artificial Intelligence in Medicine*, *Amino Acids*, *Journal of Theoretical Biology*, *Expert Systems with Applications*, *Decision Support Systems*, *PLOS ONE*, and *Interacting with Computers*, as well as in many conferences and workshops devoted to human-computer interaction and artificial intelligence.

Chapter 9

Daniela Villani is a researcher in General Psychology at the Faculty of Educational Science, Catholic University of the Sacred Heart of Milan. She received a Ph.D. in Psychology in 2008 with a thesis entitled "Virtual Experiences support real emotions: Three experimental studies". Her research focus is directed mainly in the field of Communication Psychology and to the application of mediated communication tools for the Psychology of Well-being. She has international collaborations and is author of contributions at national and international conferences as well as of national and international publications in peer-reviewed journals.

Pietro Cipresso is author and editor of several scientific publications and books such as "*Modeling Emotions at the Edge of Chaos*", "*Computing Paradigms for Mental Health*", "*The Psychology of Social Networking*" and "*Virtual Reality: Technologies, Medical Applications and Challenges*", and also an editor of international peer-reviewed scientific journals. He received his Ph.D. in Communication and new technologies, Major in Psychology, from IULM University of Milan. He has been a Visiting Researcher at Massachusetts Institute of Technology (MIT) and is Principal Investigator or Co-Investigator on several international, European, and national projects on Emotions, Psychometrics, Psychophysiology, Brain Computer Interface (BCI), Stress and Virtual Reality.

Claudia Repetto is a psychologist and cognitive psychotherapist. After working as a researcher in neuropsychology, in 2013 she obtained a Ph.D. degree in Psychology from the Catholic University of Sacred Heart of Milan. Her research interests include memory, language and new technologies. She is author of contributions at national and international conferences as well as of national and international publications in peer-reviewed journals.

Chapter 10

Anna Felnhofer is a Research Associate in the Faculty of Psychology at the University of Vienna, Austria. Her research focuses on individual differences in physical and social presence in collaborative virtual environments, as well as on the nature of the relationship between self-reported emotional states and physiological arousal such as heart rate and skin conductance level and presence.

Oswald D. Kothgassner is a Research Associate in the Faculty of Psychology at the University of Vienna, Austria. His scientific focus is on social interaction in virtual environments and related issues such physiological and hormonal changes during aversive and threatening social interactions, as well as social presence and social exclusion via media systems.

Chapter 11

Jesse Fox (M.A., University of Arizona; Ph.D., Stanford University) is an Assistant Professor in the School of Communication at The Ohio State University and the founder of the Virtual Environment, Communication Technology, and Online Research (VECTOR) Lab. Her research has appeared in *Communication Research, Media Psychology*, *Computers in Human Behavior*, and *PRESENCE*. Her current work focuses on the effects of virtual representations and social interaction on attitudes and behaviors, particularly in the contexts of health, environmentalism, and sex, gender, and sexuality.

Katheryn R. Christy (M.A., Purdue University) is a student in the Ph.D. program in the School of Communication at The Ohio State University. Her research has appeared in *Communication Methods and Measures* and the *Journal of Communication*. Her current work focuses on the use of new technologies for education and persuasion, with a special focus on issues surrounding sex and gender.

Mao H. Vang (M.A., The Ohio State University) is a student in the Ph.D. program in the School of Communication at The Ohio State University. Her research has appeared in *Cyberpsychology, Behavior, and Social Networking* and *Computers in Human Behavior*. Her current work focuses on the effects of identity, social categorization, and prejudice on user attitudes in computer-mediated contexts.

Index

Bei Fragen zur Produktsicherheit wenden Sie sich bitte an:
If you have any questions regarding product safety,
please contact:

Walter de Gruyter GmbH
Genthiner Straße 13
10785 Berlin
productsafety@degruyterbrill.com